CBD Technical Series No. 50

BIODIVERSITY SCENARIOS

Projections of 21st century change in biodiversity and associated ecosystem services

A Technical Report for the Global Biodiversity Outlook 3

Convention on Biological Diversity

UNEP WCMC

DIVERSITAS
an international programme
of biodiversity science

Published by the Secretariat of the Convention on Biological Diversity.
ISBN 92-9225-218-6
Copyright © 2010, Secretariat of the Convention on Biological Diversity

Citation
Leadley, P., Pereira, H.M., Alkemade, R., Fernandez-Manjarrés, J.F., Proença, V., Scharlemann, J.P.W., Walpole, M.J. (2010) Biodiversity Scenarios: Projections of 21st century change in biodiversity and associated ecosystem services. Secretariat of the Convention on Biological Diversity, Montreal. Technical Series no. 50, 132 pages.

For further information please contact:
Secretariat of the Convention on Biological Diversity
World Trade Centre
413 St. Jacques, Suite 800
Montreal, Quebec, Canada H2Y 1N9
Phone: 1 (514) 288 2220
Fax: 1 (514) 288 6588
E-mail: secretariat@cbd.int
Website: www.cbd.int

Photo Credits
Cover (from top to bottom): iStockphoto.com; Eric Gilman; © Center for Environmental Systems Research. University of Kassel. October 2003-Water GAP 2.1D; Frank Kovalchek, Flickr.com
Page 1: UN Photo/Ray Witlin
Page 4: courtesy of UNEP
Page 11: Joel Craycraft
Page 36: Kalovstian/UNEP
Page 38: Gaethlich, UNEP-Alpha Presse
Page 45: Anne Larigauderie

Typesetting: Em Dash Design

THIS DOCUMENT WAS PREPARED BY:

Lead Authors

Paul Leadley, *Université Paris-Sud 11/CNRS/ AgroParisTech, France*

Henrique Miguel Pereira, *Universidade de Lisboa, Portugal*

Rob Alkemade, *Netherlands Environmental Assessment Agency, Netherlands*

Juan F. Fernandez-Manjarrés, *CNRS/Université Paris-Sud 11/ AgroParisTech, France*

Vânia Proença, *Universidade de Lisboa, Portugal*

Jörn P.W. Scharlemann, *United Nations Environment Programme World Conservation Monitoring Centre, UK*

Matt J. Walpole, *United Nations Environment Programme World Conservation Monitoring Centre, UK*

Contributing Authors

John Agard, *The University of The West Indies, Trinidad and Tobago*

Miguel Araújo, *Museo Nacional de Ciencias Naturales, Spain*

Andrew Balmford, *University of Cambridge, UK*

Patricia Balvanera, *Universidad Nacional Autónoma de México, Mexico*

Oonsie Biggs, *Stockholm University, Sweden*

Laurent Bopp, *Institute Pierre Simon Laplace, France*

Stas Burgiel, *Global Invasive Species Programme, USA*

William Cheung, *University of British Columbia, Canada*

Philippe Ciais, *Laboratory for Climate Sciences and the Environment, France*

David Cooper, *CBD Secretariat, Canada*

Joanna C. Ellison, *University of Tasmania, Australia*

Juan F. Fernandez-Manjarrés, *Université Paris-Sud 11, France*

Joana Figueiredo, *Universidade de Lisboa, Portugal*

Eric Gilman, *Global Biodiversity Information Facility Secretariat, Denmark*

Sylvie Guénette, *University of British Columbia, Canada*

Robert Hoft, *CBD Secretariat, Canada*

Bernard Hugueny, *IRD, Muséum National d'Histoire Naturelle, France*

George Hurtt, *University of New Hampshire, USA*

Henry P. Huntington, *USA*

Michael Jennings, *University of Idaho, USA*

Fabien Leprieur, *IRD, Muséum National d'Histoire Naturelle, France*

Corinne Le Quéré, *University of East Anglia, UK*

Georgina Mace, *Imperial College, UK*

Cheikh Mbow, *Université Cheikh Anta Diop, Senegal*

Kieran Mooney, *CBD Secretariat*

Aude Neuville, *European Commission, Belgium*

Carlos Nobre, *Instituto Nacional de Pesquisas Espaciais, Brazil*

Thierry Oberdorff, *IRD, Muséum National d'Histoire Naturelle, France*

Carmen Revenga, *The Nature Conservancy, USA*

James C. Robertson, *The Nature Conservancy, USA*

Patricia Rodrigues, *Universidade de Lisboa, Portugal*

Juan Carlos Rocha Gordo, *Stockholm University, Sweden*

Hisashi Sato, *Nagoya University, Japan*

Bob Scholes, *Council for Scientific and Industrial Research, South Africa*

Mark Stafford Smith, *CSIRO, Australia*

Ussif Rashid Sumaila, *University of British Columbia, Canada*

Pablo A. Tedesco, *IRD, Muséum National d'Histoire Naturelle, France*

DIVERSITAS (an international program of biodiversity science) and UNEP-WCMC coordinated this synthesis for the Secretariat of the Convention on Biological Diversity as a contribution to the third Global Biodiversity Outlook (GBO-3). Paul Leadley is the co-chair and Rob Alkemade and Miguel Araujo are members of the scientific steering committee of DIVERSITAS' bioDISCOVERY core project. Georgina Mace and Bob Scholes are vice-chairs and David Cooper a member of the scientific committee of DIVERSITAS.

The lead authors would like to thank Lucy Simpson for organising the workshop, Anna Chenery and Francine Kershaw for their assistance with getting permission to reproduce the figures, Simon Blyth and Gillian Warltier for assistance with proof reading, and Kieran Mooney for photo searches.

This study was funded by the Department of the Environment, Food and Rural Affairs of the United Kingdom with additional financial assistance from the European Commission and UNEP. The views expressed herein can in no way be taken to reflect the official opinion of the these bodies, or of the Convention on Biological Diversity.

CONTENTS

1. EXECUTIVE SUMMARY

This synthesis focuses on estimates of biodiversity change as projected for the 21st century by models or extrapolations based on experiments and observed trends. The term "biodiversity" is used in a broad sense as it is defined in the Convention on Biological Diversity to mean the abundance and distributions of and interactions between genotypes, species, communities, ecosystems and biomes. This synthesis pays particular attention to the interactions between biodiversity and ecosystem services and to critical "tipping points" that could lead to large, rapid and potentially irreversible changes. Comparisons between models are used to estimate the range of projections and to identify sources of uncertainty. Experiments and observed trends are used to check the plausibility of these projections. In addition we have identified possible actions at the local, national and international levels that can be taken to conserve biodiversity. We have called on a wide range of scientists to participate in this synthesis, with the objective to provide decision makers with messages that reflect the consensus of the scientific community and that will aid in the development of policy and management strategies that are ambitious, forward looking and proactive.

KEY CONCLUSIONS

Projections of global change impacts on biodiversity show continuing and, in many cases, accelerating species extinctions, loss of natural habitat, and changes in the distribution and abundance of species and biomes over the 21st century.

▸ Combined changes in land use, exploitation of forests and marine resources, rising atmospheric CO_2 concentrations, climate change and eutrophication are projected by models to result in significant changes in the distribution and abundance of species, species groups and biomes. Many of these biodiversity transformations will involve large and sometimes highly visible modifications of ecosystems such as widespread conversion of tropical forest to pastures and croplands, climate-induced invasion of tundra by boreal forest, reductions in the abundance of top predators in marine systems, etc. Some species are projected to increase in abundance or expand their ranges, but the abundance or range size of many species will decline, often leading to substantially increased risk of extinctions.

▸ Land use change, modification of river flow, freshwater pollution, and exploitation of marine resources are currently the most important drivers of biodiversity change and are projected to remain so over the coming century. Climate change and ocean acidification will become increasingly important drivers during the 21st century.

▸ New socio-economic scenarios point to plausible development pathways of low greenhouse gas emissions and low land conversion that could lead to much lower biodiversity impacts than projected in previous studies. These optimistic scenarios require fundamental changes in development paradigms, but are coherent with known constraints on economics, resource use and human development goals.

▸ The synthesis of a broad range of global land use scenarios and models of climate change impacts on terrestrial and ocean systems shows there is much greater variability in projections of biodiversity loss compared to previous assessments. In addition, if greenhouse gas emissions continue along current trajectories, several Earth System models project that this will result in far greater climate-induced transformations of terrestrial biomes and marine biota than projected in earlier global biodiversity assessments.

- Experiments, observations of current trends and/or the paleontological record are consistent with some model projections, such as the poleward migration of boreal forest due to climate change, but other projections such as massive extinctions due to mid-century climate change have weaker support from past and present trends at least for certain taxa (e.g., some plants and insects).

- The projected changes are heterogeneous spatially and among taxonomic groups, so even moderate biodiversity losses at the global level may translate to dramatic biodiversity losses or changes at the regional level or for a given functional species group or set of vulnerable species. The largest impacts are projected to be habitat and species losses in tropical forests, biome shifts in boreal and Arctic tundra, and dramatic changes in species abundance in many freshwater and marine systems.

- Lags in the underlying socio-economic, climate and global biogeochemical drivers make acceleration in biodiversity transformations inevitable over the next several decades and require that mitigation and adaptation measures must be taken well before unacceptably large impacts on biodiversity are observed.

Thresholds, amplifying feedbacks and time-lag effects leading to "tipping points" are widespread and make the impacts of global change on biodiversity hard to predict, difficult to control once they begin, and slow and expensive to reverse once they have occurred.

- The existence of tipping-points can be anticipated with high confidence; however, specific thresholds cannot yet be predicted with adequate precision and advanced warning to allow them to be approached without high risk. This argues for a precautionary approach to human activities that are known drivers of biodiversity loss.

- Human demands for food, fiber and energy play a key role in driving many of the tipping points especially through conversion of natural and semi-natural ecosystems to farming and the overexploitation of marine resources. While global biodiversity assessments have emphasized the significance of these drivers, the potential importance of thresholds, amplifying feedbacks and time-lag effects leading to tipping-points has been underestimated. For example, previous global biodiversity assessments have not fully accounted for the extremely rapid disappearance of the Arctic polar ice cap, nor the possible widespread dieback of the Amazon forest.

- Tipping points analyses indicate that rising atmospheric CO_2 concentrations and climate change could lead to major biodiversity transformations at levels near or below the 2°C global warming defined by the IPCC as "dangerous". Widespread coral reef degradation, large shifts in marine plankton community structure especially in the Arctic ocean, extensive invasion of tundra by boreal forest, destruction of many coastal ecosystems, etc. are projected to occur below this low level of warming. Due to lags in the socio-economic, biological and physical systems of the Earth these transformations will be essentially irreversible over the next several centuries.

- Many of the tipping points occur due to complex feedback mechanisms or interactions between two or more drivers that are not accounted for in models currently used to project global change impacts on biodiversity. Because of this, the risk of catastrophic biodiversity loss as a result from interactions between two or more drivers, such as widespread Amazon forest dieback from interactions between deforestation and climate change, has been substantially underestimated in previous global biodiversity assessments.

For many important cases the degradation of ecosystem services goes hand-in-hand with species extinctions, declining species abundance, or widespread shifts in species and biome distributions. However, conservation of biodiversity and of some ecosystem services, especially provisioning services, are often at odds.

▸ Most of the biodiversity tipping points that we have identified will be accompanied by large negative regional or global scale impacts on ecosystem services and human well-being. For example, the widespread and irreversible degradation and loss of natural coastal habitats due to pollution, habitat destruction, changes in sedimentation and sea-level rise will be accompanied by increased risk of coastal damage by waves and storm surges and the loss of productivity of coastal fisheries.

▸ Biodiversity loss and the erosion of the capacity of ecosystems to deliver services often respond in similar ways to shared drivers; however, the relationship between them is not simple, and may be different for the various dimensions of biodiversity. For example, the links between local species extinctions and reduced capacity to deliver ecosystem services remain, in many cases, elusive.

▸ Experiments, observations and models indicate that changes in ecosystem services are more tightly coupled to changes in the abundance and distribution of dominant or keystone species than to species extinctions. This calls for increased awareness of the importance of shifts in species distribution and changes in local abundance as the principal drivers of change in ecosystem services. Global analyses of biodiversity change may conceal large, disproportionate local changes for some functional species groups (e.g., top predators) that have a strong influence on ecosystem services.

▸ Improvements in ecosystem services, especially provisioning services such as food, fiber and energy production, can come at the cost of habitat loss, reductions in species abundance and species extinctions. Efforts to maximize a small range of these provisioning services in the short term typically result in negative impacts on biodiversity and important sustaining, regulating and cultural ecosystem services. This calls for prudence in using ecosystem services as a blanket argument for conserving species. It also argues in favor of management that sustains a broad and balanced range of ecosystem services, including existence values, as opposed to focusing on provisioning services.

Strong action at international, national and local levels to mitigate drivers of biodiversity change and to develop adaptive management strategies could significantly reduce or reverse undesirable and dangerous biodiversity transformations if urgently, comprehensively and appropriately applied.

▸ Increasing agricultural efficiency is one of the most important keys to minimizing the destruction of natural terrestrial and freshwater habitats and limiting pressure on marine resources. There is considerable debate concerning the margin for increasing agricultural efficiency, but some recent socioeconomic scenarios require no net increase in land under cultivation at the global scale over the 21st century. Attaining this goal would require limited population growth, substantial increases in agricultural productivity and efficient use of primary production (e.g., reduction of post-harvest losses, limited meat consumption). Negative impacts of agricultural intensification on biodiversity can be minimized by appropriate agricultural practices.

▸ International regulation of fishing in non-territorial waters and improved governance at local to global scales are key to avoiding widespread modifications of marine food chains and collapse of important fisheries. Some forms of low-impact aquaculture could play an important role in preserving marine resources, but without appropriate regulation aquaculture has and will continue to lead to significant environmental problems.

▸ Climate mitigation is urgent as illustrated in many of the tipping points analyses. In particular, the target of limiting 21st century climate warming to 2°C may reach or exceed the climate change threshold for several tipping points, particularly for the Arctic ocean, Arctic tundra and coral reefs. However, mechanisms of climate mitigation should be assessed for their likely impacts on biodiversity. Potential synergies between climate mitigation and biodiversity conservation are numerous, for example the negotiations for the UNFCCC include a mechanism to encourage the reduction of emissions of greenhouse gases due to deforestation and degradation (REDD) which could preserve tropical forest biodiversity and significantly reduce global greenhouse gas emissions if appropriately implemented.

▸ Limited deployment and appropriate management of biofuels can substantially reduce competition between intensively managed ecosystems and natural habitats. Current trends and models suggest that large-scale deployment of biofuels results in net negative impacts on biodiversity. Previous biodiversity assessments have underestimated the opportunities for reducing climate change impacts on biodiversity, in part, because they relied heavily on biofuels for climate mitigation.

▸ Protected areas on land and sea are one of the most effective means of biodiversity conservation if their status is properly respected. Existing protected areas and new networks need to account for the highly dynamic nature of future biodiversity transformations, which will require much stronger integration of biodiversity conservation in and outside protected areas, especially for freshwater ecosystems.

▸ Ecosystem-based approaches can contribute to climate change mitigation and adaptation and to sustainable development more broadly. Spatial planning for ecosystem services at international, national and local levels will be an important component of ecosystem-based approaches. However, because not all elements of biodiversity are critical for ecosystem services, it is important to also target critical areas for protecting biodiversity for its own sake in spatial planning.

▸ Widespread ecological restoration, e.g. large-scale reforestation, has not been included in biodiversity projections, but could play an important role in maintaining biodiversity, and the provision of associated ecosystem services.

In the following sections we provide the details of the scientific underpinning of the conclusions outlined above (Section 2) and highlight the areas of research where significant progress must be made in order to improve the confidence in biodiversity scenarios (Section 3).

Our finding that there is greater uncertainty in projections of biodiversity change than has been acknowledged in previous global assessments should not be used as an excuse for inaction. Our message is the opposite: we find that continuing on our current development pathway leads to very high projected risks for biodiversity change and disruption of ecosystem services, and that the opportunities for conserving biodiversity are greater than previously expected.

2. TECHNICAL SUMMARY OF THE BIODIVERSITY SCENARIOS SYNTHESIS

This section synthesizes existing scenarios for biodiversity change over the 21st century. It focuses on the response of biodiversity to five main global change drivers: habitat degradation and destruction, climate change, nutrient loading, overexploitation of biological resources and biotic exchange[1]. We use "biodiversity" in a broad sense as it is defined in the Convention on Biological Diversity to mean the abundance and distributions of and interactions between genotypes, species, communities, ecosystems and biomes, and are very careful in our analyses to identify which of these components are being addressed. In addition to examining the potential impacts of global change on biodiversity, we have also identified key actions that can be taken to slow, halt or even reverse biodiversity loss.

Our work differs from previous scenario assessments such as the Millennium Ecosystem Assessment (MA 2005), the Global Environmental Outlook 4 (UNEP 2007) and the Global Biodiversity Outlook 2 (CBD 2006), because it focuses on synthesizing information from a broad range of models and scenarios. Previous assessments have relied on a single model framework for generating scenarios of biodiversity change over the 21st century, which has the advantage of providing fully integrated and internally coherent projections of the indirect and direct drivers of biodiversity and their effects on biodiversity. The disadvantage of using a single model framework is that it may underestimate uncertainty, since models differ greatly in their underlying assumptions and their projections of biodiversity change. In addition, we have attempted to confront projections with observations and experimental data in order to evaluate the degree of certainty in model projections. Our synthesis relies primarily on global and large regional scale projections, and to the extent possible is

based on research published in peer-reviewed scientific journals. A wide range of scientists participated in the preparation of this synthesis by contributing text, especially for the tipping points analyses, by participating in a scoping workshop and by providing ample comments on drafts of this synthesis.

This synthesis of biodiversity scenarios is organized by major realms: terrestrial, freshwater and marine systems. Within each realm we present model projections for biodiversity change at the global scale and for specific ecosystem types or regions, with a focus on biodiversity tipping points (Box 1). Our analyses of tipping points cover several regions of the world (Figure 1) which are a subset of a much wider list of potential tipping points.

TERRESTRIAL SYSTEMS

Global biodiversity models project that terrestrial species extinctions, loss of natural habitat, and changes in the distribution and abundance of species, species groups and biomes will continue throughout this century, with land use change being the main threat in the short term, and climate change becoming progressively much more important over the next several decades.

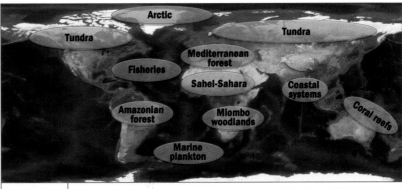

| FIGURE 1 | MAP OF THE DISTRIBUTION OF TIPPING POINTS OF GLOBAL IMPORTANCE. |

Base map is the NASA Blue Marble Next Generation, a MODIS-derived 500m true color earth dataset. Source: onearth.jpl.nasa.gov/.

A relatively broad definition of tipping point has been used in the context of the GBO3 biodiversity scenarios synthesis. It includes situations where changes in ecosystem functioning are significant enough to have important impacts on biodiversity or ecosystem services at regional to global scales, and that meet any one of the following four criteria:

1. The overall effect of a global change driver is amplified by positive feedback loops;

2. There is a threshold beyond which an abrupt shift between alternate ecological stable states occurs;

3. The changes induced by the driver are long lasting and hard to reverse;

4. There is a significant time lag between the dynamics of the drivers and the expression of impacts, causing great difficulties in ecological management.

Tipping points are a major concern for scientists, managers and policy makers because of their potentially large impacts on biodiversity, ecosystem services and human well-being and the difficulty in adapting coupled human-environmental systems to rapid and potentially irreversible regime shifts. While it is almost certain that tipping points will occur in the future, the dynamics in most cases cannot yet be predicted with enough precision and advance warning to allow for secure and adequate approaches to avoid or mitigate impacts. This reality argues for a precautionary approach to human activities which are known to drive biodiversity loss.

For the GBO3 a diverse, but not exhaustive, range of biodiversity and ecosystem services tipping points has been selected. The tipping points selected cover examples from terrestrial, freshwater and marine systems and differ in terms of the main drivers of the underlying mechanisms and of the extent of their spatial distribution. We have not considered all potentially policy-relevant tipping points, and the selection presented should not be regarded as a prioritization of tipping points with respect to their relevance for biodiversity and ecosystem services. This selection aims to provide an overview of tipping points of global importance and to raise the awareness about these phenomena and their consequences. All tipping point descriptions are accompanied by a diagram summarizing the main drivers and mechanisms involved. Pictures illustrating the current condition and the potential future state are also shown.

IMPACT OF DRIVERS

Drivers:
Habitat change
Climate change
Overexploitation
Invasive species
Pollution

Impacts:
High   Low

TIPPING POINT MECHANISMS

Positive/amplifying feedback

Irreversibility

Threshold

Time lag

In general, land use change has been the main driver of terrestrial biodiversity loss during the past century. Land use change, climate change and to a lesser extent nutrient loading, have been predominantly selected over other drivers to explore projections of terrestrial biodiversity change at the global scale. The effects of species invasions and overexploitation, although suspected to be important are still underexplored due to a lack of adequate global datasets and models[2].

Models of terrestrial biodiversity response to global change vary considerably in the methods of modeling biodiversity responses to drivers and in measures of biodiversity change, which greatly complicates the task of synthesis. Methods for modeling biodiversity responses are particularly diverse and include niche-based models[3], dose-response relationships[4], species-area relationships[5], empirical estimates of vulnerability based on IUCN criteria[6], global vegetation models[7] and various combinations of these and other models. We have focused on four key measures of biodiversity change – (i) species extinctions[8], (ii) changes in species abundance[9], (iii) habitat loss[10] and (iv) changes in the distribution of species, functional species groups[11] or biomes[12].

SPECIES EXTINCTIONS – Projections of 21st century terrestrial species extinctions, also referred to as

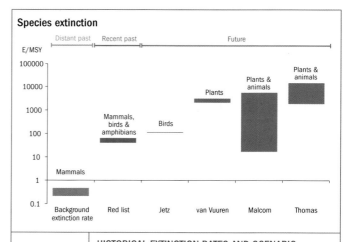

Species extinction

FIGURE 2 | HISTORICAL EXTINCTION RATES AND SCENARIO PROJECTIONS FOR **THE** 21ST CENTURY.

Extinctions per million species years (E/MSY) for distant past, recent past and future. "Distant past" refers to the background extinction rate of mammals obtained from the fossil record (MA 2005). "Recent past" refers to documented extinctions registered in the 20th century, by the Red List — mammals (upper bound), amphibians (lower bound) and birds (in between) (Baillie et al. 2004). "Future" refers to projections of species "committed to extinction" according to different global scenarios: birds (Jetz et al. 2007, for the period of 2000-2050), vascular plants (van Vuuren et al. 2006 for the period 1995-2050) and various taxa (Thomas et al. 2004 for the period 2000-2050 and Malcolm et al. 2006 for the period 2000-2100). This figure shows that projected extinction rates have large uncertainties (both intra and inter-study), but are nonetheless higher than recent extinction rates.

TABLE 1 Characteristics of models of extinction risks for terrestrial species presented in Figure 2.

	Thomas et al. (2004)	van Vuuren et al. (2006)	Malcolm et al. (2006)	Jetz et al. (2007)
Global change drivers	Climate change	Land use & climate change	Climate change	Land use & climate change
Socio-economic scenario	Various GHG emissions scenarios	MA 2005 socio-economic scenarios	Broad range of GHG emissions scenarios (see Neilson et al. 1998)	MA 2005 socio-economic scenarios
Climate models	Hadley centre climate model	IMAGE climate model (Bouwman et al. 2006)	Several (Neilson et al. 1998)	IMAGE climate model
Habitat or species range model	Synthesis of regional projections of species ranges using niche-based models	Habitat loss based on land use change & the IMAGE global vegetation model (Bouwman et al. 2006) response to climate.	Habitat loss based on two global vegetation models.	Habitat loss based on land use change & the IMAGE global vegetation model response to climate.
Species extinction model	Species-area curves and IUCN status	Species-area curves.	Species-area curves	IUCN status. (Extinction = 100% habitat loss)
Species groups considered	Various plants and animals	Plants	All species in biodiversity "hotspots"	Birds
Periods for projections	2050	2050 & 2100	2050 & 2100	2050 & 2100

"species loss", have been the focus of several recent studies, which is understandable because extinctions constitute an irrevocable loss of unique life forms. We have summarized these projections in Figure 2 and Table 1[13].

The majority of these studies project that a very large fraction of species will be "committed to extinction" in the 21st century due to land use and climate change (Figure 2, Table 1). These projected rates are, with one exception, two orders of magnitude higher than observed extinction rates in the second half of the 20th century, which are already approximately two orders of magnitude higher than in the Cenozoic fossil record.

Projected species loss varies substantially across biomes in all studies. For example, the Jetz et al. study indicates that birds in tropical regions are the most sensitive, due to large-scale deforestation in these biomes that are characterized by exceptional species richness and narrow geographical ranges of species (Figure 3). In contrast, van Vuuren et al. rank warm mixed forests, temperate deciduous forests and savannahs as being the most sensitive to global change (Figure 4). Part of this divergence is due to the focus on percent species loss in van Vuuren et al. versus numbers of species extinctions in Jetz et al., highlighting the importance of global patterns in species richness as a critical determinant of future species extinctions.

Land use change typically remains the dominant driver of species loss at the global scale throughout the 21st century in projections that account for both land use and climate change. In all studies based on the Millennium Assessment (MA) socio-economic scenarios, the regions most heavily impacted by land use change are grasslands, savannas and tropical forest in Central and Southern Africa (also see tipping points in Box 5 and Box 6), the Atlantic coastal regions of South America which include megadiverse Atlantic forests, and parts of Southeast Asia (Figure 3). Habitat loss accounts for more than three quarters of global species loss at 2050 in van Vuuren et al., although climate change impacts predominate in high latitude biomes (Figure 3). Surprisingly, the highest projections of species loss come from models that only account for climate change (Thomas et al. and Malcolm et al. in Figure 2). Large differences in methods and species groups studied make it difficult to determine why this occurs[14].

Socio-economic scenarios with high population growth rates and low value placed on public goods have the highest projected species loss (i.e., the "Order from Strength" scenario in studies based on the MA (2005), Table 1), but in general there are

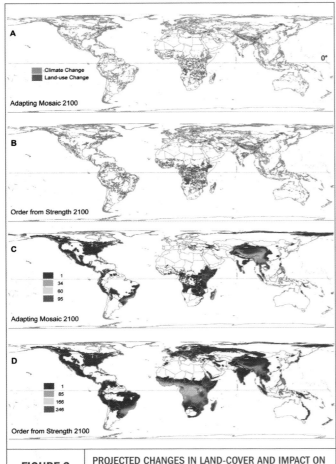

FIGURE 3	PROJECTED CHANGES IN LAND-COVER AND IMPACT ON BIRDS FOR 2100.

A) and B) Projected land cover changes due to land use and climate change for two contrasting socio-economic senarios, with the "Adapting Mosaic" being environmentally proactive and the "Order from Strength" being environmentally reactive. C) and D) Pattern of richness of species with projected range declines >=50%. The map represents the summed occurrences of qualifying species across a 0.5° grid. Source: Jetz et al. 2007.

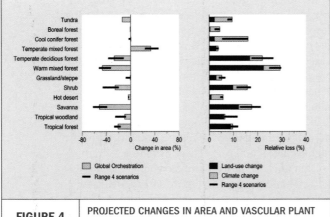

FIGURE 4	PROJECTED CHANGES IN AREA AND VASCULAR PLANT DIVERSITY FOR EACH BIOME IN 2050.

Values are given for the "Global orchestration" socio-economic scenario and black bars indicate the range of projections based on the four MA (2005) socio-economic scenarios. Relative loss of vascular plant diversity indicates the percentage of species "committed to extinction" per biome. All values are relative to 1995 values. Source: van Vuuren et al. 2006.

only modest differences between socio-economic scenarios in many studies of species loss (e.g., Figure 4) despite important differences in human population growth, greenhouse gas emissions, environmental technologies, etc. The absence of large differences in impacts on species across scenarios appears to be the result of complex compensatory effects of development pathways on land use and climate change impacts[15]. We delve into potential explanations for this in the "Species Abundance" section below.

There is growing concern that projections of species extinctions, especially those based on species-area relationships, rely on insufficiently tested hypotheses and are incoherent with recent historical extinctions and the paleontological record[16]. It should also be kept in mind that most models project the proportion of species that are "committed to extinction" at some future time because their habitat or range size shrinks, but the lag time between becoming "committed to extinction" and actually going extinct may range from decades to many millennia[17]. Interestingly, in our analysis, the model that does not use species-area curves (Jetz et al. 2007) forecasts only slightly higher extinction rates compared to those observed over the last century, while the remaining models project extinction rates that are as much as two orders of magnitude higher (Figure 2). Arguably, the Jetz et al. model may be too optimistic as it only projects extinctions when the entire habitat of a species has been modified[18]. Furthermore, habitat loss often makes species more vulnerable to other drivers of extinction such as exploitation, as is the case for large mammals, or disease, as is currently the case for Central American amphibians[19]. In addition, future extinctions could be worse than projected in the most pessimistic scenarios in Figure 2, because the non-linear dynamics of tipping points have not been fully accounted for (see below). The above considerations clearly illustrate that there is far more uncertainty in projections of species extinctions than previous assessments have suggested, and therefore it is incumbent on the scientific community, biodiversity managers and policy makers to make concerted efforts to better understand this uncertainty and to develop plans of action accordingly.

SPECIES ABUNDANCE – Population sizes of species, also referred to as "species abundance", are an important and sensitive indicator of the intensification or alleviation of pressures on species and their habitats. Changes in species abundances of well-studied terrestrial and marine vertebrates are the basis of the Living Planet Index (LPI), one of the most widely used measures of global biodiversity status. Models have recently been developed to project changes in

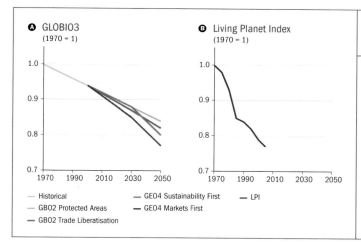

| FIGURE 5 | OBSERVED CHANGES AND SCENARIO PROJECTIONS TO 2050 IN ABUNDANCE OF TERRESTRIAL SPECIES. |

A) Modelled changes in terrestrial mean species abundance (MSA) using the GLOBIO model (Alkemade et al. 2009) for the GEO4 and GBO2 scenarios from 1970 to 2050. B) The Living Planet Index (LPI) for terrestrial species is based on observed changes in the population sizes of well-studied terrestrial vertebrates from 1970 to 2005 (Source: Jonathan Loh, WWF). These two indicators assess changes in species abundances, but are calculated differently so they are not directly comparable. Nevertheless, they suggest that species abundances have been declining globally, and will continue to do so in the examined scenarios. The scenario that has the least biodiversity loss is the one where effective protected areas are implemented and expanded globally.

terrestrial species abundance over the 21st century at regional and global scales, where change in species abundance is defined as the loss of species between a "natural" or relatively undisturbed reference ecosystem and a transformed ecosystem in these studies[20]. We present the two published global projections of species abundance (GEO4 and GBO2), both based on the GLOBIO model, and compare them with recent trends in the LPI for terrestrial species.

Global models project that mean species abundances will decrease during the first half of the century between 9% and 17% (Figure 5A). Observed trends in the Living Planet Index (LPI) for terrestrial ecosystems also show strong reductions in abundance for vertebrate species (Figure 5B), although considerable caution must be exercised when comparing observed and projected trends because of important methodological differences[21]. Despite these differences in methods, observations and model-based projections indicate that populations of many species, especially those that depend on natural habitats, can be expected to decline rapidly over the next several decades at the global scale. Projections from the GEO4 even suggest that species abundances will decline at increasing rates (Figure 5A).

One of the novel aspects of the analyses of the GBO2 is that specific policy and development pathways were examined individually to study their impacts on biodiversity (Figure 6B), making analysis for policy action easier than with complex socio-economic storylines (e.g., MA and GEO4 scenarios). Substantial increases in protected areas are projected to have the greatest positive impact on biodiversity by 2050 compared to the baseline scenario[22]. Sustainable meat production also has beneficial effects on biodiversity through reduced pressure on land use for pastures and crops. Concerted efforts to alleviate poverty have a negative effect on species abundances, primarily due to increased demand for food and energy production in this option[23]. Surprisingly, the climate mitigation option results in lower species abundance than in the baseline scenario, primarily

because this option relies heavily on large-scale conversion of natural systems for biofuels. Large-scale deployment of biofuels is also a key element of "environmentally friendly" socio-economic scenarios used by the MA (i.e., "Technogarden") and GEO4 (i.e., "Sustainability first") and explains in part why these scenarios don't lead to more favorable outcomes for biodiversity[24]. A second important explanation is that climate mitigation will have relatively small impacts on global warming by 2050 because of long time lags in the Earth system[25]. Climate mitigation is expected to play an extremely important role in limiting biodiversity change by the end of the century, in the absence of large-scale deployment of biofuels (see examples "Shifts in the distribution of species, species groups and biomes" below).

Species abundance models avoid some of the pitfalls of projecting species extinctions, because they are anchored in observations of environmental impacts on species. However, they do have some important limitations. In particular, defining the reference ecosystem can be problematic, especially when few pristine ecosystems remain or are not a relevant baseline[26]. It has been suggested that long-term population monitoring data provides a much stronger basis for a species abundance approach[27], but this is strongly limited by the lack of data for many regions and species groups (cf. LPI). An additional caveat is that these models have not been validated at large regional or global scales, so we do not know if the limited number of local-scale measurements of species response to environmental impacts used in constructing the models can correctly capture trends at these large scales.

HABITAT LOSS – Conversion of relatively undisturbed terrestrial ecosystems to agricultural, urban systems or other highly human dominated systems, also referred to as "habitat loss", is currently the main driver of changes in species abundance globally. All models that we have analyzed project a substantial loss of natural habitats over the coming century

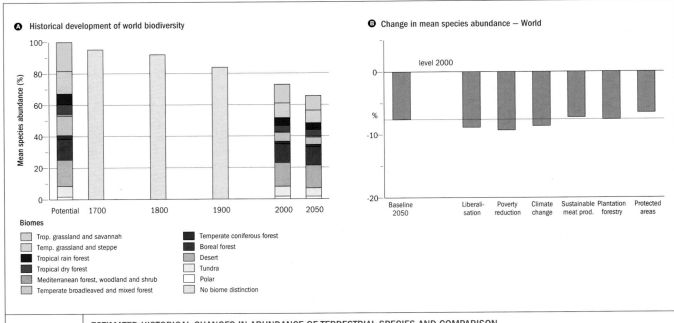

FIGURE 6 ESTIMATED HISTORICAL CHANGES IN ABUNDANCE OF TERRESTRIAL SPECIES AND COMPARISON OF PROJECTED CHANGES IN 2050 FOR DIFFERENT SUSTAINABILITY POLICIES.

A) Historical and projected changes for a "Business as Usual" scenario in Mean Species Abundance. B) Comparison of scenarios examining the effect of different policy options on Mean Species Abundance for 2050 as compared to the Baseline projection. Projections were made using the GLOBIO model. Source: ten Brink et al. 2007.

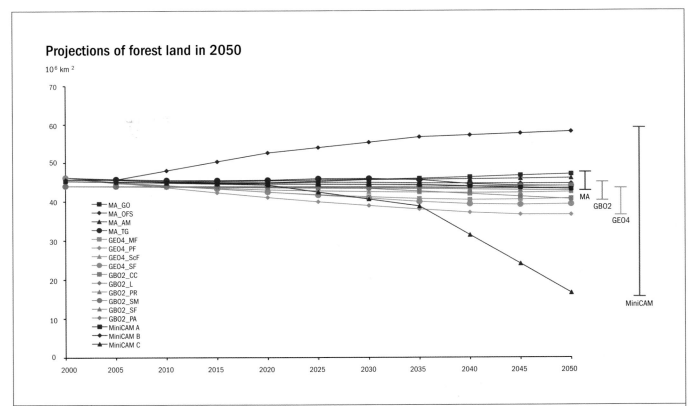

FIGURE 7 PROJECTED CHANGES IN THE EXTENT OF FORESTS TO 2050 IN DIFFERENT GLOBAL SCENARIOS.

Data sources: MA scenarios (Sala et al. 2005), GBO2 scenarios (ten Brink et al. 2007), GEO4 scenarios (UNEP 2007) and MiniCAM scenarios (Wise et al. 2009). For the MA, GBO2 and GEO 4 (all based on IMAGE (Bouwman et al. 2006)), forest includes mature forest, regrowth forest and wood plantations (for timber or carbon sequestration), but excludes woody biofuel crops. The MiniCAM scenarios uses different categories, and forest includes managed and unmanaged forest. The MiniCAM scenarios show that there is a much wider range of possible futures for forest, depending on the policies and societal choices, than had been previously anticipated in other scenario assessments. An increase in forest area can be achieved by increasing crop yields in developing countries, limiting meat consumption, and avoiding large-scale deployment of biofuels.

primarily due to conversion for crop or bioenergy production, or due to climate change (e.g., Figure 3 and Figure 4).

Deforestation is the most important cause of habitat loss at the global scale, so we have used a simple index — the area of natural and semi-natural forest globally — to provide an overview of model-based projections of habitat loss. Most models project loss of forests globally, but some best-case scenarios result in an increase in forest area by 2050 (Figure 7). The relative importance of land use and climate change in driving these losses or gains varies in different scenarios (Figure 3), with climate change growing in importance over time in all scenarios. The strongest negative impacts of land-use change are projected to occur in the tropical forests, while boreal forests will be mainly affected by climate change (Figure 3), although global vegetation modeling studies (see below) and our tipping points analyses suggest that climate change impacts in temperate and tropical forests could be much greater than previous biodiversity assessments have suggested.

The range of habitat loss projections across studies suggests that the differences between future pathways may be much greater than previously anticipated. Within most previous studies, there are relatively small differences in projected forest area change arising from the various socio-economic scenarios (Figure 7, GEO4, GBO2 and MA studies). This has been attributed to compensating mechanisms, two of the most important being related to bioenergy production and agricultural productivity[28]. As discussed above, most "environmentally friendly" socio-economic scenarios achieve only minor reductions in habitat loss in comparison with other development pathways, in part because climate mitigation relies on large-scale deployment of bioenergy production. In contrast, some recent socio-economic scenarios suggest that climate mitigation can be plausibly achieved with modest reliance on bioenergy (Figure 7, miniCAM B). Second, most scenarios require large-scale conversion of natural habitats to croplands, either because crop yield improvements are low or because food consumption rises rapidly[29]. Some recent scenarios suggest that substantially increased crop yields in developing countries is plausible (though this is hotly debated), and when combined with limited meat consumption can substantially reduce the conversion of natural habitats to croplands[30] (Figure 7 — miniCAM B). At the opposite extreme, plausible scenarios combining large-scale deployment of biofuels and rapidly rising food consumption lead to a loss of forests that far exceeds the worst scenarios in previous

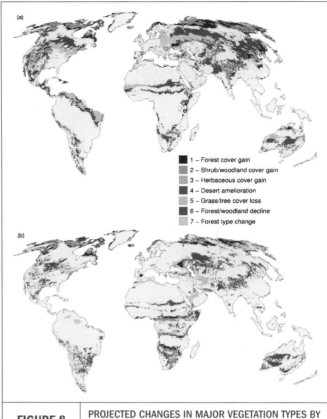

| FIGURE 8 | PROJECTED CHANGES IN MAJOR VEGETATION TYPES BY 2100 DUE TO CLIMATE CHANGE. |

(a) High CO_2 emissions scenario from the IPCC (A1 SRES) and (b) Low emissions scenario (B2 SRES). Vegetation shifts are shown only if they exceed 20% in a given grid cell. Projections done with the LPJ global vegetation model and relative to 2000. Source: Fischlin et al. 2007.

biodiversity assessments (Figure 7 — miniCAM C). One of the key lessons drawn from this analysis is that differences in socio-economic development pathways can have a tremendous impact on habitat loss as well as on biodiversity at other levels, but that the suite of storylines that have been used for most global biodiversity assessments are not well adapted to demonstrating the potential impacts of policy choices on biodiversity.

SHIFTS IN THE DISTRIBUTION OF SPECIES, SPECIES GROUPS AND BIOMES – Shifts in the spatial distribution of species, vegetation types or biomes have been projected at the regional and global scales by a wide range of models, especially niche-based models and global vegetation models that focus on climate change as the main driver. We have not made an exhaustive review of these models and their projections, but have chosen to focus on representative examples of recent work with global vegetation models.

As shown in Figure 8 and Figure 9, climate driven shifts in the ranges of species and biomes could be many 100's of km poleward over the next century. These shifts in the distribution of species, vegetation types or biomes are important biodiversity

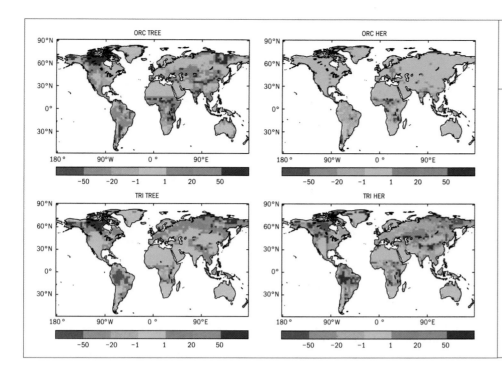

Trees (TREE, panels on the left) and herbaceous species (HER, panels on the right) from 1860 to 2099 based on two global vegetation models that simulate terrestrial vegetation dynamics and ecosystem function (ORC = Orchidee, TRI = Triffid). Colors indicate projected percentage cover changes. These projections are based on scenarios of the highest levels of greenhouse gas emissions considered by the IPCC (SRES A1FI) and use a common climate model. Note that areas in blue or red indicate vegetation shifts that are large enough to be qualified as changes in biome type[109]. For this study, only climate change impacts on vegetation were simulated. Source: Sitch et al. 2008.

changes even when they do not result in substantially increased extinction risk, declining species abundance or net habitat loss. Northern hemisphere forests provide a salient example of the importance of species and biome shifts. Boreal forest species are projected to move northward into arctic tundra as climate warms, and at their southern edge they are projected to die back and give way to temperate conifer or mixed forest species (Figure 8, and see Tundra tipping point in Box 2). These range shifts of boreal species are likely to cause substantial disruptions in the provisioning of key ecosystem services including wood harvests and climate regulation, even though it does not lead to high levels of habitat loss (Figure 4), species extinctions (figure 3 C & D) or reductions in species abundance (Figure 6A). A wide range of studies at regional scales with a broad range of model types all indicate that large scale vegetation shifts are likely to occur in the 21st century due to climate change[31]. The paleontological record clearly demonstrates that past climate change has resulted in large-scale shifts in the distribution of species and vegetation types, and observations indicate that species have been moving poleward and up in altitude in response to climate warming over the last several decades[32].

The primary uncertainty is not whether species and biome range shifts will happen in response to climate change, but rather the rate and extent to which these shifts will occur. These uncertainties have been underestimated in previous global biodiversity assessments. The IMAGE model used in most of these assessments falls in the mid-range of climate sensitivity of global vegetation models, and therefore projects modest climate change impacts

on vegetation distributions (Figure 3, Figure 4). Some other global vegetation models also foresee modest vegetation shifts even under high climate warming scenarios (Figure 9, Orchidee model), but several widely-used models project dramatic vegetation shifts including the collapse of the Amazon forest, large-scale invasion of tundra by boreal forest and widespread dieback at the southern edge of boreal and temperate forest ranges (Figure 8A, Figure 9-Triffid model, and see Box 4 and Box 2). The moderate sensitivity of the IMAGE global vegetation model to climate change means that climate mitigation brings about only modest reductions in biodiversity change in this model. Other widely used, well-tested models suggest that strong climate mitigation is absolutely essential in order to avoid large-scale displacement of species and biomes over the 21st century (compare Figure 8B, based a low greenhouse gas emissions scenario, with Figure 8A, based on a high emissions scenario).

Terrestrial tipping points will hit regions with developing economies the hardest. Most tipping points will be difficult to predict because of the complex interactions between global change factors that drive them, but will have exceptionally large impacts on human well-being if they occur.

The terrestrial tipping points are summarized in Boxes 2 to 8 and described in greater detail in the Appendices. This is not an exhaustive list of terrestrial tipping points: for example many arid systems have tipping points similar to those described for the Sahel, invasive species lead to tipping points in many terrestrial systems other than islands, etc.[33] We have focused on a representative sample of tipping points mediated by a range of global change

BOX 2   ARCTIC TUNDRA*

TIPPING POINT MECHANISMS

Climate warming has been and will be stronger in the Arctic than in other parts of the globe with projected increases of 3°C to 8°C for the Arctic region by the end of the 21st century. Climate warming will cause the widespread melting of permafrost, leading to emissions of very large quantities of greenhouse gases from organic tundra soil. Transformations from tundra to boreal forest are also predicted to decrease albedo (i.e., increase the fraction of light absorbed by the land surface) and change aerosol emissions. These changes in tundra systems are projected to further aggravate regional and global climate warming. Due to lags in the earth system, global warming is predicted to persist for several centuries even if greenhouse gas emissions decline substantially, making this biome shift inevitable and irreversible over the 21st century.

IMPACTS ON BIODIVERSITY AND ECOSYSTEM SERVICES

Experiments, observations and models clearly show that all plausible climate scenarios will lead to continued and widespread increases in dominance of deciduous shrubs in tundra communities and decreases in abundance of herbaceous, bryophyte and lichen species. Most models project that boreal forest will heavily invade tundra over large areas by the end of the century, as has occurred during warm periods in the recent past (e.g., 6000 years BP). The risk of 21st century extinctions is modest given the large, contiguous ranges of many tundra species. Permafrost melting and changes in game availability have already heavily impacted some indigenous populations and these impacts are likely to become widespread and severe over the coming decades.

UNDERSTANDING OF MECHANISMS

High — Processes are generally well understood and modelled, with some notable exceptions such as climate feedbacks from cloud formation and migration rates of boreal forest species.

CERTAINTY IN PROJECTIONS

High — Models, experiments and observations are qualitatively coherent concerning the direction of change. Uncertainty is related to rates and extent of permafrost melting and boreal forest expansion.

KEY ACTIONS

Because of long lags in the earth system we have probably already passed a tipping point for long-term, widespread permafrost degradation and invasion of tundra by boreal forest, but aggressive climate mitigation could slow these processes. Adaptive management to conserve tundra systems is not feasible outside of very small areas. At local scales, grazing by large herbivorous could be managed to reduce the rate of tree encroachment. Relocation of indigenous populations is currently a viable adaptation strategy for preserving traditional livelihoods, but long-term adaptation will require cultural adjustments.

---

* The original text for this tipping point was prepared by Juan Fernandez (Université Paris-Sud XI, juan.fernandez@u-psud.fr) and Paul Leadley (Université Paris-Sud XI, paul.leadley@u-psud.fr) and is available in Appendix 1. Further reading: Bigelow et al. 2003, Folley 2005, Wahren et al. 2005, Lucht et al. 2006, McGuire et al. 2009.

BOX 3   MEDITERRANEAN FOREST*

TIPPING POINT MECHANISMS

Land use scenarios foresee a decrease in cropland due to rural abandonment, and an increase of naturally regenerated vegetation and forest plantations in the Mediterranean region. In addition, climate models project increasing temperatures and decreasing precipitation for the region, leading to more frequent periods of drought and high fire risk as the vegetation becomes more flammable. An increase in fire disturbance due to climate and land use change is projected to lead to the expansion of early successional communities, such as shrublands. Shrublands, in turn, promote the recurrence of fire due to their high flammability.

IMPACTS ON BIODIVERSITY AND ECOSYSTEM SERVICES

Shrublands are species poor compared to natural forests and extensively managed farmland, so this tipping point is projected to lead to a significant reduction in species diversity. Many areas of the Mediterranean region are also currently characterised by a high heterogeneity in land use, leading to high landscape level species diversity, which will be reduced if fire brings about more uniform vegetation cover. Fire associated with expansion of early successional communities will also result in higher costs of fire control and negative impacts on infrastructure and health, as well as reductions in a broad range of regulating ecosystem services such as watershed protection and carbon storage.

UNDERSTANDING OF MECHANISMS

High — This tipping point is already occurring in many areas and the ecological feedback mechanisms in this tipping point are well documented and modelled.

CERTAINTY IN SCENARIOS

Moderate to low — A large majority of climate models predict hotter and drier climates and most land use scenarios project substantial land abandonment for the Mediterranean region. However, changes in forest management are difficult to foresee and will play a determinant role in controlling this tipping point.

KEY ACTIONS

It is important to accelerate natural succession towards native broadleaved forest by adopting appropriate forest management practices. A shift to new forest management paradigms focusing on multifunctional forests is needed to provide multiple ecosystem services and to create forests that are more resistant to fire disturbance than current fire prone plantations. At the same time, it is important to persist in raising public awareness regarding fire prevention and the value of forests in providing a broad range of ecosystem services. At the global scale, climate change mitigation is also important.

---

* The original text for this tipping point was prepared by Vânia Proença (University of Lisbon, vaniaproenca@fc.ul.pt) and Henrique M. Pereira (University of Lisbon, hpereira@fc.ul.pt) and is available in Appendix 2. Further reading: Schroter et al. 2005, Vallejo et al. 2006, Palahi et al. 2008, Pausas et al. 2008.

BOX 4 | AMAZONIAN FOREST*

TIPPING POINT MECHANISMS

Two interacting tipping points could result in widespread dieback of humid tropical forest in the Amazon. 1) Forest conversion to agricultural land and burning alter regional rainfall and increase drought. Forest fragmentation and drought are projected to increase the susceptibility of forests to fire and dieback, leading to a vicious cycle in which fire and dieback become widespread. 2) Some climate models project substantial reductions in rainfall for the Amazon. Reduced rainfall combined with rising temperatures result in forest dieback and reduced transfer of water to the atmosphere in some vegetation models, setting off feedbacks that lead to a drier climate in which humid tropical forest is permanently replaced by shrub and grass dominated vegetation. A recent study of the combined impacts of these two processes suggests that parts of the Amazon may already be close to a forest dieback tipping point.

IMPACTS ON BIODIVERSITY AND ECOSYSTEM SERVICES

The Amazon forest, especially at its western edge, is one of the most species rich areas of the world. Widespread dieback of humid tropical forest would lead to much higher reductions in species abundance and extinctions of plants and animals than foreseen in previous global biodiversity assessments. Moreover, widespread fires and forest dieback could lead to massive degradation of sustaining and regulating ecosystem services, such as losses of carbon stored in vegetation and soils that would be large enough to significantly influence atmospheric CO_2 concentrations and global climate.

UNDERSTANDING OF MECHANISMS

Moderate – Many of the biophysical mechanisms are reasonably well understood, but the response of forests to drought and fire less so. Some observations and experiments lead credence to predictions of dieback, but others suggest that humid tropic forest is less sensitive to drought than some models predict. The response of forests to rising CO_2 is a critical determinant of projected dieback, but is not well understood.

CERTAINTY IN PROJECTIONS

Moderate to Low – There is substantial uncertainty in the land use tipping point mechanism, but several modeling studies suggest there is a significant risk of dieback when deforestation exceeds 20% – 40% of original forest area. For the global climate change mechanism, there are large differences between climate and vegetation models concerning future precipitation regimes and impacts on forests.

KEY ACTIONS

A precautionary approach would suggest that deforestation should not exceed 20% of original forest area, fire for clearing should be minimized and global climate warming should be kept below 2°C in order to avoid this tipping point. This will require concerted efforts to implement sustainable agricultural practices, establish large protected areas, reduce of national and global pressures for increased meat and feed production, etc. Application of REDD+ initiatives could lead to a win-win situation for biodiversity and climate if appropriately implemented. As current trends will likely take cumulative deforestation to 20% of the Brazilian Amazon at or near 2020, a programme of significant forest restoration would be a prudent measure to build in a margin of safety.

* The original text for this tipping point was prepared by Carlos Nobre (Instituto Nacional de Pesquisas Espaciais, nobre@cptec.inpe.br), Paul Leadley (Université Paris-Sud XI, paul.leadley@u-psud.fr) and Juan Fernandez (Université Paris-Sud XI, paul.leadley@u-psud.fr) and is available in Appendix 3. Further reading: Betts et al. 2008, Malhi et al. 2008, Nepstad et al. 2008, Nobre and Borma 2009. World Bank. 2010.

---

drivers. We discuss below some of the common lessons that can be drawn from the analysis of these tipping points.

UNCERTAINTIES ARE HIGH FOR MOST TERRESTRIAL TIPPING POINTS, BUT THE POTENTIAL CONSEQUENCES OF INACTION ARE GREAT – Of the terrestrial tipping points we examined, only the Arctic Tundra tipping point is widely accepted as highly likely to occur and to affect very large areas. This high confidence is based on the strong coherence of evidence provided by experiments, observations and models. There is little doubt that the Coastal sea level rise tipping point will occur as there is very good evidence that sea level is rising and will continue to do so. However, the extent of the areas affected and the degree of impacts on biodiversity and ecosystem services will depend on several factors with high uncertainty (e.g., sea level rise, sedimentation rates, land use, etc). Projections of future sea level rise have recently been revised upwards[34], leaving little hope that the extent of the areas heavily impacted will be small. The invasive species tipping point is ongoing and nearly linear trends in naturalized invasives on islands over the last 100–150 years suggest that there is not much hope in stopping invasions in the near future, resulting in large

impacts on global species extinctions. The Mediterranean tipping point will almost certainly occur in the future in the absence of good land use management, because it has already occurred in the past in some areas with negative impacts on biodiversity and local ecosystem services. However, the extent of areas affected by these tipping points in the future is difficult to forecast because of the importance of land management decisions in controlling them. The West Africa tipping point for land degradation has already been passed on several occasions with dramatic consequences for human well-being. There are, however, very large uncertainties concerning the future of this tipping point because of diametrically opposed climate model projections of rainfall and because the evolution of governance is exceptionally difficult to foresee for this region. There is relatively high uncertainty concerning the Amazon tipping point, but if the widespread dieback of the Amazonian forest occurred over the course of the next several decades it would have overwhelming large negative impacts on biodiversity, regional rainfall and global climate. One of the most uncertain is the Miombo tipping point, but the high potential for extremely large impacts on species and habitat loss in the near future make this region of great concern.

BOX 5	WEST AFRICA: THE SAHARA, SAHEL AND GUINEAN REGION*

TIPPING POINT MECHANISMS

Coupled human-environment systems in West Africa, extending from the southern Sahara, down through the Sahel and into the Guinean Forest, are vulnerable to three strongly interacting tipping points. 1) "Desertification" processes in the semi-arid portions of this region are driven by the overuse of marginally productive lands leading to degradation in vegetation and soils that is difficult to reverse. 2) Models suggest that regional climate is highly unstable, and models variously project a switch to either drier or wetter regimes as a result of global warming. 3) Social and political instability promotes the unregulated use of natural resources and drives human migrations to regions already under environmental stress, often triggering further social and political disruption. Together, these processes can set off vicious cycles in which drought, overuse of resources and political instability has led and is projected to lead to widespread land degradation, destruction of natural habitats and catastrophic impacts on human well-being. At the other extreme, virtuous cycles set off by favourable climate, good governance and improved agricultural practices have led and could continue to lead to a reversal of land degradation, reduced impacts on natural habitats and improvements in human well-being.

IMPACTS ON BIODIVERSITY AND ECOSYSTEM SERVICES

Many studies have documented the reduction in species richness due to land degradation in the semi-arid areas of this region, as well as the tremendous difficulty of restoring lands once they have been degraded due to soil compaction, erosion and salinization. In addition, land use scenarios for this area foresee very large rates of land use conversion in the next several decades, in particular the destruction of highly diverse Guinean forests that are characterized by high endemism (e.g., 38% of amphibians and 21% of mammals are endemic). Ecosystems in this region are a major source of environmental capital for local populations as most local economies are based on direct exploitation of ecosystems. Therefore, ecosystem degradation will have direct negative impacts on human well being.

UNDERSTANDING OF MECHANISMS

Moderate to low – Land degradation and habitat destruction in this region are occurring and the mechanisms are well documented. The regional climate tipping point mechanism and social processes are complex and difficult to model

CERTAINTY IN PROJECTIONS

Low – The complexity of the interactions between drivers, diametrically opposed climate projections and high political instability make the future of this region very uncertain, even though a large number of people could be affected.

KEY ACTIONS

Strategies for improving governance often fail due to political instability and conflict, but are urgently needed to limit unregulated use of natural resources including inside protected areas. International regulations should control the international demand for local resources, thus diminishing the unregulated exporting of raw products and supporting non-destructive use of biodiversity. REDD+ initiatives could help protect Guinean forests if appropriately implemented.

* The original text for this tipping point was prepared by Cheikh Mbow (Université Cheikh Anta Diop, cmbow@ucad.sn), Mark Stafford Smith (CSIRO, mark.staffordsmith@csiro.au) and Paul Leadley (Université Paris-Sud XI, paul.leadley@u-psud.fr) and is available in Appendix 4. Further reading: Ludeke et al. 2004, African Environmental Outlook 2 2006, Cooke and Vizy 2006, Reynolds et al. 2007, Mbow et al. 2008.

MOST OF THE TERRESTRIAL TIPPING-POINTS RESULT FROM COMPLEX MECHANISMS AND INTERACTIONS THAT ARE NOT ACCOUNTED FOR IN MODELS – Sala et al. (2005) identified interactions between a broad range of global change drivers as one of the most important unknowns in modeling future biodiversity changes. However, models treat only a small range of global change drivers and rely on methods that, at best, only partially account for interactions between drivers. Of the tipping points that we have identified, only the Tundra tipping point is reasonably well accounted for in models, because it depends almost entirely on interactions between global climate change, broad vegetation shifts and physical and greenhouse gas feedbacks to global climate, which are processes incorporated in many models (Figure 8 and Figure 9). One of the Amazon tipping point mechanims, is rarely accounted for in global models (but see Figure 9, Triffid), because most models do not account for dynamic feedbacks between vegetation and regional climate. Fire and its interactions with land management are key drivers of several of the tipping points (see the Amazon, Mediterranean, Miombo, and West Africa tipping points). For example, several global and regional models include fire[35], but accounting for its interaction with land management remains a difficult task. Invasive species are rarely accounted for in biodiversity scenarios even though they have large impacts on biodiversity in many terrestrial ecosystems[36] and are one of the main drivers of biodiversity loss on islands. Governance, or lack thereof, plays a critical role in all of the tipping points. Sensible regulation of construction in coastal areas would limit some of the impact of sea level rise on biodiversity; regional land use planning could help strike a balance between the need for provisioning services on one hand and biodiversity conservation on the other hand, etc. This type of local and regional governance is exceptionally difficult to include in global models, but is often the key to avoiding many of the tipping points. These and multiple other examples in our tipping points analyses show that we are far from having a predictive understanding of most tipping points. This does not mean that we are unable to foresee these tipping points with some confidence: it does, however, mean that we often cannot provide decision makers with quantitative thresholds beyond which the system is likely to switch to an undesirable state.

AVOIDING TIPPING POINT CATASTROPHES REQUIRES CONCERTED ACTION AT LOCAL TO GLOBAL SCALES – Strong local intervention is necessary to avoid passing thresholds

before & after: Robert Höft

BOX 6 | MIOMBO WOODLANDS*

TIPPING POINT MECHANISMS

The belt of moist savannas, the 'miombo woodlands', stretching south of the Congo rainforests from Angola to Tanzania, is one of the largest remaining near-intact ecosystems in the world. Socio-economic and ecological tipping points will be key determinants of the future of these savannas. 1) If population growth exceeds economic growth over the next few decades, it is projected that the region will be trapped in a vicious cycle of agricultural extensification and poverty resulting in widespread destruction of miombo woodlands. A virtuous cycle of sustainable intensification of agriculture and poverty alleviation could minimize destruction, and is foreseeable if strong economic growth and good governance occur soon. 2) Miombo ecosystems are also characterized by high instability in tree cover, where climate change, rising CO_2, and altered fire regimes and herbivory could shift these savannas, which are grasslands with sparse woody cover, to dense forest.

IMPACTS ON BIODIVERSITY AND ECOSYSTEM SERVICES

The miombo biome is vast (over 3 million km^2), harbours about 8500 plant species and is characterised by a high level of endemism. All MA and GEO4 socio-economic scenarios foresee massive miombo woodland conversion to agriculture in the next few decades, making it the area of the world that is projected to be most heavily impacted by land use change. Land use change is projected to cause very high rates of extinctions of vertebrates and plants and reduce the abundance of a wide range of species characteristic of woodlands by more than 20% by 2050. In addition, climate change and rising CO_2 are generally projected to increase tree cover and decrease the abundance of grasses in areas not converted to agriculture. These changes in land cover will have large negative impacts on ecosystem services such as carbon storage, and water supply which is expected to become more variable and of lower quality.

UNDERSTANDING OF MECHANISMS

Moderate to Low—The "poverty trap" at the root of the socio-economic tipping point is well described, but its causes and impacts on land use are complex. The mechanisms that maintain the delicate tree-grass balance of savannas are reasonably well understood, but modelling the key drivers, fire and large herbivores, remains difficult.

CERTAINTY IN PROJECTIONS

Low—The land use tipping point is highly dependant on the relative rates of population vs. economic growth that cannot be projected with confidence far into the future. Many global vegetation models project an increase in tree cover for this region, but the degree and extent of change vary greatly.

KEY ACTIONS

Moderate and sustainable intensification of agriculture coupled with good land-use planning that includes large protected areas should allow biodiversity and ecosystem services to be preserved, while also making great strides in alleviating poverty. Application of REDD+ initiatives in miombo woodland could be win-win for biodiversity and climate if appropriately implemented. Education, large improvements in agriculture and good governance are keys to avoiding this tipping point, with projections suggesting that the window of opportunity for altering the trajectory of land conversion this region is rapidly closing.

---

* The original text for this tipping point was prepared by Robert J Scholes (Council for Scientific and Industrial Research, bscholes@csir.co.za)and Reinette Biggs (Stockholm Resilience Centre, oonsie.biggs@stockholmresilience.su.se) and is available in Appendix 5. Further reading: Frost et al. 1996, Desanker et al. 1997, Scholes and Biggs 2004, Biggs et al. 2008.

---

for most tipping points. The very large range of local actions needed makes them difficult to summarize. However, using well known sustainable land management practices and sound land use planning would go a long way in alleviating local pressures in most tipping points. For example, moderate, but sustainable intensification of agriculture and good spatial planning of agricultural and conservation areas in Miombo woodlands could improve human wellbeing and preserve biodiversity. Putting these simple ideas into action is socially and economically complex because they rely on improved education, good governance, poverty reduction, etc and constructive changes in global pressures on national and local economics and policy[37].

Local action must be combined with global action to avoid passing thresholds for most tipping points. Global climate change is of particular importance since it is a key driver in many of the tipping points; however, clearly defined thresholds can only be identified for a few examples. The tundra system has probably already passed its climate tipping point, but models strongly suggest that climate mitigation could play a major role in reducing the rate and extent of biome shifts at high latitudes. The Amazon has a global warming tipping point may be as low as 2°C, so climate change could push the Amazonian forest beyond its threshold despite strong national and local efforts to limit deforestation. In other systems, climate change plays an important role, but has complex interactions with other drivers making it difficult to identify thresholds. Clearly, the most reasonable course of action is to limit climate change through strong international policy. Other coordinated international efforts must be enhanced to limit the exchange of potentially invasive species, improve agricultural practices especially in developing countries, support the conservation and sustainable use of forests, etc.

Scenarios suggest that provisioning of food and fiber will often continue to increase at the expense of many other ecosystem services and biodiversity. Beyond certain thresholds, however, global change is projected to cause dramatic degradation of biodiversity and all types of ecosystem services.

The idea that biodiversity is related to human wellbeing through ecosystem services is an extremely powerful framework for demonstrating to the public and policy makers that biodiversity matters[38]. A

TIPPING POINT MECHANISMS

The introduction of a small number of individuals of key invasive species (e.g., cats, rats, snakes, goats, a wide variety of plant species, etc.), followed by the expansion of their populations (referred to as "naturalization") has and will continue to cause severe degradation of biodiversity and ecosystem services on islands. Island systems are particularly vulnerable to invasive species because the biota of these insular communities evolves in isolation and often lack defences against external pathogens, competitors, and predators. In addition, invasive species can trigger a cascading set of extinctions and ecosystem instabilities, making islands even more vulnerable to succeeding invasions. To make matters worse, most invasive species are costly and difficult to eradicate once they have become established and their eradication can often have unexpected negative effects on biodiversity and ecosystem services.

IMPACTS ON BIODIVERSITY AND ECOSYSTEM SERVICES

Species dispersion and establishment in new habitats is a natural process, but the current rates of human-caused geographic translocation of plants and animals have reached unprecedented levels. In the short term, the co-existence of invasives and native species increases species richness on most islands. However, invasive predators often eliminate local fauna — with a particularly heavy toll on birds. Because islands are the global hotspot for endemic species local eliminations often constitute global extinctions. Of the roughly 90 documented vertebrate extinctions that can be attributed to invasive species worldwide, more than 70 occurred on islands. Plants are much less susceptible to extinction, but all recorded global extinctions due to invasives have been on islands. There are few projections of invasions on islands, but the lack of control of biotic exchange and the high number of latent populations of invaders is projected to lead to a continuation of the current linear increase in the number of naturalized invasive plant species on islands. There is also concern that many island plant and animal endemics are "condemned to extinction" due to long-term effects of invasives on their populations. A wide variety of studies have illustrated large negative impacts of many invasive species on ecosystem services such as plant productivity, nutrient cycling, water supply, etc.

UNDERSTANDING OF MECHANISMS

Moderate — Many of the worst animal invaders are relatively well known, but the pathways of introduction are not fully understood, especially for plants. Eradication efforts too often lead to unpleasant surprises due to a lack of understanding of community dynamics.

CERTAINTY IN PROJECTIONS

Moderate — Current trends and projected increases in globalization leave little reason to believe that invasions on islands can be controlled in the near future.

KEY ACTIONS

Management options consist of two main approaches, the prevention of species invasion, which requires a strong effort in the identification and regulation of potential invasion pathways, and the control or eradication of invasive species, which is not always effective due to the difficulty of effectively removing established invasive species.

---

* The original text for this tipping point was prepared by Michael Jennings (University of Idaho, jennings@ uidaho.edu). A long description of this tipping point prepared by Stas Burgiel (Global Invasive Species Programme, s.burgiel@gisp.org) is available in Appendix 6. Further reading: Mooney et al. 2005, Nentwig 2007, Sax and Gaines 2008.

---

new study on "The Economics of Ecosystems and Biodiversity" (TEEB) is beginning to provide concrete illustrations of the link between biodiversity, ecosystem services and economics and we refer the reader to TEEB documents for excellent case studies of the value of biodiversity and related ecosystem services[39]. Below we provide an overview of the key issues related to projections of biodiversity and ecosystem services.

NOT ALL ECOSYSTEM SERVICES RESPOND IN THE SAME WAY TO CHANGES IN BIODIVERSITY. — Nearly all scenarios suggest that provisioning services such as food and fiber production cannot be met for large and growing human populations without converting natural habitats to croplands or managed forests[40]. Historically this has often come at the cost of reductions in species abundance, increased risk of species extinctions and degradation in other ecosystem services, particularly regulating services such as nutrient retention, clean water supply, soil erosion control and ecosystem carbon storage[41]. A new quantitative analysis of projections from IMAGE and GLOBIO models suggests that this tradeoff is likely to continue at the global scale, using as an example the relationship between species abundance,

agricultural productivity and a key regulating service, ecosystem carbon storage (Figure 10). For the "business as usual" development pathway, agricultural productivity is projected to go up as the abundance of species characteristic of natural systems and carbon storage go down. Regulating services that are dependent on the configuration or spatial pattern of the landscape, for example pest control or pollination, show more complex relationships. For these services a mixture of natural vegetation and agricultural land seems to be optimal[42]. Cultural services may also have a complex relationship with biodiversity, as some of these services[43], such as recreation are related to human access, which can in turn have a negative effect on biodiversity[44].

PUSHING TERRESTRIAL SYSTEMS PAST THRESHOLDS COULD RESULT IN LARGE NEGATIVE IMPACTS ON BIODIVERSITY AND A WIDE RANGE OF ECOSYSTEM SERVICES. — Our terrestrial tipping points analyses suggest the tradeoffs between provisioning services, biodiversity and other ecosystem services are viable only up to certain thresholds. There is a high risk of dramatic biodiversity loss and accompanying degradation of a broad range of ecosystem services if terrestrial systems are pushed beyond these thresholds.

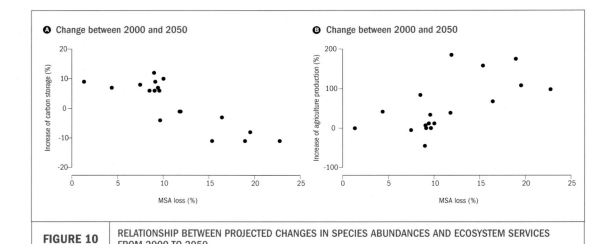

| FIGURE 10 | RELATIONSHIP BETWEEN PROJECTED CHANGES IN SPECIES ABUNDANCES AND ECOSYSTEM SERVICES FROM 2000 TO 2050. |

A) Projected changes in ecosystem carbon storage (a regulating service)[110] versus projected changes in Mean Species Abundance (MSA) (r = -0.84). B) Projected changes in agricultural productivity (estimated using net primary productivity) versus projected changes in MSA (r = 0.63). MSA was calculated using the GLOBIO model (Alkemade et al. 2009) and ecosystem services using the IMAGE model (Bouwman et al. 2006). Each point corresponds to a world region in the IMAGE model. All projections are based on the scenario for the OECD Environmental Outlook (OECD 2008).

Combinations of deforestation, fire and global climate change in the Amazon could lead to forest dieback, massive species extinctions, increased global warming, and regional reductions in rainfall that could compromise the sustainability of regional agriculture (Box 4). Rapid sea level rise accompanied by habitat conversion could lead to a substantial increase in the degradation of coastal ecosystems and biodiversity, making coasts more vulnerable to erosion and reducing the productivity of coastal marine systems (Box 8). Interactions between climate, land-use and social dynamics have and could continue to cause loss of biodiversity and shortages of food, fiber and water in the Sahel region of Western Africa (Box 5). This same mix of drivers may promote wildfires leading to ecosystem change and degradation in the Mediterranean Basin (Box 3) and African Miombo Woodlands (Box 6). In all cases, feedbacks and long time lags could make these transitions essentially irreversible over decades to centuries. All of these scenarios indicate that excessive pressure on ecosystems to increase provisioning services may actually shift the system into a state where the provisioning services themselves are compromised.

PROVISIONING, SUPPORTING AND REGULATING SERVICES MUST NOT BE OVERSOLD AS THE SOLE MOTIVATION FOR CONSERVING BIODIVERSITY. – We have identified, especially in our tipping points analyses, a number of win-win situations in which the protection of biodiversity goes hand-in-hand with the protection of key provisioning and regulating services. However, in cases where important thresholds are not passed, there are many scenarios in which biodiversity conservation does not result in such win-win solutions[45]. We use a study of the links between global conservation strategies and ecosystem services to illustrate

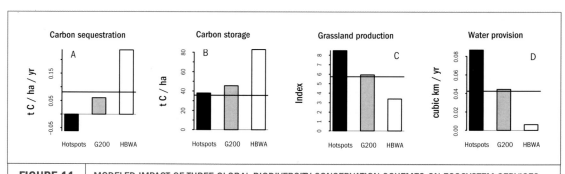

| FIGURE 11 | MODELED IMPACT OF THREE GLOBAL BIODIVERSITY CONSERVATION SCHEMES ON ECOSYSTEM SERVICES. |

The "Hotspots" conservation scheme focuses on global biodiversity hotspots, the "G200" scheme focuses on conserving representative ecoregions of the world and the "HBWA" scheme focuses on high-biodiversity wilderness areas. (A) Carbon sequestration. (B) Carbon storage. (C) Grassland production of livestock. (D) Water provision. Horizontal lines represent the global mean for each service. Values for ecosystem services are per unit area within protected areas. Source: Naidoo et al. 2008. Copyright (2008) National Academy of Sciences, U.S.A.

TIPPING POINT MECHANISM

Based on monitoring, experiments and modelling, sea level rise may be the greatest future threat to tidal wetlands and beaches. A tipping-point occurs when the surface elevation of a coastal ecosystem does not keep pace with the rise in sea-level; i.e., the balance between sea-level rise and sedimentation rates results in flooding. When this tipping-point occurs, the coastal ecosystem can be rapidly reduced in area to a point where it is reduced to a narrow fringe or is lost. Additional non-climate stressors on coastal ecosystems, such as reduction of sediments reaching coastal zones due to dams, changes in river beds, etc., and pollution increase the vulnerability of coastal ecosystems to sea-level rise. Earth system models project sea level rise of 20–60 cm or more by the end of the century, and that sea level rise will continue for many centuries after all CO_2 emissions have ceased.

IMPACTS ON BIODIVERSITY AND ECOSYSTEM SERVICES

Rising seas will likely have the greatest impacts on coastal wetlands experiencing net reductions in sediment elevation, and where there is limited area for landward migration due to the physiographic setting or obstacles from urban development. The impacts on biodiversity will be large due to the loss of nesting, nursery and forage habitat for numerous species groups, including fish, shellfish, seabirds, waterbirds, sea turtles, crocodiles, manatees and dugongs. For example, the majority of mangrove sites studied have not been keeping pace with current rates of relative sea-level rise. As a result, sea level rise is projected to contribute to 10 to 20% of total estimated losses of mangroves on Pacific Islands by the end this century. Reduced coastal ecosystem area and condition will increase coastal hazards to human settlements, reduce coastal water quality, release large quantities of stored carbon, etc.

UNDERSTANDING OF MECHANISMS

High to medium—The mechanisms of sea-rise due to thermal expansion of seawater and glacial melt are understood well enough to predict the direction and to a lesser extent the rate of sea-level rise, including a very small probability of catastrophic (several meter) sea-level rise by the end

of the century. Some mechanisms driving sedimentation rates are well understood, others less so.

CERTAINTY IN PROJECTIONS

High—Sea level rise is already occurring and causing damage in low-lying regions, and all trends and models point to increasing impacts over the coming century. Uncertainties concern the rate and extent to which damage to coastal ecosystems will occur.

KEY ACTIONS

Resistance and resilience of coastal ecosystems to rising seas can be improved through coastal planning to facilitate landward migration, 'no regrets' reduction of addition stressors, including catchment management to minimize disturbance to sedimentation processes, rehabilitation of degraded areas and increases in protected areas that include functionally linked coastal ecosystems. At the global level, aggressive climate change mitigation measures are essential. Establishing coastal ecosystem monitoring will enable a better understanding of coastal ecosystem responses to sea level rise and global climate change.

---

* The original text for this tipping point was prepared by Eric Gilman (Global Biodiversity Information Facility Secretariat, egilman@gbif.org) and Joanna C. Ellison (University of Tasmania, joanna.ellison@utas.edu.au) and is available in Appendix 7. Further reading: Morris et al. 2002, Cahoon et al. 2006, Gilman et al. 2008.

---

this point (Figure 11). Global conservation priority schemes that focus low-human density wilderness areas are predicted to result in improved benefits to the global community through increased carbon storage and sequestration (Figure 11-HBWA). At the other extreme, focusing conservation efforts on densely populated biodiversity hotspots does a much poorer job of serving the global community in terms of carbon storage and sequestration, but a much better job of ensuring water provision and grassland production of livestock that benefit local communities (Figure 11–Hotspots). Conservation strategies must be motivated by examining a broad range of ecosystem services including cultural services related to aesthetic, spiritual, etc. values of biodiversity. Sustainable conservation will depend on ensuring an appropriate and socially acceptable balance between a full set of services.

THE ABUNDANCE AND DISTRIBUTION OF KEYSTONE SPECIES, FUNCTIONAL SPECIES GROUPS AND BIOMES PROVIDES THE CLEAREST LINK BETWEEN TERRESTRIAL BIODIVERSITY AND REGULATING AND PROVISIONING SERVICES. – Links between the reduction of species richness within communities and ecosystem services have been demonstrated, but only at small spatial and

temporal scales for a limited range of ecosystems and ecosystem services. Yet, we are currently unable to scale up these relationships to regional or global levels or use them in projections[46], and therefore we do not have enough information to address general relationships between species loss and ecosystem services.

"Keystone species" are species or groups of species that play particular roles in controlling ecosystem services. Some of the most important keystone species groups are predators such as large carnivores; mutualists such as pollinators; and species that play the role of "engineers" in ecosystems by modifying their structure and functioning such as dominant plant species. Human activities have disproportionately large impacts on some of these groups, especially large terrestrial predators and mutualists. For example, a decline in the diversity and abundance of pollinators has been detected in several regions in the world, for example the decline of honeybees in North America and bumbles in Europe. Pollinators play a key role in maintaining species diversity and functioning in natural ecosystems, but are also responsible for the pollination of many crops. At global scales expected reductions in total global food production derived from pollination decline range from 3 to 8% and with a loss of between 190 and 310 billion dollars per year[47].

A wide variety of analyses with process-based ecosystem models (e.g., GVMs) show that major changes in the abundance or distribution of plant functional types due to land use or climate change will significantly alter river flow, regional rainfall, fire regimes, ecosystem carbon storage, global climate, etc[48]. The effects of major transformations of terrestrial vegetation types are overwhelmingly larger than the reductions in species richness per se. We have relied heavily on global vegetation modeling studies in our tipping points analyses to make the link between biodiversity and regulating services (see especially the Amazon and Tundra tipping points). Similarly, much of the economic valuation of the impact of global change on terrestrial ecosystem services has focused on major ecosystem transformations characterized by changes in key plant or animal species, functional species groups or vegetation types as opposed to changes in species richness or species extinctions[49].

Scenarios where a proactive, sustainable attitude towards the environment is used have greater success in halting biodiversity loss and negative changes in ecosystem services.

LAND MUST BE USED MORE EFFICIENTLY TO FEED, HOUSE, CLOTHE AND PROVIDE ENERGY FOR THE WORLD'S POPULATION. — Current trends and model projections all agree that land use is and will remain the most important driver of changes in biodiversity and ecosystem services. Improving agricultural yields using sustainable best-practices, reducing post-harvest losses, modifying diets to include fewer animal products, and widely applying sustainable forestry practices are essential to decrease habitat loss and preserve biodiversity. In addition, promoting lower human population growth reduces the pressure on land. The strongest pressures on land are projected to be in the tropics, so particular attention must be paid to alleviating local, national and international pressures on land use in these regions.

MITIGATION OF CLIMATE CHANGE IS URGENT. — If greenhouse gas emissions are maintained at current levels, virtually all models project extremely large negative impacts on biodiversity and ecosystem services. Extensive shifts in the ranges of species and biomes and tipping points are likely to occur near or even before the 2°C global warming target suggested by the IPCC. However, considerably more attention must be given to the side effects of climate change mitigation strategies on biodiversity and ecosystem services other than climate regulation[50]. In particular, avoiding extensive cultivation of bio-energy crops is essential for minimizing habitat destruction and species loss. Plausible development pathways suggest that the opportunities for climate mitigation without large-scale deployment of biofuels are much greater than previously anticipated. This is partially due to the fact that massive deployment of biofuels may be counterproductive for reducing GHG emissions goals because of direct and indirect impacts on habitat that cause terrestrial carbon emissions[51].

PAYMENTS FOR ECOSYSTEM SERVICES MAY HELP TO PROTECT BIODIVERSITY IF APPROPRIATELY APPLIED. — Initiatives such as REDD (reduced deforestation and degradation), which aims to keep carbon out the atmosphere by protecting intact tropical forests through avoided deforestation, are good examples of how payments for ecosystem services could help conserve biodiversity[52]. However, such schemes must be applied with considerable caution since protecting ecosystem services and conserving biodiversity are not the same thing, and can sometimes be conflicting, particularly when only a narrow set of ecosystem services is considered.

PROTECTED AREAS, COMBINED WITH EFFECTIVE PROTECTION MEASURES WILL BE A KEY COMPONENT OF BIODIVERSITY CONSERVATION. — Observations and models strongly agree that protected areas, if properly managed, are one of the most effective ways to protect terrestrial biodiversity. Species and biome shifts due to climate change will raise serious challenges for protected areas, and requires broad regional visions of where efforts should be placed and how networks of protected areas will function. In addition to reinforcing the global network of protected areas, the management of biodiversity in human dominated landscape needs greater attention, in part because of the vital role that these systems will play as corridors between protected areas and as harbors of biodiversity, especially as species and communities migrate due to climate change[53, 54].

THERE ARE OPPORTUNITIES FOR 'REWILDING' LANDSCAPES IN SOME REGIONS. — For example, farmland abandonment will free about 20 million ha by 2050 in Europe under scenarios that do not include large-scale deployment of biofuel production[55]. Pilot projects suggest that some of this area could be used to recreate self-sustaining ecosystems with little need for further human intervention. Ecological restoration including managing fire regimes, supporting succession pathways and reintroducing large herbivores and carnivores, will be important in creating these self-sustaining ecosystems.

BOX 9	SNOW AND GLACIER MELT*

TIPPING POINT MECHANISM

Climate change is altering freshwater ecosystems that depend on snowpack and glacial meltwater, and these effects are projected to accelerate over the coming century. Globally, the majority of glaciers are shrinking and annual snowpacks persist for less time due to climate change. Observations and models suggest that global warming impacts on glacier and snow-fed streams and rivers will pass through two contrasting phases. In a first phase, stream and river flow will generally increase due to intensified melting. In a second phase, a threshold is crossed when snowfields melt so early and glaciers have shrunken to the point that late-summer stream flow is severely reduced. Streams and rivers fed by glaciers and snowpacks near their altitudinal limits are projected to experience large reductions in late-summer stream flow in the next few decades.

IMPACTS ON BIODIVERSITY AND ECOSYSTEM SERVICES

In the phase of increased stream-flow, the overall diversity and abundance of species may increase. However, changes in water temperature and stream-flow are projected to have negative impacts on narrow range endemics, such as cold water adapted fish. The second phase of reduced late-summer stream flow is projected to have much broader negative impacts on freshwater species, particularly in headwaters because species will be unable to shift their ranges to suitable habitats. Changes in stream and river-flow are likely to have a large range of highly negative impacts on ecosystem services when late-summer flows become undependable.

UNDERSTANDING OF MECHANISMS

High to moderate – Climate change impacts on glacier melt are relatively well understood, although feedbacks that accelerate glacial sliding are not fully understood. Projections of species responses are based on empirical models that account for only a few of the mechanisms driving species diversity and distributions.

CERTAINTY IN PROJECTIONS

High to Moderate – It is difficult to predict the fate of some glaciers, especially where increased snowfall could counterbalance melting. There is high certainty that changes in snow and glacier melt will impact freshwater diversity, but species-specific responses are uncertain.

KEY ACTIONS

Addressing climate change and reducing green house gases is paramount, but for freshwater ecosystems minimizing additional non-climate stressors, such as dams, pollution, water extraction and habitat loss, is just as important as it reduces the vulnerability of aquatic ecosystems and species. Assisted migration should be considered when species are at risk of global extinction.

---

* The original text for this tipping point was prepared by James C. Robertson (The Nature Conservancy, jrobertson@tnc.org) and Carmen Revenga (The Nature Conservancy, crevenga@tnc.org). Further reading: Poff et al. 2002, Lemke et al. 2007.

FRESHWATER SYSTEMS

Scenarios and projection of recent trends suggest that a combination of climate change, water withdrawal, pollution, invasive species, and dam construction will further deteriorate the current state of freshwater biodiversity. The particular vulnerability of freshwater species to global changes reflects the fact that both fish and freshwater are resources that have been heavily managed.

Scenarios for freshwater biodiversity are limited compared to terrestrial and marine biodiversity. Global scenarios tend to address water resources for people, but rarely include models of freshwater biodiversity[56]. Those that do, model a limited number of drivers and lack or treat only qualitatively major drivers such as dam construction, eutrophication and invasive species[57].

Habitat loss and/or fragmentation are among the greatest threats to biodiversity worldwide, and this certainly holds true for riverine fish. It is almost certain that disturbances to freshwater ecosystems, such as dams, reservoirs and diversions for irrigation and industry, will endanger or extinguish many freshwater fish species in the future, by creating physical barriers to normal movements and migration of the biota and by decreasing habitat availability[58].

Currently it is difficult to make precise predictions about how climate change will affect fish biodiversity, however climate niche modelling suggests that locally the number of warm-water species may increase in temperate areas even as some cryophil (i.e. cold-water) species may regionally vanish[59]. Narrow endemic riverine fishes can be particularly threatened by climate change[60]. The biggest problems occur in basins which have an East-West configuration, while in basins with a North-South configuration, there will be more opportunities for migration and adaptation, as long as the rivers are not blocked by dams. Models also project that in shallow lakes in northern latitudes there will be summer fish kills of cold-water species due to both increased water temperatures and decreased dissolved oxygen[61]. Other negative impacts of climate change on freshwater ecosystems are changes in snow melt timing and flow volumes (Box 9).

Global climate scenarios have been applied to known relationships between fish diversity and river discharge[62]. Results predict decreased freshwater biodiversity in about 15% of the world's rivers in 2100 (Figures 12 and 13) from a combination of reduced run-off (caused by climate change) and increased water withdrawals for human use. However, these predictions should be considered with great caution, as the approach does not provide true extinction rates but

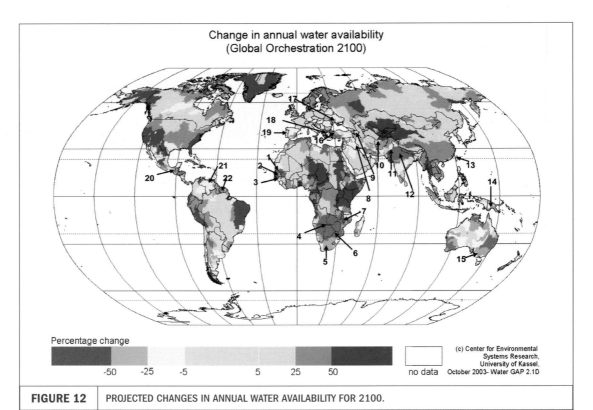

FIGURE 12   PROJECTED CHANGES IN ANNUAL WATER AVAILABILITY FOR 2100.

Percentage changes in annual water availability for each river basin, projected for the Global Orchestration Scenario using the Water GAP model. A negative change (red to yellow) means that a region is drying, while a positive change (green) means that a region is becoming wetter. Numbers indicate the location of river basins used in Figure 13. Source: Sala et al. 2005. © Center for Environmental Systems Research. University of Kassel. October 2003-Water GAP 2.1D.

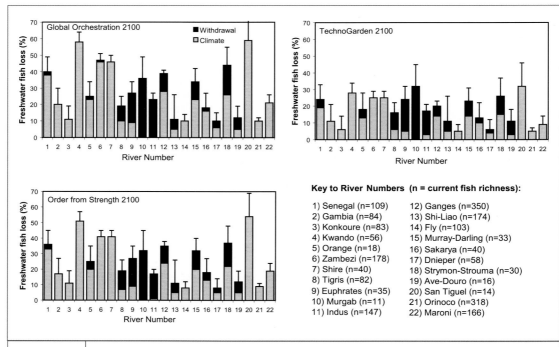

Key to River Numbers (n = current fish richness):

1) Senegal (n=109)
2) Gambia (n=84)
3) Konkoure (n=83)
4) Kwando (n=56)
5) Orange (n=18)
6) Zambezi (n=178)
7) Shire (n=40)
8) Tigris (n=82)
9) Euphrates (n=35)
10) Murgab (n=11)
11) Indus (n=147)
12) Ganges (n=350)
13) Shi-Liao (n=174)
14) Fly (n=103)
15) Murray-Darling (n=33)
16) Sakarya (n=40)
17) Dnieper (n=58)
18) Strymon-Strouma (n=30)
19) Ave-Douro (n=16)
20) San Tiguel (n=14)
21) Orinoco (n=318)
22) Maroni (n=166)

FIGURE 13   PROJECTED FISH SPECIES EXTINCTIONS IN 2100 FROM DECREASES OF RIVER DISCHARGE DUE TO CLIMATE CHANGE AND WATER WITHDRAWAL.

Mean percentage species extinctions plus 95% confidence intervals for three MA scenarios. Projections based on a species discharge relationship[111]. Proportion of species losses associated with changes in river discharge from climate change (grey); proportion of species losses associated with changes in river discharge from water withdrawals by humans (black). The location of each river is given in Figure 12. Source: Sala et al. 2005. From *Ecosystems and Human Well-Being: Scenarios*, by the Millennium Ecosystem Assessment. Copyright © 2005 Millennium Ecosystem Assessment. Reproduced by permission of Island Press, Washington, D.C.

BOX 10 | **LAKE EUTROPHICATION***

TIPPING POINT MECHANISM

Freshwater eutrophication refers to the build-up of nutrients in freshwater ecosystems such as lakes, reservoirs and rivers, leading to excessive plant growth or algal blooms. Decay of dead algae in eutrophic lakes leads to depletion of oxygen levels in the water that in severe cases kills rooted plants, invertebrates, fish, etc. The main driver of freshwater eutrophication is phosphorus pollution from agricultural fertilizers, sewage effluent and detergents. Beyond a certain threshold of phosphorous accumulation, recycling mechanisms are activated which can keep the system locked in a eutrophic state even when phosphorus inputs are substantially decreased.

IMPACTS ON BIODIVERSITY AND ECOSYSTEM SERVICES

At moderate levels of eutrophication, native, often highly desirable fish that require high dissolved O_2 levels are replaced by less desirable species and invasives. Eutrophication often leads to blooms of toxic cyanobacteria, making water unfit for drinking or recreation. Phosphorus inputs in freshwater systems are declining and are projected to continue to decline in most socio-economic scenarios for industrialized countries; in contrast, projected large increases in untreated sewage and fertilizer use will lead to increased eutrophication of lakes over the next several decades for much of Latin America, Asia and Africa.

UNDERSTANDING OF MECHANISMS

Moderate — The mechanisms leading to eutrophication of freshwater ecosystems are very well understood. However, the degree of reversibility from eutrophic to oligotrophic conditions varies greatly and is not fully understood.

CERTAINTY IN PROJECTIONS

Moderate — New management options for eutrophication, e.g., manipulations of food webs to control algal blooms, use of natural water filters, and growing awareness of the negative impacts of eutrophication, raises that possibility that developing countries will use these tools to minimize eutrophication and its impacts on lakes.

KEY ACTIONS

The main management option, both for prevention and restoration, is to reduce phosphorous inputs from sewage, detergents and intensive agriculture. Other options are the reforestation of watersheds to reduce erosion and nutrient runoff from the soils, the restoration of wetlands and the development of technology and economic incentives to close the nutrient cycle at the local level, especially on farms.

---

* The original text for this tipping point was prepared by Reinette Biggs (Stockholm University, oonsie.biggs@stockholmresilience.su.se) and Juan Carlos Rocha Gordo (Stockholm University, aguilajk@gmail.com). Further reading: Scheffer et al. 1993, Carpenter 2003, Smith and Schindler 2009.

---

instead a percentage of species "committed to extinction" with an unspecified time lag. These predictions also do not include other current stresses on freshwater fish, such as pollution or river fragmentation.

Based on the established relationship between the number of non-native fish species and human activity we expect that river basins of developing countries will host an increasing number of non-native fish species as a direct result of economic development[63]. Furthermore impoundments and climate change may facilitate the expansion of invasive species and diseases associated with lake ecosystems[64].

Pressure on freshwater ecosystem services and wetland degradation will increase leading to the deterioration of regulating services such as regulation of water quality and flood protection.

The combination of population growth, increasing water use and climate change will lead to an increase in human population living in river basins facing severe water stress (Figure 14). This will not only increase the risks of chronic water shortages in these regions but will also cause major negative impacts on freshwater ecosystems[65].

Eutrophication of freshwater systems will increase in the developing world, as fertilizer use and untreated sewage effluents continue to increase (Figure 15)[66]. This may be further exacerbated in some regions

by decreasing precipitation and increasing water stress[67]. The transition to eutrophic conditions is in some instances difficult to reverse and can lead to loss of fish species, loss of recreational value, and in certain cases health risks for humans and livestock (Box 10).

Loss of wetlands due to over-extraction of groundwater, drainage for human uses (reclamation), reduced runoff[68], and increasing sea level rise (Box 8), will reduce biodiversity and negatively impact the regulation services of wetlands such as water purification and flood mitigation.

There is uncertainty on the prospects for fish production from inland waters, both wild harvested fish and aquaculture, due to the projected degradation of freshwater ecosystems[69]. This is important because approximately 10% of wild harvested fish are caught from inland waters, and these frequently make up large fractions of dietary protein for people, particularly the rural poor[70].

The management of freshwater ecosystems can be improved and there are opportunities for restoring degraded freshwater habitats to functioning ecosystems delivering a wide range of services to human populations.

Scenarios suggest that there is a large potential to minimize impacts on water quality through sewage

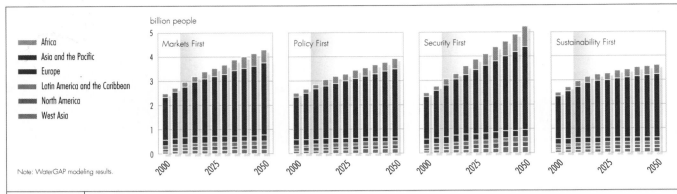

FIGURE 14 | PROJECTED POPULATION LIVING IN RIVER BASINS FACING SEVERE WATER STRESS FROM 2000 TO 2050.

Severe water stress is defined as a situation were withdrawals exceed 40% of renewable sources. It is assumed that the higher the water stress the more likely that chronic or acute water shortages will occur. Projections for GEO4 scenarios calculated using the WaterGAP model. Source: UNEP 2007.

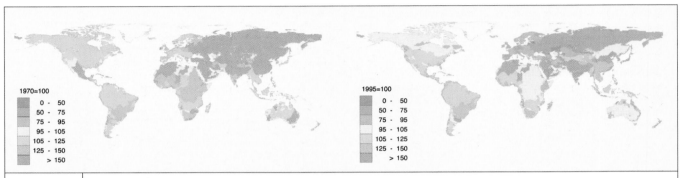

FIGURE 15 | ESTIMATED CHANGES IN TOTAL RIVER NITROGEN LOAD DURING 1970–1995 AND 1995–2030.

Total river nitrogen loads are estimated for each individual river basin from point (sewage effluents, including wastewater from households and industrial activities) and non-point sources (agriculture and atmospheric deposition). Note that from 1995 to 2030 the nutrient load is projected to decrease in Europe and Former Soviet Union, and increase in Northern Africa and Southern Asia. Source: Bouwman et al. 2005

treatment, wetland protection and restoration, and control of agricultural run-off, particularly in the developing world.[71] Further potential exists for improvement of water use efficiency, particularly in agriculture and industry[72]. These actions will minimize the trade-offs between increasing freshwater provisioning services and protecting freshwater regulating services.

There is an opportunity to develop an integrated ecosystem approach in the management of freshwater systems, favouring restoration of freshwater ecosystems in order to improve ecosystem services; such approach includes reopening fish habitat, reconnecting floodplains, managing dams to mimic natural flow patterns and restoring riparian forests and wetlands.[73] Spatial planning of ecosystem services and biodiversity in each basin is a key component of an integrated ecosystem approach to the management of freshwater systems. Many services produced upstream (run-off regulation, timber production, carbon sequestration, etc.) benefit communities downstream, so it is important to develop spatial planning that assures the flows of these ecosystem services[74]. Payments for ecosystem services could also be implemented to reward

the communities, which assure the delivery of ecosystem services[75]. Finally, spatial planning is best developed when it considers the linkages between terrestrial, freshwater and marine systems through fluxes of energy, nutrients and services.

Freshwater biodiversity is not adequately represented in existing protected area systems. Therefore there is an opportunity to establish a network of protected areas designed to convey protection to essential processes in rivers and wetlands[76]. Particularly important is the protection of still unfragmented rivers from further development.

Climate change increases the frequency of extreme events such as floods and droughts. Thus the importance of using wetlands and floodplains for flood mitigation and water cycle regulation will increase[77]. Another consequence of climate change is that it may render hydroelectric power less reliable in some regions.[78] Nonetheless, the need to develop renewable energy increases the demand for hydroelectric power. It will be important to design, operate and better place dams that allow for more natural flow patterns and for fish to reach spawning grounds, as well as perform robustly under climatic uncertainties.

MARINE SYSTEMS

Scenarios show that human population growth, income growth and increasing preferences for fish will likely cause increases in fishing effort leading to the continuation of marine biodiversity loss. Immediate action to tackle overfishing is needed to reduce marine biodiversity loss.

Most scenarios project an increase in demand for fish, as the world population grows and increasing average income allows for increasing the proportion of fish in the diet, particularly in the developing world. In response to the increasing demand, scenarios forecast an increase in fishing effort and an increase in aquaculture production.[79]

Most scenarios using the EcoOcean model (a mass-balance model developed at the University of British Columbia) forecast an increase in fish landings at the cost of declining marine biodiversity (Figure 16).[80] The marine trophic index measures the mean trophic level of fish landings and is an indicator of marine biodiversity. For many marine regions, scenarios project the continuation of the decline in the marine trophic index and the disappearance of large-bodied fish, demersal and pelagic. This process is known as "fishing down the food web". Increased fish landings are achieved by harvesting species not currently exploited commercially such as species from secondary ground fish groups and invertebrates.[81] The projected increase in fish landings may also be a result of incorrect estimates of fishing effort and population dynamics of pelagic fishes and should be interpreted with caution. In

reality, there is probably no room to increase catches and manage fisheries sustainably at the same time. Therefore the increasing trends in catches from 2000 onwards should not be interpreted as a possible management strategy.

One result of "fishing down the food web" is the disappearance of top marine predators, which can cause major ecosystem changes (Box 11). Furthermore, over-exploitation can cause significant extinction risk for marine species[82]. For example, overfishing contributes to the listing of 20 species of groupers and 11 ocean pelagic shark and ray species as threatened with extinction (critically endangered, endangered or vulnerable)[83].

One projection based on a regression model from catch trends over the last 50 years for a wide range of fisheries suggests that there is a high risk of regional collapses in the first half of this century[84]. Another study has suggested that harvesting levels on reef island fisheries will increase to triple of the maximum sustainable yields by 2050, increasing the risk of collapse of those fisheries[85]. Such regional collapses will have dramatic consequences for human well-being, including unemployment and economic losses in the regions affected. For instance, after the Newfoundland fisheries collapsed, an estimated 18000 fishermen lost jobs and 30000 jobs in the fish processing industry became under threat.[86] If current trends in fishing and climate change continue, some models project that fish populations will redistribute away from tropical countries[87], precisely where food security is a critical issue.

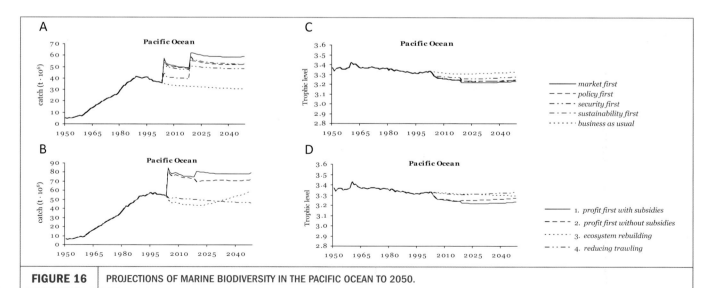

| **FIGURE 16** | PROJECTIONS OF MARINE BIODIVERSITY IN THE PACIFIC OCEAN TO 2050. |

Projections from scenarios for marine biodiversity in the Pacific Ocean developed for the Global Environmental Outlook 4 (top) and the International Assessment for Agricultural Science, Technology and Development (bottom), using the EcoOcean model. Total fish landings (left); Marine Trophic Index (right).
Source: Alder et al. 2007.

BOX 11 | MARINE FISHERIES*

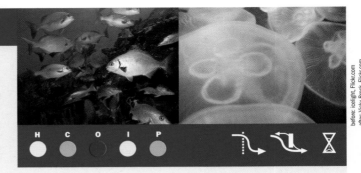

TIPPING POINT MECHANISM

Two well-documented tipping points occur in marine fisheries driven primarily by overfishing and pollution. 1) The collapse of the populations of many economically important marine fish has resulted from overfishing, and often feedbacks prevent populations from recovering despite strong restrictions on fishing. Current trends (see Christensen (2007)) and scenarios suggest that fishing effort will increase over most areas of the ocean, leading to more widespread collapse of fisheries. 2) Profound modifications of the structure of marine food webs are occurring due to overexploitation of large fish, eutrophication due to high nitrogen inputs and habitat degradation, especially in coastal areas. In a growing number of cases, combinations of these factors have resulted in the conversion of species rich, productive ecosystems to those dominated by resilient species such as jellyfish and micro-organisms. These radical transformations of food webs are often characterized by important thresholds, e.g., development of anoxic "dead zones", and are often very difficult to reverse. Ocean warming and acidification may aggravate these effects.

IMPACTS ON BIODIVERSITY AND ECOSYSTEM SERVICES

Unsustainable fishing has pushed many populations of large fish to critically low levels, e.g. nearly 50% of shark and ray species are considered to be vulnerable or threatened with extinction. Coastal "dead zones" have approximately doubled every decade since the 1960s, and are now reported in more than 400 systems affecting a total area of around 250000 km^2. Impacts on biodiversity include habitat loss, the death of immobile, oxygen-dependent species, and disruption of dispersal paths of mobile species. Projections for most world regions foresee substantially increased fishing pressure and nitrogen inputs to estuaries and oceans, raising the specter of even more extensive degradation. In addition to biodiversity impacts, these tipping points reduce the catch of nutritionally and commercially important fisheries for a large proportion of the world population.

UNDERSTANDING OF PROCESSES

Moderate—There is considerable disagreement on the level of fishing that can be maintained without significantly increasing the risk of population collapses or modifications of marine food webs. Critical loads of nitrogen are difficult to determine due to interactions with climate and ocean currents. The feedbacks that prevent recovery of fish populations, or that maintain jellyfish populations are not fully understood.

CERTAINTY IN PROJECTIONS

Moderate—Current trends and scenarios indicate that pressures on marine fisheries will continue over the next several decades. The incapacity of models to predict the collapse and non-recovery of North Atlantic cod populations is a clear illustration of the limits of projections and the dangers of approaching ecological thresholds.

KEY ACTIONS

Development of international treaties regulating fishing in international waters is urgently needed, as is strong climate change mitigation. At the national scale, illegal and unregulated fishing must be stopped, marine resources must be appropriately managed and subsidies promoting overfishing eliminated. Large marine protected areas, if appropriately enforced appear to be an effective mechanism for maintaining biodiversity and ecosystem services. Coastal dead zones need to be reduced by improving agricultural practices with less fertilizer use. The restoration of upstream and coastal wetlands will also help to reduce nutrient loading in coastal areas.

---

* The original text for this tipping point was prepared by U. Rashid Sumaila (University of British Columbia, r.sumaila@fisheries.ubc.ca), William W.L. Cheung (University of East Anglia, william.cheung@uea.ac.uk) and Sylvie Guénette (University of British Columbia, guenette@agrocampus-ouest.fr) and is available in Appendix 9. D. Cooper contributed with text on the dead zones. Further reading: Cheung et al. 2002, Pauly et al. 2002, Worm et al. 2006, Alder et al. 2007, Richardson et al. 2009.

Atmospheric CO₂ content (ppm)

FIGURE 17

TEMPERATURE, ATMOSPHERIC CO_2 AND CARBONATE-ION CONCENTRATIONS FOR THE PAST 420,000 YEARS AND POSSIBLE FUTURE SCENARIOS FOR CORAL REEFS.

The thresholds for major changes to coral communities are indicated for thermal stress (+2°C) and carbonate-ion concentrations ([carbonate] = 200 µmol kg^{-1}, $[CO_2]_{atm}$ = 480 ppm). These thresholds are based on the relatively narrow range of conditions in which coral reefs have occurred over the last 420 000 years (blue dots). Source: Hoegh-Guldberg et al. 2007.

Tackling overfishing requires a combination of several strategies[88]: improving the management of fishing activities including stopping illegal, unreported and unregulated fishing; the creation of effective marine reserves or no-take areas[89]; cutting catches; gear restrictions and modification; establishing access rights for fishers[90]; ecosystem restoration[91]; and a resource-efficient / low-impact aquaculture. Scenarios suggest that if fisheries management focuses on rebuilding ecosystems instead of maximizing economic returns and if benthic trawling and other destructive fishing practices are reduced, stocks can recover and the decline of marine biodiversity could be stopped[92]. Aquaculture can partially help meet the increasing sea-food demand but it has its own environmental and productivity limitations, such as the use of fishmeal for farming piscivore species, the increased risks of disease propagation to wild species, and local pollution[93].

Climate change will increase ocean acidification and sea surface temperature, which is likely to cause major coral reef losses and change the distribution and relative abundances of marine organisms.

BOX 12 | TROPICAL CORAL REEFS*

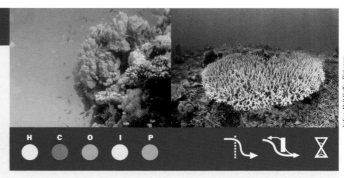

TIPPING POINT MECHANISMS

Scientists are increasingly concerned that tropical coral reefs may cross two important thresholds over the next several decades. 1) Higher than normal sea surface temperatures can cause bleaching and death of corals. Bleaching and degradation of coral communities becomes severe when temperatures rise more than ca. 2°C above current temperatures. 2) Ocean acidification caused by rising atmospheric CO_2 concentrations reduces the capacity of hard corals to form carbonate-based skeletons. Ocean chemistry models project that sea water will be too acid for coral reef growth in many regions when 450 ppm CO_2 in the atmosphere is reached, and far too acid for nearly all coral reefs when 550 ppm is reached.

IMPACTS

Bleaching and reduced calcification may affect corals in several ways: it may lead to a reduction in coral reef building, it may affect the quality of coral skeletons, and it may reduce their fitness. In degraded coralline communities, corals often lose their dominance to algae. Degradation of hard corals leads to broader reductions in biodiversity, since an exceptionally diverse and productive community of fish and invertebrates depend on corals for shelter and feeding. Negative impacts on ecosystem services include declines in locally important fisheries, reduction of protection of coasts from storm surges and loss of tourism revenues.

UNDERSTANDING OF MECHANISMS

High to moderate — There is general agreement about the negative impacts of ocean warming and acidification on hard corals based on experiments, observations and models. However, the capacity of coral communities to adapt to rising temperatures and ocean acidification is not well understood, and, although communities are expected to change, there might be a potential for adaptation and therefore resistance to warming and recolonization of damaged habitats.

CERTAINTY IN PROJECTIONS

High — Several episodes of high sea surface temperatures over the last two decades have already severely damaged coral reefs in many regions. Even best case climate mitigation scenarios will result in widespread damage to tropical coral reefs, according to available models.

KEY ACTIONS

Reducing the influence of local stressors, especially destructive fishing, coastal pollution or the overexploitation of herbivores, such as sea urchins and herbivorous fish, reduces the vulnerability of corals to ocean acidification and climate warming. As such, marine protected areas appear to be an important tool for reducing vulnerability. The coral reef tipping point is a strong argument in favor of strict climate mitigation goals (<450 ppm atmospheric CO_2 and <2°C warming).

---

* The original text for this tipping point was prepared by Joana Figueiredo (University of Lisbon, jcfigueiredo@fc.ul.pt) and is available in Appendix 10. Further reading: Bellwood et al. 2004, Hughes et al. 2005, Hoegh-Guldberg et al. 2007, Donner 2009.

Sea surface warming and the acidification of oceans will drive the corals outside the conditions they have experienced for the last half million years (Figure 17) and can lead to widespread degradation of coral reefs. Coral bleaching is the breakdown of the endo-symbiosis between corals and zooxanthellae[94] and occurs when there is one month of sea surface temperatures 1°C above historical average[95]. These conditions are predicted to become very common by mid century in most reef regions leading to annual or biannual bleaching events (Figure 18). Ocean acidification reduces the availability of carbonate for calcification, slowing coral growth. The degradation of corals is a tipping point and will cause major ecosystem changes (Box 12)[96]. Ocean acidification can also have negative impacts on other calcifying organisms in the oceans[97], and there could be major changes in the distribution and abundance of phytoplankton (Box 13).

Marine species may respond to ocean warming by shifting their latitudinal and depth ranges[98]. Such species responses may lead to local extinctions and invasions, affecting patterns of species diversity, particularly in the tropics, polar regions and semi-enclosed seas (Figure 19). These shifts can cause major rearrangements of the food webs. A good example of these dynamics is the Arctic which may be largely ice free in the summer within one or two decades. This will cause a decline of ice-associated

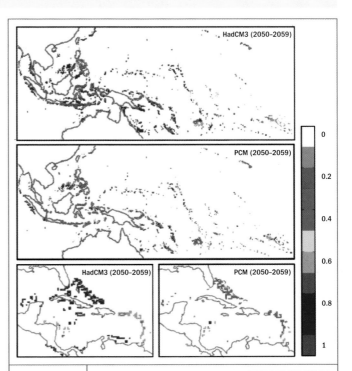

| FIGURE 18 | PROJECTIONS OF CORAL REEF BLEACHING FREQUENCY FOR THE CARIBBEAN AND THE INDO-PACIFIC IN 2050-2059. |

Probability that annual degree heating month >1 in 2050-2059 for each 36 km grid cell in the Indo-Pacific (Top) and Caribbean (Bottom) containing coral reefs, under SRES A2 for two climate models HadCM3 and PCM. Source: Donner et al. (2005).

species, with some species likely to become extinct and to be replaced by subarctic species (Box 14). Changes in the abundance of plankton species can propagate to higher levels of the marine food web, and even to terrestrial ecosystems, given that many birds and mammals link the dynamics of the two systems[99]. The rapid loss of sea ice leaves even less time for corrective action in the form of addressing global climate change or for adaptation by biota and humans to the new conditions in the Arctic.

Based on limited monitoring, experiments and modeling of climate change outcomes, relative sea-level rise may be the greatest future threat to tidal wetlands and beaches (Box 8). Reduced coastal ecosystem area and health will increase coastal hazards to human settlements, reduce coastal water quality, release large quantities of stored carbon, and eliminate nesting, nursery and forage habitat for numerous species groups, including fish, shellfish, seabirds, waterbirds, sea turtles, crocodiles, manatees and dugongs. Rising seas are likely to have the greatest impact on coastal wetlands experiencing net relative lowering in sediment elevation, and where there is limited area for landward migration due to the physiographic setting or obstacles from development.

Climate change needs to be limited in order to protect marine biodiversity, and while any significant increases in global mean temperature may have negative impacts on marine biodiversity, values above 2°C are likely to have dramatic consequences[100]. Adaptation measures should also be taken to increase the resilience of marine and coastal ecosystems to climate change. In the case of coral reefs, there is a need to address overfishing, better planning of coastal development, and decrease pollution sources[101]. Better land planning is also essential to allow for space for the landward migration of coastal habitats in response to sea level rise, which should be complemented with the restoration of coastal habitats and better catchment management to minimize disturbances to sedimentation processes. Finally, there is a need for an international agreement for the development of stringent regulation of human activity in Arctic waters to avoid additional stressors on species and ecosystems (Box 14).

Scenarios suggest that there is a wide range of futures for coastal water pollution, depending on the evolution of agricultural land, fertilizer use, and sewage treatment. Some scenarios project an increase in global trade with increasing risks of expansion of invasive species.

In coastal waters, increasing nutrient loads and pollution, in association with climate change will stimulate eutrophication and increase the number and extent of dead zones (Box 11). Dead zones are areas without oxygen where no fish can survive. They have negative impacts on aquaculture, fisheries, and recreation[102]. In scenarios where there is less expansion of agricultural land, less fertilizer use, more sewage treatment, better management of freshwater ecosystems (in particular the restoration of wetlands), the current trend for an increase in dead zones is halted.[103]

Several scenarios predict increasing globalization[104], including an increase in marine transportation of goods in transoceanic trips. Ships use ballast water to maintain balance, and marine organisms such as plankton and small invertebrates are contained in ballast water. When the ballast water is taken from one region and discharged in another region, biotic exchange occurs and there is the potential for the establishment of invasive species.[105] Measures to control this problem require international collaboration. These are already on-going and include the IMO convention and strategies aiming at: minimizing the uptake of organisms during ballasting, minimizing the build-up of sediments in ballast tanks (which may harbor organisms) and treating ballast water to kill organisms. A similar problem which needs further attention is hull-fouling, i.e. the transport of organisms which attach themselves to the hull of a ship.

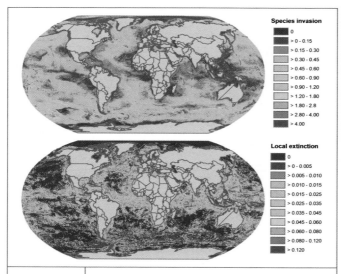

Species invasion
■ 0
▨ > 0 - 0.15
▨ > 0.15 - 0.30
▨ > 0.30 - 0.45
▨ > 0.45 - 0.60
▨ > 0.60 - 0.90
▨ > 0.90 - 1.20
▨ > 1.20 - 1.80
▨ > 1.80 - 2.8
▨ > 2.80 - 4.00
■ > 4.00

Local extinction
■ 0
▨ > 0 - 0.005
▨ > 0.005 - 0.010
▨ > 0.010 - 0.015
▨ > 0.015 - 0.025
▨ > 0.025 - 0.035
▨ > 0.035 - 0.045
▨ > 0.045 - 0.060
▨ > 0.060 - 0.080
▨ > 0.080 - 0.120
■ > 0.120

FIGURE 19	PROJECTED CHANGES IN MARINE BIODIVERSITY DUE TO CLIMATE CHANGE.

Biodiversity impact in 2050 under the IPCC SRES A1B scenario expressed in terms of: number of new species moving from other regions (top) and local extinction intensity (bottom). The projections are based on bioclimate envelope models for 1,066 species of fish and invertebrates. Source: redrawn from Cheung et al. 2009.

BOX 13 | MARINE PHYTOPLANKTON*

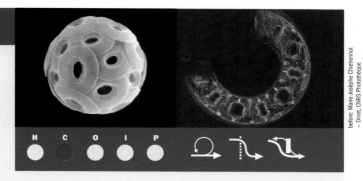

before: Marie-Josèphe Chrétiennot – Dinet, CNRS Photothèque
after : Leanne Armand, CNRS Photothèque, KEOPS

TIPPING POINT MECHANISM
Global warming and rising atmospheric CO_2 concentrations will alter the biodiversity and functioning of oceans through two phytoplankton tipping points. 1) Climate models predict sea surface warming of 2-6°C over the next century. This is projected to enhance ocean stratification at low latitudes reducing nutrient supply from deeper layers, and decrease the mixing layer depth at high latitudes increasing light availability. Both of these will have large effects on phytoplankton productivity and diversity. 2) Rising atmospheric CO_2 concentrations have already reduced ocean pH ("ocean acidification"). Continued ocean acidification is projected to alter the productivity and abundance of phytoplankton that form carbonate-based skeletons. These two processes are projected to lead to feedbacks to global warming due the importance of phytoplankton in driving oceanic carbon sequestration. These shifts are not projected to be abrupt, but the impacts will be planetary in scale and are irreversible over the course of the coming century due to long time lags in the earth system.

IMPACTS ON BIODIVERSITY AND ECOSYSTEM SERVICES
Phytoplankton distributions are already shifting poleward in response to ocean warming and these shifts are projected to accelerate throughout this century. Some functional groups may be favored by ocean acidification, such as diatoms that form silicate-based skeletons, while others may be reduced, especially those that form carbonate-base skeletons like coccolithophores, although there is high uncertainty in this response. Marine phytoplankton play a central role in biogeochemical cycles and in climate regulation, for example by sequestering carbon in dead phytoplankton that sink to the bottom of the ocean. Changes in phytoplankton productivity may cause bottom-up impacts on marine trophic webs affecting marine biodiversity and fisheries. Ocean biogeochemical models predict a global decrease in marine primary productivity of up to 20% in the next century relative to pre-industrial times. Additional anthropogenic impacts on marine phytoplankton will arise from overfishing, pollution and invasive species, especially near highly populated coastal regions.

UNDERSTANDING OF MECHANISMS
Low—Among key unknowns are the physiological response of carbonate-based phytoplankton to ocean acidification, the role of competition and trophic interactions in controlling phytoplankton community dynamics, and the mechanisms of interactions between global change drivers.

CERTAINTY IN PROJECTIONS
Low—Models, observations and experiments are in qualitative agreement that ocean warming and acidification are very likely to have large impacts on phytoplankton and carbon sequestration by oceans; however, the speed, direction and distribution of these impacts are highly uncertain.

KEY ACTIONS
Long-term, global monitoring programs are needed to better understand the effects of environmental change on ocean phytoplankton and the propagation of impacts in food-webs up to fisheries. Despite high uncertainties, strong climate change mitigation measures must be considered given that negative impacts on ocean biodiversity, productivity or carbon sequestration would have planetary scale implications. Adaptation measures are not currently considered feasible.

---

* The original text for this tipping point was prepared by Laurent Bopp (Institute Pierre Simon Laplace, Laurent.Bopp@cea.fr) and Corinne Le Quéré (University of East Anglia/British Antarctic Survey). Further reading: Bopp et al. 2001, Hays et al. 2005, Rost et al. 2008, Alvain et al. 2008, Riebesell et al. 2009.

BOX 14 | ARCTIC OCEAN*

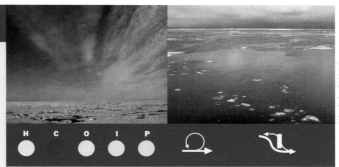

before & after: Patrick Kelley, U.S. Coast Guard, Flickr.com

TIPPING POINT MECHANISM
Arctic summer sea ice extent is decreasing rapidly, indeed more quickly than recent models projected, reaching a record low in September 2007. Sea ice is thinning and most multi-year ice has been lost, setting the stage for further rapid reduction in extent and raising the possibility of an ice-free Arctic summer within a few decades. Because open water reflects much less solar radiation than sea ice, the loss of sea ice accelerates regional and global warming.

IMPACTS ON BIODIVERSITY AND ECOSYSTEM SERVICES
The arctic marine environment is rapidly becoming a subarctic environment, with consequent threats to arctic species but opportunities for subarctic ones. Ice-dependent species are rapidly losing habitat, creating key mismatches in timing of seasonal events such as food availability and reproduction, or in spatial relationships such as feeding and resting areas for marine mammals. Where sea ice is a platform and a provider of ice-associated species, ecosystem services will decline. Where sea ice is a barrier to human activity, development may increase, including perhaps provisioning services such as fisheries, but may also lead to increased conflict among users and potential users.

UNDERSTANDING OF MECHANISMS
High—While models failed to correctly predict recent rates of ice cover loss, the drivers and feedback mechanisms are broadly well understood. Biodiversity responses can be projected with some certainty based on current trends and knowledge of environmental constraints on arctic and subartic organisms.

CERTAINTY IN PROJECTIONS
High—This tipping point is already occurring and all models agree that ice cover will continue decline substantially over the coming century. Major uncertainties are rates of ice cover change and the speed and direction of change in biotic communities.

KEY ACTIONS
Aggressive mitigation of climate change is urgent. Clear international regulatory regimes must be defined to control the future impacts of additional stressors, such as fisheries and pollution.

---

* The original text for this tipping point was prepared by Henry P. Huntington (hph@alaska.net) and is available in Appendix 8. Further reading: Holland et al. 2006, Winton 2006, Greene et al. 2008, Moore and Huntington 2008.

3. THE WAY FORWARD FOR BIODIVERSITY MODELS AND SCENARIOS

MODELS OF THE FUTURE OF BIODIVERSITY AND ECOSYSTEM SERVICES CONTRIBUTE TO OUR SCIENTIFIC UNDERSTANDING AND CAN INFORM POLICY. – Quantitative models should not be viewed as capable of predicting the future state of biodiversity and ecosystem services. Large uncertainties in the future trajectories of indirect and direct drivers of biodiversity and ecosystem services exclude the possibility of making multi-decadal predictions. There has, however, been tremendous progress in modeling biodiversity and its relationship with ecosystem services over the last decade, and the scientific community is now poised to use models as tools to: comprehend the mechanisms that have led to current patterns of biodiversity, understand the processes that underlie the response of biodiversity to global change, synthesize a wide range of disparate sources of information, provide insight into the effectiveness of mitigation and adaptation strategies, etc. In particular, quantitative models, when used wisely, are exceptionally good at addressing "what if" questions that decision makers frequently are confronted with. These questions can be explored by examining the impact of a variety of socio-economic scenarios on biodiversity. For example, models have recently played a crucial role in demonstrating that plans for large-scale deployment of biofuels are unsound, both for the environment and biodiversity.

MODELS SHOULD INCLUDE INTERACTIONS AND FEEDBACKS THAT LINK BIODIVERSITY, ECOSYSTEM FUNCTIONING, ECOSYSTEM SERVICES AND SOCIO-ECONOMIC PROCESSES. – Although our understanding of direct and indirect links between biodiversity and ecosystem services is limited, models of the better-understood aspects of ecosystem services could be incorporated in scenario studies, e.g. carbon sequestration, hydrological cycles, regulation of nutrients, pollination, production of food and fiber, etc. However, models that do a good job at simulating these ecosystem services often have poor representations of biodiversity and vice versa. Links between

biodiversity and ecosystem services to human well-being can be modeled, for instance using economic valuation or links to human health and the TEEB initiative has made great strides in moving towards model-based valuation of ecosystem services. One of the challenges is the frequent spatial disconnect between where services are produced and where people benefit from those services (e.g., people downstream benefit from forest services upstream). Thus, there is the need to develop models that can map the spatial and temporal flows of ecosystem services. A daunting task will be to include a broader range of ecosystem services, especially cultural services that are very different from other ecosystem services and will require new conceptual frameworks to be developed.

MODELS NEED TO INCORPORATE MULTIPLE DRIVERS AFFECTING BIODIVERSITY AND ECOSYSTEM SERVICES AND INTEGRATE INTERACTIONS BETWEEN REALMS. – Important drivers that are currently missing or only partially treated in current models include: invasive species and overexploitation in terrestrial systems; dam construction, pollution and invasive species in freshwater systems; and habitat degradation and pollution in coastal and marine systems. Challenges to incorporate these drivers in the models used in biodiversity scenarios include the lack of general and scalable relationships between those drivers and biodiversity change. More basic research into these relationships is needed, using standard indicators of biodiversity change, such as the ones adopted by the CBD for the 2010 targets. Models for terrestrial, freshwater and marine biomes need to be integrated so that interactions and feedbacks among these systems can be accounted for[106].

IDEALLY MODELS OF BIODIVERSITY AND ECOSYSTEM SERVICES SHOULD INCORPORATE DYNAMICS AND BE PROCESS-BASED INSTEAD OF THE CURRENTLY AVAILABLE STATIC, PATTERN-MATCHING MODELS. – Process-based models could incorporate evolutionary, ecological and physical processes and, thereby, provide quantitative simulations of the dynamics of the multiple dimensions of biodiversity (genes, species and ecosystems). By incorporating feedbacks, interactions and key processes, such as food webs or dispersal, models could help to uncover and describe important "tipping points". This will require the development of a new generation of models that cover a much broader range of processes than existing models. Such models might also provide better estimates of the dynamics of biodiversity change such as the time to extinctions, the speed at which novel ecosystems are likely to be created (for example due to climate change), etc.

MODELS OF BIODIVERSITY AND ECOSYSTEM SERVICES MUST BE EVALUATED USING A STANDARD SET OF INDICATORS TO ASSESS THE VALIDITY AND LIMITATIONS OF THE PROJECTIONS. – Models can be evaluated in several ways, good examples of which are model evaluations undertaken by the global climate modeling community. Model inter-comparisons, the systematic comparison of outputs generated by different models, and sensitivity analyses are powerful means for estimating uncertainty in model projections, but are too rarely undertaken by the biodiversity modeling community. Further, model inter-comparisons can help to identify and correct errors, as has been demonstrated by IPCC climate model intercomparisons[107]. Testing the ability of models to simulate past and present conditions against observed conditions of past and current biodiversity and ecosystem services is an essential part of model evaluation. Models of biodiversity change have too rarely been benchmarked using observational or experimental datasets. Improving this situation will require models to output standardized variables that can be compared against agreed datasets on biodiversity and ecosystem services, such as the biodiversity indicators adopted by the CBD. The development of a Global Biodiversity Observation Network by the Group on Earth Observations (GEO-BON)[108] opens an opportunity to harmonize biodiversity data to use in developing and testing scenario models.

SCENARIOS CAN INFORM THE DEFINITION OF POST-2010 TARGETS, BOTH GLOBALLY AND REGIONALLY. – The discussion on post-2010 targets has started recently (e.g. UNEP-WCMC 2009). It is possible to compare recent trends in some CBD indicators with the output of models (Figure 7 and Figure 16). As such, models could help to set targets that are informed by current trends and to assess the feasibility of reaching targets by comparing various socio-economic scenarios. Different target timelines could be defined for different indicators, with indicators that have a slower time dynamics receiving longer-term targets (i.e. 2030), such as the red list index, and indicators with faster dynamics receiving shorter-term targets (2015) such as forest area extent. Given the heterogeneity of biodiversity loss patterns across the world (Figure 3), regional or national biodiversity targets could be defined in the context of plausible scenarios. For instance, in areas where there are strong trends for biodiversity decline the targets could be more permissive, while in areas where pressures are reduced the targets could be more stringent, and in some cases, targets may even involve improving biodiversity condition relative to the baseline, through ecological restoration.

IPBES, AN IPCC-LIKE MECHANISM FOR BIODIVERSITY AND ECOSYSTEM SERVICES, COULD PROVIDE THE STIMULUS FOR THE MAJOR EFFORT NEEDED TO EVALUATE AND IMPROVE MODELS. – The work outlined above to evaluate and improve models will require an unprecedented effort on the part of the socio-economic, climate, ecosystem and biodiversity modeling communities to work together. The IPCC has clearly demonstrated that an independent, but government recognized international assessment body is a powerful mechanism for mobilizing the scientific community. The time is ripe for a similar assessment mechanism for biodiversity and ecosystem services, because huge strides have recently been made in modeling and in creating global and regional databases. As such, dramatic improvements in scope, quality and political relevance of biodiversity and ecosystem service projections for the 21st century are within reach in the next few years. IPBES, an intergovernmental science-policy platform on biodiversity and ecosystem services, could be the key to unlocking this potential.

iStockphoto.com

ENDNOTES

1 MA — Millennium Ecosystem Assessment 2005.

2 Sala et al. 2005.

3 Niche-based models (NBM) — NBMs are based on statistical relationships between spatial distributions of plant or animal species and key environmental factors controlling their distribution such as temperature, precipitation, etc. The resulting model of the environmental "niche" of a species can be used to simulate future distributions when combined with projections of changes in environmental drivers. This is a powerful approach for projecting climate change impacts at the species level because it can be used for any species for which there are maps of their distribution and corresponding environmental factors. Limitations of NBMs generally include the lack of species migration, inter-specific interactions, key environmental factors controlling distributions (e.g., rising CO_2 concentrations for plants) and adaptive mechanisms. NBMs are often referred to as "bioclimatic" or "climate envelope" models when only climate variables are used to predict species range. See Thuiller et al. (2008) for a critical overview of niche-based modelling.

4 Dose-response relationships — Observational data and experiments can be used to generate empirical relationships between the intensity of a global change driver (i.e., the dose) and species loss, changes in species abundance, etc. (i.e., the response). The development of dose-response relationships requires significant efforts to synthesize observational and experimental studies. The advantage of these models is that they are solidly anchored in measured responses of biodiversity to global change drivers. One key drawback of this approach is that it is difficult to account for interactions between global change drivers that are likely to occur in the future. See MA (2005) and Alkemade et al. (2009) for discussions of the development and limitations of this approach.

5 Species-area relationships — The relationship between geographical or habitat area and species richness is one of the best-studied correlations in ecology. In nearly all systems, the number of observed species increases asymptotically with increasing geographical or habitat area. Based on this relationship, the loss of habitat area has been interpreted to imply a loss of species. This use of the species-area relationship to predict species extinctions is, however, poorly tested at large spatial scales and the lag time between the loss of habitat and the resulting loss of species is unknown in most cases. The Sala et al. (2005) and van Vuuren et al. (2006) provide a comprehensive overview of the use of species-area curves to project species loss at the global scale.

6 Empirical models using IUCN status — The IUCN has developed criteria for assessing species extinction risk for their Red List of the conservation status of plant and animal species. One of the key components of these criteria is the change in geographical distribution of a species. Hence, models that simulate changes in species range size, e.g., niche models, can be combined with IUCN classifications to determine the fraction of species that are at high risk of future extinction (Thomas et al. 2004, Thuiller et al. 2005). The IUCN status was not, however, designed for this use, so projections of species extinctions based on this method have a high degree of uncertainty (Akcakaya et al. 2006).

7 Global vegetation models (GVM or DGVM) — GVMs use mathematical descriptions of plant photosynthesis, respiration, etc., coupled with descriptions of the functioning of soils to simulate vegetation dynamics and biogeochemical cycling (e.g., carbon storage and fluxes, water use by plants, runoff, etc.). These models are widely used to investigate the impacts of global change on regional and global biogeochemical cycling. The use of biomes or a very small number of plant functional types (often 10 or less for the entire planet) and the absence of animals currently prohibits their use for directly modelling distributions of species or species richness. GVMs have, however, been used in combination with species-area or dose-response relationships to estimate species loss at regional and global scales. The IMAGE model described in Alcamo et al. (2005b) contains a GVM that simulates biome distributions. Most recent GVMs simulate the distribution of plant functional types (e.g., Sitch et al. 2008).

8 Species extinctions are also frequently referred to as "species loss" in biodiversity assessments. In this synthesis we use both terms interchangeably to refer to the global extinction of species (as opposed to local extinctions).

9 Species abundance is used to refer to the population size of a species. We also use the term Mean Species Abundance, which has a slightly different meaning and refers to the difference in mean species population sizes between relatively pristine ecosystems and systems where these pristine ecosystems have been transformed by human activities.

10 Habitat loss is a relatively broad term that we use to describe a major transformation of relatively pristine ecosystems by human activities and is usually equated with a major transformation of vegetation type, land cover or land use; e.g., the transformation of relatively intact forest to cropland constitutes habitat loss as defined in most previous biodiversity assessments. Technically this is an incorrect use of the word "habitat" because the loss of habitat for one group of species is always habitat gain for another group.

11 Functionally similar groups of species are often referred to as "functional groups". This refers to groups of species that either respond to environmental signals or perturbations in a similar way, or have similar effects on ecosystem functioning; e.g., "temperate deciduous trees" is a commonly used plant functional group used in global vegetation models.

12 Biome is often equated with the dominant type of vegetation for terrestrial ecosystems; e.g., the "savanna" biome can be found on several continents, but is typically defined as grassland with sparse tree cover. We use the terms "vegetation type" and "biome" interchangeably. Biome definitions nearly always differ between studies: we have attempted to use the biome definitions given in the MA (2005) when possible.

13 The global scale projections of terrestrial species extinctions that are presented have focused on the impacts of climate and/or land use change. All of these projections rely on a complex, multi-step process that includes 1) scenarios of global socio-economic development that include greenhouse gas (GHG) emissions, land use change (i.e., "habitat" change), etc., 2) climate models that translate GHG emissions into projections of climate change, 3) models of shifts in the range of species or vegetation types (i.e., "habitats") in response to climate change and 4) models that scale from changes in habitat or species range sizes to global species extinctions. We have not included the Sala et al. (2005) projections in Figure 2 because they are very similar in methodology and results to van Vuuren et al. (2006), nor the global biodiversity projections of Sala et al. (2000), because they estimated impact of global change drivers on biodiversity using a qualitative index of "biodiversity change" that cannot be compared with other studies.

14 See discussion in van Vuuren et al. (2006).

15 Sala et al. 2005.

16 Species-area relationships assume that loss of habitat area leads to greatly increased risk of long-term extinction; however, loss of habitat area and contractions in species range size have often not been good predictors of species extinctions in the paleontological and recent historical record (Ibanez et al. 2006, Botkin et al. 2007, Willis and Bhagwat 2009). For example, large contractions in range size or habitat modifications of many species during Quarternary glaciations appear to have resulted in few plant species extinctions (Botkin et al. 2007, Willis and Bhagwat 2009) and may only partially explain mass extinctions of large vertebrates (Koch and Barnosky 2006): many species appear to have escaped extinction by taking refuge in small areas of favorable environments, or in environments that differ substantially from where they currently occur (Botkin et al. 2007, Willis et al. 2007, Willis and Bhagwat 2009). More recently, large scale deforestation in the Eastern US — 50% of forest area had been cleared by the mid-19th century — should have led to very high extinction rates based on habitat area considerations, but observed plant extinctions were much lower and indigenous bird extinctions considerably higher than would have been predicted based on species-area relationships (Ibanez et al. 2006). Observations show that some species groups are capable of long-term survival as small populations or can successfully adapt to non-native habitats (Prugh et al. 2008, Willis and Bhagwat 2009) which may explain why projections of species extinctions based on habitat loss are not coherent with large observed differences in vulnerability to extinction across species groups (Stork et al. 2009).

17 Sala et al. 2005.

18 It is tempting to explain low species extinction probabilities in Jetz et al. (2007) compared to other global projections, because extinctions are projected only when species lose their entire current habitat. However when similar criteria to Thomas et al. (2004) are used (e.g., assuming a 15-75% probability of extinction for bird species with >50% habitat loss based on IUCN criteria), projected species loss due to climate change alone in Jetz et al. (2007) are still significantly lower than those in Thomas et al. (2004). Another difference between the two works is that Jetz et al. (2007) used a model of biome shifts as the basis of calculating future range size, while Thomas et al. used climate-based niche models. Also note that even the projections in Jetz et al. (2007) may be overly pessimistic because they assume that birds are stationary and cannot move in response to land use or climate change.

19 Pounds et al. 2006.

20 We have summarized the responses of two studies that have examined the future impacts of global change on species abundance, the UNEP (2007) and ten Brink et al. (2007). In both studies, changes in Mean Species Abundance (MSA) were simulated using the GLOBIO model (Alkemade et al. 2009), which is an IMAGE based model (Bouwman et al. 2006) that simulates the impact of multiple pressures on biodiversity using empirical data from published studies to establish a relation between the magnitude of pressures and the magnitude of the impacts, i.e., "dose-response" models (Rothman et al. 2007). The baseline scenario was a "business as usual" scenario, meaning one that was not influenced by any specific policy scenario besides the ones presently implemented. It is driven by moderate socio-economic development. The baseline scenario predicts a decline in MSA from 70% in 2000 to 63% in 2050 (100% corresponds to the total natural capital in 1700 AD). See Biggs et al. (2008) for use of this type of approach at regional scales.

21 There are two important methodological differences between the Mean Species Abundance used in Figure 5A and the LPI used in Figure 5B. First, LPI is based on long-term population trends for a small range of species, while MSA uses comparisons of a broad range of species populations between disturbed and undisturbed reference habitats. Second, the Living Planet Index uses the geometric means of trends in species abundance across realms to calculate average terrestrial trends (WWF 2008), in contrast to the GLOBIO model that uses arithmetic means to calculate Mean Species Abundance at all scales (MSA, Alkemade et al. 2009). Both approaches can easily be justified.

22 The success of this option depends heavily on the ability to appropriately enforce the status of protected areas and to integrate the management of protected areas and non-protected areas (Brooks et al. 2009).

23 The relationship between poverty alleviation and biodiversity conservation is hotly debated. Improvements in human welfare have historically been accompanied by the conversion of natural systems to human dominated systems with lower diversity (MA 2005). There are some development pathways that allow for substantial increases in human welfare, yet do a far better job of preserving biodiversity than is currently the case in many regions (Chan et al. 2007).

24 Kok et al. (2008) provide a very insightful synthesis of previous global change assessments.

25 van Vuuren et al. 2006, IPCC 2007.

26 Nielsen et al. 2007, Froyd and Willis 2008.

27 Nielsen et al. 2007.

28 Kok et al. 2008.

29 van Vuuren et al. 2006, Kok et al. 2008

30 Stehfest et al. (2009) provide a detailed analysis of the effects of diets based on "healthy" levels of meat consumption and clearly illustrate the large impacts of high levels of meat consumption on global land use. See also Kok et al. (2008) and Alkemade et al. (2009).

31 IPCC (2007) provides an excellent summary of these model projections.

32 See exhaustive review by Perry et al. (2005). See also Fischlin et al. (2007).

33 See Reynolds et al. (2007) for a thorough review of desertification and land degradation processes in arid and semi-arid regions. See Pejchar and Mooney (2009) for a review of species invasions and their impacts on a broad range of ecosystems.

34 Overpeck and Weiss 2009.

35 Bond et al. (2005) provide a global analysis of fire impacts on terrestrial ecosystems using the Sheffield DGVM.

36 But see Thuiller et al. (2005).

37 Walker et al. 2009.

38 The MA (2005) provides a comprehensive discussion of the relationships between biodiversity, ecosystem services and human well-being.

39 TEEB 2009 — The Economics of Ecosystems and Biodiversity for National and International Policy Makers – Summary: Responding to the Value of Nature 2009. See also the TEEB web site at www. teebweb.org.

40 Wise et al. (2009) have published the only global scenarios in which land dedicated to crops and intensively managed forest declines over the coming century. See discussion of Figure 2.7 for more detail.

41 MA 2005, Carpenter et al. 2009.

42 Chan et al. 2006, Nelson et al. 2009.

43 Balmford et al. 2009.

44 But see Lindemann-Mathies et al. (2010) who showed that aesthetic appreciation is positively related to biodiversity in Switzerland.

45 Naidoo et al. 2008.

46 There is good experimental and theoretical evidence that species loss can degrade some ecosystem functions; however, these effects are most pronounced at low levels of species richness and reductions in species richness are often considerably less important than changes in key species or species groups that dominate ecosystem functioning (Loreau et al. 2001, Gaston 2010). In addition, most studies of the relationship between biodiversity and ecosystem function in terrestrial ecosystems have focused on species loss in grasslands (Balvanera et al. 2006), although some studies have focused on other ecosystems such as forests (Oelmann et al. 2010). Most studies show that a reduction in species richness has negative effects on some key measures of ecosystem services (Balvanera et al. 2006), but since many of these studies are based on random species loss and carried out at very small spatial scales they are extremely difficult to extrapolate to projected changes in biodiversity at larger spatial scales (Hillebrand and Matthiessen 2009).

47 Kremen et al. 2007, Aizen et al. 2008, Aizen et al. 2009, Gallai et al. 2009. Based on text prepared by P. Balvanera.

48 For examples of the use of GVMs to model ecosystem functions and services see: river flow (Ishidaira et al. 2008), regional rainfall (Betts et al. 2008), fire regimes (Bond et al. 2005, Bar Massada et al. 2009), ecosystem carbon storage (Schaphoff et al. 2006, Sitch et al. 2008), global climate (Gullison et al. 2007, Davin and de Noblet-Ducoudre 2010).

49 TEEB 2009. See www.teebweb.org.

50 Paterson et al. 2008.

51 See reviews by Gullison et al. (2007) and Howarth and Bringezu (2008).

52 Grainger et al. 2009.

53 Heller and Zavaleta 2009.

54 See Ranganathan et al. (2008) for good examples of the importance of improving biodiversity management in human dominated landscapes.

55 Calculations based on the MA scenarios output from IMAGE, using the total food crop area, grass & fodder area, and biofuel crop area in 2050 relative to 2000.

56 For instance the scenarios in GEO4 (UNEP 2007) and GEO3 (UNEP 2002) analyse prospects for population facing severe water stress and for the volume of untreated domestic and municipal wastewater but only analyse terrestrial biodiversity. Similarly, the scenarios of Crossroads of Planet Earth's Life (ten Brink et al. 2006) only look at terrestrial biodiversity.

57 The importance of these drivers has been reviewed in Finlayson and D'Cruz (2005).

58 Nilsson et al. (2005) do a global overview of dam-based impacts on large river systems. They found that more than half of large river systems are affected by dams. The push for reducing emissions by using hydropower is driving the construction of thousands of new dams, some of them in river systems not yet fragmented by dams.

59 Reviews of the impacts of climate change on freshwater biodiversity can be found in Poff et al. (2002), Fischlin et al. (2007), Heino et al. (2009).

60 Climate change is expected to force species distributions towards higher latitudes, leading to potential extinctions of species whose future habitable climate space becomes too small or too isolated from their current geographical ranges. Because of the insular nature of rivers for freshwater fishes (Oberdorff et al. 1999), endemic species may be at a higher risk of extinction as they cannot adapt to new climatic conditions and cannot shift their geographic ranges. Since endemic taxa are not replaceable from elsewhere, and are usually part of global conservation priorities, their extinction will have a global scope and will translate in net biodiversity loss at the global level. The protection of river basins holding endemic species may not be sufficient to avoid extinction. Therefore a possible mitigation option would consist on the translocation of these species to alternative river basins. However, species translocations also pose serious risks to conservation, since they may cause unexpected and undesirable shifts on ecosystem functioning (Richardson et al. 2009). Based on text prepared by T. Oberdorff.

61 Fang et al. (2004a,b,c) looked at $2xCO_2$ scenarios for water temperature and dissolved oxygen in North American lakes and found that the number of lakes with suitable cool-water fish habitat will decrease by 30% and most shallow water lakes will experience summerkill of cold-water fish due to elevated water temperatures. Jankowski et al. (2006) do an analysis of the impacts of 2003 European heat wave on hipolimnetic oxygen and its implications for the effects of climate change.

62 Sala et al. (2005) developed global scenarios using a species-discharge curve, which predicts fish species diversity as a function of mean annual discharge. This regression model was built with data from 237 rivers across the world. Using the WaterGAP model they estimated current and future discharge for the Millennium Ecosystem Assessment scenarios, considering separately the effects of water withdrawal and climate change. The scenarios predict major changes in water availability in river basins across the world, with an increase in availability in Northern Europe and North America, and a reduction in availability in the Mediterranean, Australia, Southern Africa and India (Figure 12). Therefore, Sala et al. predict major declines in freshwater biodiversity in the rivers of the latter regions, up to 65% in one case (Figure 13). These will not be compensated in the short term by increased water availability in other parts of the world, as extinction occurs in ecological time while speciation occurs in evolutionary time. In these scenarios the main cause of change in water availability and ultimately the cause of fish extinctions is climate change, with a minor role played by water withdrawal (Figure 13). Therefore the scenario where freshwater biodiversity is least affected is the scenario where climate change is minimized (Technogarden). The same authors performed a similar modelling exercise for two IPCC SRES scenarios and found that 15% of the rivers would lose more than 20% of fish species (Xenopoulos et al. 2005). There are significant uncertainties and limitations associated with the scenarios of Sala et al. (2005) and Xenopoulos et al. (2005). There is still limited empirical evidence for extinctions associated with decrease in river discharge. The species-discharge model is based on a snapshot of the distribution of fish diversity across many river basins, and the slope of the relationship could differ if an analysis of the consequences of river discharge for fish diversity was performed over time within a river basin. Finally there are important limitations associated with the estimates and projections of the WaterGAP model.

63 Leprieur et al. (2008) studied the spatial variation in non-native species richness globally. They found that indicators of propagule pressure and habitat disturbance (i.e. gross domestic product, human population density and the percentage of urban area) accounted for most of the global variation in non-native fish species richness. Based on these results, they predicted that river basins of developing countries will host an increasing number of non-native fish species as a direct result of economic development.

64 Dam construction facilitates biological invasions of the impounded water bodies and of nearby natural lakes (Johnson et al. 2008). Climate change may facilitate the invasion by exotic species of systems previously limited by minimum winter temperatures (Schmitz et al. 2003).

65 Most scenarios in the MA (Alcamo et al. 2005) and GEO 4 (UNEP 2007) predict increasing water withdrawals, as consequence of population growth, agricultural demand, and industry demand. Globally, increased precipitation is expected to increase water availability but not as fast as withdrawals. Furthermore in some arid regions precipitation will decrease. Overall population under severe water stress will increase (Figure 14).

66 Bouwman et al. (2005) projected river nutrient loads up to 2030 based on projections for food production and wastewater effluents.

67 Sala et al. (2005) developed qualitative scenarios for eutrophication and acidification on freshwater ecosystems and discussed implications for biodiversity. They used return flows from WaterGAP (i.e. flows returned by human water uses) as proxy

for eutrophication. For acidification they used an index of aerial SOx deposition from IMAGE. They found that almost all areas with large increases in return flows are also areas with decrease discharge (caused by changes in precipitation and water use). Some of these areas (e.g. Middle East) also experience increasing acid deposition. The scenario where pro-active environmental measures are taken at the global scale (Technogarden) was the scenario with the brightest outlook for biodiversity.

68 Alcamo et al. (2005a) discuss the impacts on wetlands and their services caused by land reclamation and by changes in river runoff induced by climate change and water withdrawals.

69 Gopal (2005) describes how intensive aquaculture has been developed in some places in Asia to compensate for declininig fish catches from dry and polluted rivers. However, aquaculture also degrades water quality and reduces biodiversity, and in some cases eutrophication has occurred to such extent that the aquaculture farms become unviable. Lake and Bond (2007) developed narrative scenarios for the future of freshwater ecosystems in Australia. In one of their scenarios, where economic growth receives priority, agriculture expands increasing water usage, leading to increases in salinity, restriction of fish migration through dam construction for irrigation, and increase in nutrient loads and other pollutants. As a consequence there are significant losses of biodiversity.

70 Approximately 10% of wild harvested fish are caught from inland waters (Wood et al. 2005) and inland aquaculture production further increases the significance of freshwater ecosystems as a major source of protein for a large part of the world´s population (Finlayson and D'Cruz 2005).

71 See Alcamo et al. (2005).

72 Minimizing water use is shown to be a key issue in both the MA scenarios (Alcamo et al. 2005) and GEO 4 scenarios (UNEP 2007).

73 See Palmer et al. (2008).

74 Heal et al. (2001) proposed the concept of Ecosystem Service Districts to develop a spatial planning system based on ecosystem services.

75 Payments for ecosystem services of freshwater ecosystems are discussed in Bohlen et al. (2009) and Leclerc (2005).

76 Abell et al. (2008) discuss the lack of broadscale planning efforts for freshwater systems and propose an ecoregion approach for the development of conservation strategies.

77 The role of wetlands on flood mitigation is reviewed by de Guenni et al. (2005). The role of wetlands on water purification is reviewed by Finlayson and D'Cruz (2005).

78 See Fischlin et al. (2007).

79 Alder et al. (2007) develop fishing policy scenarios for the four scenarios of the Global Environmental Outlook 4 up to 2050, all of them forecasting an increase in fishing effort due to an increasing human population and fish consumption. Alder et al. (2007) also explored four scenarios of the International Assessment of Agricultural Science Technology and Development (IAASTD), with fishing effort increasing in two of them. The scenarios explored in the MA up to 2020 exhibit similar dynamics (Alcamo et al. 2005) and project a substantial increase of aquaculture production. FAO (2009) analysed the prospects for aquaculture to 2015, suggesting that, given the overall stagnation of fisheries landings over the last two decades, the increase in demand for fish will lead to growth in aquaculture production.

80 The EcoOcean model projects changes in biomass for 43 functional groupings, including 25 groups of fish, 3 groups of marine mammals, 1 group of marine birds, 11 groups of invertebrates, 2 groups of primary producers and 1 detritus group. The sub-models (one for each FAO area, the poles excepted) are adjusted to fit biomass and catch, using the fishing effort of five fleets as drivers for the period 1950 to 2000. Scenarios are developed by defining a set of weights for the following criteria associated with fisheries: value, jobs, ecosystem structure and subsidies. These criteria are then used to calculate optimal fishing efforts over the time period for each scenario. Results are reported using indicators such as total landings per functional group, the marine trophic index (which measures the distribution of landings relative to their position in the food web, Pauly et al. (2003)), and the depletion index (representing the relative level of species depletion by fishing, Cheung and Sumaila (2008)).

81 Alder et al. 2007.

82 The level of this risk is not consensual and has been discussed by Hutchings and Reynolds (2004).

83 See Baillie et al. (2004). See also Cheung et al. (2007) who found that species with higher intrinsic vulnerability (slow growth and late maturity) are more impacted by overfishing. Dulvy et al. (2004) review available methods to assess extinction risk in marine fishes.

84 Worm et al. (2006) analysed data on fish and invertebrate catches from 1950 to 2003 from 64 large marine ecosystems reaching from estuaries and coastal areas to the seward boundaries of continental shelves. They plotted the number of collapsed fish and invertebrate taxa over time, this is, taxa where catches dropped below 10% of the recorded maximum. They found that about 1/3 of currently fished species had collapsed by 2003. Projecting the collapses trend (using a power equation) into the future they forecasted a global collapse of marine fisheries by 2050. The use of this kind of extrapolation and other aspects of the paper have been criticized by some scientists (Holker et al. 2007).

85 Newton et al. (2007) studied the prospects for island coral reef fisheries up to 2050. Based on an estimate of maximum sustainable yields, they estimated the current ecological footprint of coral reef fisheries was 164%, which means that we would need 64% more reef area than exists in the world. They found that human population size on the islands was a significant predictor of the ecological footprint on the islands reef fisheries.

Using this relationship, and UN projections for population growth up to 2050, they predict that by that time, we would need almost three times the existing reef area.

86 Ruitenbeek 1996.

87 Cheung et al. 2009.

88 See Beddington et al. (2007) and Worm et al. (2009) and for an overview of strategies to improve fisheries management.

89 Marine reserves and no-take zones have been shown to increase species diversity of target and non-target species within their boundaries (Worm et al. 2006) and depending on design, location and size, can increase adjacent fish catches (Roberts et al. 2001), and increase tourism revenue, a cultural service (Worm et al. 2006).

90 One way in which this can be done is by tradable catch shares or individual transferable quotas, TURFs etc (Beddington et al. 2007, Costello et al. 2008), whereby each fishermen or community is guaranteed a proportion of the total allowable catch. See also the discussion of property rights in Berkes et al. (2006).

91 Roughgarden and Smith (1996) have argued that in order to avoid collapses, stocks should be managed so that the target stock is above the producing maximum sustainable yield and harvested at less than the maximum sustainable yield.

92 Alder et al. 2007.

93 Pauly and Alder 2005.

94 Dinoflagelates produce 95% of the energy available to the corals (Hoegh-Guldberg et al. 2007).

95 Donner et al. 2005.

96 Some researchers have expressed doubts about the gloomier scenarios of the impacts of climate change on coral reefs (Hughes et al. 2003, Maynard et al. 2008). They argue that there is evidence for coral capacity to adapt at least partially to increases in sea surface temperature and acidification, and that it is likely we will see great changes in coral reef communities but these will not be necessarily catastrophic.

97 This includes calcifying phytoplankton species (Riebesell et al. 2000), pteropods living in high-latitude oceans (Orr et al. 2005), cold-water reefs, and other calcifying marine organisms (Raven et al. 2005, Fischlin et al. 2007). But some species may benefit from the interaction between ocean acidification and warming, such as seastars (Gooding et al. 2009).

98 Perry et al. 2005, Dulvy et al. 2008, Whitehead et al. 2008, Cheung et al. 2009.

99 Stempniewicz et al. (2007) developed a scenario of how changes in marine biodiversity in the Arctic can affect the biogeochemical cycle of nutrients in the tundra. Seabirds transport organic matter from the nutrient-rich sea to the nutrient-poor land, by feeding on marine life and depositing guano in seabird colonies. Arctic waters are usually dominated by large zooplankton species, which support plankton-eating seabirds (e.g. little auk), which nest a few kilometres inshore. Climate warming will favour instead the dominance of small species of zooplankton from Atlantic waters, which support plankton-eating fish species and in turn fish-eating birds (e.g. guillemots). Fish-eating guillemots nest on rocky cliffs at the coast, and therefore the transport of nutrients to inland will decrease, with negative impacts on primary productivity of tundra plant communities affecting tundra-dependent mammals and birds

100 Hoegh-Guldberg et al. (2007) describe two thresholds above which corals have not been found over the last half a million years: a thermal threshold of 2°C and a carbonate ion concentration of 200 μmol kg^{-1} (Figure 17).

101 Hughes et al. (2003) suggested that addressing overfishing may also improve the resilience of coral reefs to climate changes and other human pressures. Other measures to improve the conditions and resilience of coral reefs include controlling pollution sources and coastal development Perry et al. 2005, Dulvy et al. 2008. The coral reef crisis also opens economic opportunities. Given the rates of degradation of many coral reefs across the world, we believe that the islands that will best manage their reefs will be able to reap the economic benefits associated with nature tourism in the short-term (in one of the MA scenario storylines this is explored, Cork et al. 2005).

102 Diaz and Rosenberg 2008.

103 See Cork et al. (2005).

104 Cork et al. 2005, UNEP 2007.

105 Barry et al. 2008.

106 IEEP et al. 2009.

107 Randall et al. 2007.

108 http://www.earthobservations.org/geobon_a.shtml

109 A biome shift from tundra to boreal forest in North America is projected by both models as evidenced by the increase in % tree cover (blue) and decline in % herbaceous cover (red). The TRIFFID model predicts the replacement of tropical forests by herbaceous vegetation, especially in the Amazon, which is in stark contrast to the moderate increases in tree cover projected by the Orchidee model. TRIFFID also predicts boreal forest replacement of tundra in Asia, while the Orchidee model projects much more modest changes. It is important to note that neither of these models includes migration limitations on plants, so they may overestimate the extent to which boreal forest colonizes tundra in the 21st century. Sitch et al. (2008) also explored the response of two additional global vegetation models, LPJ and Hyland not presented here.

110 An explanation of the calculation of carbon storage in IMAGE is given in van Minnen et al. (2009). For a description of IMAGE see Bouwman et al. (2006).

111 Xenopoulos and Lodge 2006, Xenopoulos et al. 2005.

LIST OF ACRONYMS

CBD	Convention on Biological Diversity
DGVM	Dynamic global vegetation model
GBO2	Global Biodiversity Outlook 2
GBO3	Global Biodiversity Outlook 3
GEO-BON	Global Biodiversity Observation Network by the Group on Earth Observations
GEO4	Global Environment Outlook 4
GHG	Greenhouse gases
GVM	Global vegetation model
IAASTD	International Assessment for Agricultural Science, Technology and Development
IPBES	Intergovernmental Science-Policy Platform on Biodiversity and Ecosystem Services
IPCC	Intergovernmental Panel on Climate Change
IUCN	The International Union for Conservation of Nature
LPI	Living Planet Index
MA	Millennium Ecosystem Assessment
MSA	Mean Species Abundance
MTI	Mean Trophic Index
NBM	Niche-based models
OECD	Organisation for Economic Co-operation and Development
REDD	Reduced Emissions from Deforestation and Degradation
REDD+	Reduced Emissions from Deforestation and Degradation including through forest conservation, sustainable management of forests and enhancement of forest carbon stocks in developing countries
TEEB	The Economics of Ecosystems and Biodiversity
TURF	Territorial use rights in fisheries
UNEP	United Nations Environment Programme
UNFCCC	United Nations Framework Convention on Climate Change

REFERENCES

Abell, R., M. L. Thieme, C. Revenga, M. Bryer, M. Kottelat, N. Bogutskaya, B. Coad, N. Mandrak, S. C. Balderas, W. Bussing, M. L. J. Stiassny, P. Skelton, G. R. Allen, P. Unmack, A. Naseka, R. Ng, N. Sindorf, J. Robertson, E. Armijo, J. V. Higgins, T. J. Heibel, E. Wikramanayake, D. Olson, H. L. López, R. E. Reis, J. G. Lundberg, M. H. Sabaj Pérez, and P. Petry. 2008. Freshwater Ecoregions of the World: A New Map of Biogeographic Units for Freshwater Biodiversity Conservation. BioScience 58:403-414.

African Environmental Outlook 2: Our Environment, Our Wealth. 2006. United Nations Environment Programme, Nairobi, Kenya, (www.unep.org/dewa/Africa).

Aizen, M. A., L. A. Garibaldi, S. A. Cunningham, and A. M. Klein. 2009. How much does agriculture depend on pollinators? Lessons from long-term trends in crop production. Annals of Botany 103:1579-1588.

Aizen, M., L. Garibaldi, S. Cunningham, and A. Klein. 2008. Long-Term Global Trends in Crop Yield and Production Reveal No Current Pollination Shortage but Increasing Pollinator Dependency. Current Biology 18:1572-1575.

Akcakaya, H., S. Butchart, G. Mace, S. Stuart, and C. Hilton-Taylor. 2006. Use and misuse of the IUCN Red List Criteria in projecting climate change impacts on biodiversity. Global Change Biology 12:2037-2043.

Alcamo, J., D. van Vuuren, and W. Cramer. 2005a. Changes in ecosystem services and their drivers across scenarios. Pages 297-373 in S. R. Carpenter, L. P. Prabhu, E. M. Bennet, and M. B. Zurek (eds) Ecosystems and Human Well-Being: Scenarios. Millennium Ecosystem Assessment. Island Press, Washington DC.

Alcamo, J., van Vuuren, D. and Ringer, C. 2005b. Methodology for developing the MA scenarios. Pages 145-172 in S.R. Carpenter, L. P. Prabhu, E. M. Bennet & M. B. Zurek (eds) Ecosystems and Human Well-Being: Scenarios. Millennium Ecosystem Assessment. Island Press, Washington DC.

Alder J., S. Guénette, J. Beblow, W. Cheung and V. Christensen. 2007. Ecosystem-based global fishing policy scenarios. Fisheries Centre Research Reports 15 (7).

Alkemade, R., M. van Oorschot, L. Miles, C. Nellemann, M. Bakkenes, and B. ten Brink. 2009. GLOBIO3: A Framework to Investigate Options for Reducing Global Terrestrial Biodiversity Loss. Ecosystems 12:374-390.

Alvain, S., C. Moulin, Y. Dandonneau, and H. Loisel. 2008. Seasonal distribution and succession of dominant phytoplankton groups in the global ocean: A satellite view. Global Biogeochemical Cycles 22:GB3001.

Baillie, J. E. M., C. Hilton-Taylor, and S. N. Stuart. 2004. 2004 IUCN Red List of Threatened Species. A Global Species Assessment. IUCN, Gland, Switzerland.

Balmford, A., J. Beresford, J. Green, R. Naidoo, M. Walpole, and A. Manica. 2009. A Global Perspective on Trends in Nature-Based Tourism. PLoS Biology 7: e1000144.

Balvanera, P., A. Pfisterer, N. Buchmann, J. He, T. Nakashizuka, D. Raffaelli, and B. Schmid. 2006. Quantifying the evidence for biodiversity effects on ecosystem functioning and services. Ecology Letters 9:1146-1156.

Bar Massada, A., Y. Carmel, G. Koniak, and I. Noy-Meir. 2009. The effects of disturbance based management on the dynamics of Mediterranean vegetation: A hierarchical and spatially explicit modeling approach. Ecological Modelling 220:2525-2535.

Barry, S. C., K. R. Hayes, C. L. Hewitt, H. L. Behrens, E. Dragsund, and S. M. Bakke. 2008. Ballast water risk assessment: principles, processes, and methods. ICES J. Mar. Sci. 65:121-131.

Beddington, J. R., D. J. Agnew, and C. W. Clark. 2007. Current Problems in the Management of Marine Fisheries. Science 316:1713-1716.

Bellwood, D. R., T. P. Hughes, C. Folke, and M. Nyström. 2004. Confronting the coral reef crisis. Nature 429:827–833.

Berkes, F., T. P. Hughes, R. S. Steneck, J. A. Wilson, D. R. Bellwood, B. Crona, C. Folke, L. H. Gunderson, H. M. Leslie, J. Norberg, M. Nystrom, P. Olsson, H. Osterblom, M. Scheffer, and B. Worm. 2006. Globalization, Roving Bandits, and Marine Resources. Science 311:1557-1558.

Betts, R. A., Y. Malhi, and J. T. Roberts. 2008. The future of the Amazon: new perspectives from climate, ecosystem and social sciences. Philosophical Transactions of the Royal Society B-Biological Sciences 363:1729-1735.

Bigelow, N. H., L. B. Brubaker, M. E. Edwards, S. P. Harrison, I. C. Prentice, P. M. Anderson, A. A. Andreev, P. J. Bartlein, T. R. Christensen, W. Cramer, J. O. Kaplan, A. V. Lozhkin, N. V. Matveyeva, D. F. Murray, A. D. McGuire, V. Y. Razzhivin, J. C. Ritchie,

B. Smith, D. A. Walker, K. Gajewski, V. Wolf, B. H. Holmqvist, Y. Igarashi, K. Kremenetskii, A. Paus, M. F. J. Pisaric, and V. S. Volkova. 2003. Climate change and Arctic ecosystems: 1. Vegetation changes north of 55 degrees N between the last glacial maximum, mid-Holocene, and present. Journal of Geophysical Research-Atmospheres 108:D19.

Biggs, R., H. Simons, M. Bakkenes, R. J. Scholes, B. Eickhout, D. van Vuuren, and R. Alkemade. 2008. Scenarios of biodiversity loss in southern Africa in the 21st century. Global Environmental Change – Human and Policy Dimensions 18:296-309.

Bohlen, P. J., S. Lynch, L. Shabman, M. Clark, S. Shukla, and H. Swain. 2009. Paying for environmental services from agricultural lands: an example from the northern Everglades. Frontiers in Ecology and the Environment 7:46-55.

Bond, W. J., F. I. Woodward, and G. F. Midgley. 2005. The Global Distribution of Ecosystems in a World without Fire. New Phytologist 165:525-537.

Bopp, L., P. Monfray, O. Aumont, J. Dufresne, H. Le Treut, G. Madec, L. Terray, and J. Orr. 2001. Potential impact of climate change on marine export production. Global Biogeochemical Cycles 15:81-99.

Botkin, D. B., H. Saxe, M. B. Araújo, R. Betts, R. H. W. Bradshaw, T. Cedhagen, P. Chesson, T. P. Dawson, J. R. Etterson, D. P. Faith, S. Ferrier, A. Guisan, A. S. Hansen, D. W. Hilbert, C. Loehle, C. Margules, M. New, M. J. Sobel, and D. R. B. Stockwell. 2007. Forecasting the Effects of Global Warming on Biodiversity. BioScience 57:227.

Bouwman, A.F., T. Kram, and K. Klein Goldewijk (eds) 2006. Integrated modelling of global environmental change. An overview of IMAGE 2.4. Report no. 500110002, Netherlands Environmental Assessment Agency, Bilthoven, The Netherlands. ISBN 9069601516, pp 228.

Bouwman, A., G. Van Drecht, J. Knoop, A. Beusen, and C. Meinardi. 2005. Exploring changes in river nitrogen export to the world's oceans. Global Biogeochemical Cycles 19: GB1002.

Brooks, T., S. Wright, and D. Sheil. 2009. Evaluating the Success of Conservation Actions in Safeguarding Tropical Forest Biodiversity. Conservation Biology 23:1448-1457.

Cahoon DR, Hensel PF, Spencer T, Reed DJ, McKee KL, Saintilan N. 2006. Coastal wetland vulnerability to relative sea-level rise: wetland elevation trends and process controls. Pages 271-292, In: J. T. A. Verhoeven, B. Beltman, R. Bobbink, and D. Whigham (eds). Wetlands and Natural Resource Management. Ecological Studies, Volume 190, Springer-Verlag Berlin & Heidelberg.

Carpenter, S. R. 2003. Regime shifts in lake ecosystems: pattern and variation. International Ecology Institute, Oldendorf/Luhe.

Carpenter, S. R., H. A. Mooney, J. Agard, D. Capistrano, R. S. DeFries, S. Díaz, T. Dietz, A. K. Duraiappah, A. Oteng-Yeboah, H. M. Pereira, C. Perrings, W. V. Reid, J. Sarukhan, R. J. Scholes, and A. Whyte. 2009. Science for managing ecosystem services: Beyond the Millennium Ecosystem Assessment. Proceedings of the National Academy of Sciences 106:1305-1312.

CBD - Secretariat of the Convention on Biological Diversity. 2006. Global Biodiversity Outlook 2. Page 81+vii in UNO-Secretariat of the Convention on Biological Diversity. Montreal. Montreal.

Chan, K., M. Shaw, D. Cameron, E. Underwood, and G. Daily. 2006. Conservation planning for ecosystem services. PLoS Biology 4:2138-2152.

Chan, K., R. Pringle, J. Ranganathan, C. Boggs, Y. Chan, P. Ehrlich, P. Haff, N. E. Heller, K. Al-Krafaji, and D. Macmynowski. 2007. When Agendas Collide: Human Welfare and Biological Conservation. Conservation Biology 21:59-68.

Cheung, W. W. L., R. Watson, T. Morato, T. J. Pitcher, and D. Pauly. 2007. Intrinsic vulnerability in the global fish catch. Marine Ecology Progress Series 333:1-12.

Cheung, W. W., and U. R. Sumaila. 2008. Trade-offs between conservation and socio-economic objectives in managing a tropical marine ecosystem. Ecological Economics 66:193-210.

Cheung, W. W., V. W. Lam, J. L. Sarmiento, K. Kearney, R. Watson, and D. Pauly. 2009. Projecting global marine biodiversity impacts under climate change scenarios. Fish and Fisheries 10:235-251.

Christensen, V., K. A. Aiken, and M. C. Villanueva. 2007. Threats to the ocean: on the role of ecosystem approaches to fisheries. Social Science Information Sur Les Science Sociales 46:67-86.

Cook, K. H., and E. K. Vizy. 2006. Coupled model simulations of the West African monsoon system: Twentieth- and twenty-first-century simulations. Journal of Climate 19:3681-3703.

Cork, S., G. Peterson, G. Petschel-Held, J. Alcamo, J. Alder, E. Bennet, E. R. Carr, D. Deane, G. C. Nelson, and T. Ribeiro. 2005. Four Scenarios. Pages 223-294 in S. Carpenter, L. P. Prabhu, E. M. Bennet, and M. Zurek, editors. Ecosystems and Human Well-Being: Scenarios. Island Press, Washington DC.

Costello, C., S. D. Gaines, and J. Lynham. 2008. Can Catch Shares Prevent Fisheries Collapse? Science 321:1678-1681.

Davin, E., and N. de Noblet-Ducoudre. 2010. Climatic Impact of Global-Scale Deforestation: Radiative versus Nonradiative Processes. Journal of Climate 23:97-112.

de Guenni, L., M. Cardoso, J. Goldammer, G. Hurtt, and L. J. Mata. 2005. Regulation of Natural Hazards: Floods and Fires. in Ecosystems and Human Well-Being: Current State and Trends. Island Press, Washington DC.

Desanker, P.V., P.G.H. Frost, C.O. Justice, and R.J. Scholes. 1997. The Miombo Network: Framework for a Terrestrial Transect Study of Land-Use and Land-Cover Change in the Miombo Ecosystems of Central Africa. IGBP Report 41, Stockholm, Sweden.

Diaz, R. J., and R. Rosenberg. 2008. Spreading Dead Zones and Consequences for Marine Ecosystems. Science 321:926-929.

Donner SD. 2009. Coping with Commitment: Projected Thermal Stress on Coral Reefs under Different Future Scenarios. Plos One 4:e5712.

Donner, S., W. Skirving, C. Little, M. Oppenheimer, and O. Hoegh-Guldberg. 2005. Global assessment of coral bleaching and required rates of adaptation under climate change. Global Change Biology 11:2251-2265.

Dulvy, N. K., S. I. Rogers, S. Jennings, Stelzenmü, V. ller, S. R. Dye, and H. R. Skjoldal. 2008. Climate change and deepening of the North Sea fish assemblage: a biotic indicator of warming seas. Journal of Applied Ecology 45:1029-1039.

Dulvy, N., J. Ellis, N. Goodwin, A. Grant, J. Reynolds, and S. Jennings. 2004. Methods of assessing extinction risk in marine fishes. Fish and Fisheries 5:255-276.

Fang, X., H. G. Stefan, J. G. Eaton, J. H. McCormick, and S. R. Alam. 2004a. Simulation of thermal/dissolved oxygen habitat for fishes in lakes under different climate scenarios: Part 1. Cool-water fish in the contiguous US. Ecological Modelling 172:13-37.

Fang, X., H. G. Stefan, J. G. Eaton, J. H. McCormick, and S. R. Alam. 2004b. Simulation of thermal/dissolved oxygen habitat for fishes in lakes under different climate scenarios: Part 2. Cold-water fish in the contiguous US. Ecological Modelling 172:39-54.

Fang, X., H. G. Stefan, J. G. Eaton, J. H. McCormick, and S. R. Alam. 2004c. Simulation of thermal/dissolved oxygen habitat for fishes in lakes under different climate scenarios: Part 3. Warm-water fish in the contiguous US. Ecological Modelling 172:55-68.

FAO. 2009. The State of World Fisheries and Aquaculture 2008. FAO.

Finlayson, C. M., and R. D'Cruz. 2005. Inland Water Systems. p. 551-584 in Hassan R., R. Scholes and N. Ash (eds). Ecosystems and Human Well-Being: Current State and Trends, Volume 1. The Millennium Ecosystem Assessment. Island Press, Washington DC.

Fischlin, A., G. F. Midgley, J. Price, R. Leemans, B. Gopal, C. Turley, M. Rounsevell, P. Dube, J. Tarazona, and A. Velichko. 2007. Ecosystems, their properties, goods and services. Page 211 in M. Parry, O. Canziani, J. Palutikof, P. van der Linden, and C. Hanson, editors. Climate Change 2007: Impacts, Adaptation and Vulnerability. Contribution of Working Group II to the Fourth Assessment Report of the IPCC. Cambridge University Press, Cambridge.

Folley, J. A. 2005. Tipping points in the tundra. Science 310:627-628.

Frost, P.G.H. 1996. The Ecology of Miombo Woodlands. In: Campbell B. (ed.), The Miombo in Transition: Woodlands and Welfare in Africa. Centre for International Forestry Research (CIFOR), Bogor, Indonesia, pp. 11-55.

Froyd, C., and K. Willis. 2008. Emerging issues in biodiversity & conservation management: The need for a palaeoecological perspective. Quaternary Science Reviews 27:1723-1732.

Gallai, N., J. Salles, J. Settele, and B. Vaissiere. 2009. Economic valuation of the vulnerability of world agriculture confronted with pollinator decline. Ecological Economics 68:810-821.

Gaston, K. 2010. Valuing Common Species. Science 327:154-155.

Gilman, E., J. Ellison, N. Duke, C. Field. 2008. Threats to mangroves from climate change and adaptation options: A review Aquatic Botany 89: 237-250.

Gooding, R. A., C. D. G. Harley, and E. Tang. 2009. Elevated water temperature and carbon dioxide concentration increase the growth of a keystone echinoderm. Proceedings of the National Academy of Sciences 106:9316-9321.

Gopal, B. 2005. Does inland aquatic biodiversity have a future in Asian developing countries? Hydrobiologia 542:69-75.

Grainger, A., D. H. Boucher, P. C. Frumhoff, W. F. Laurance, T. Lovejoy, J. McNeely, M. Niekisch, P. Raven, N. S. Sodhi, O. Venter, and S. L. Pimm. 2009. Biodiversity and REDD at Copenhagen. Current Biology 19:R974-R976.

Greene, C. H., A. J. Pershing, T. M. Cronin, and N. Ceci. 2008. Arctic climate change and its impacts on the ecology of the North Atlantic. Ecology 89:S24-S38.

Gullison, R. E., P. C. Frumhoff, J. G. Canadell, C. B. Field, D. C. Nepstad, K. Hayhoe, R. Avissar, L. M. Curran, P. Friedlingstein, C. D. Jones, and C. Nobre. 2007. Tropical Forests and Climate Policy. Science 316:985-986.

Hays, G. C., A. J. Richardson, and C. Robinson. 2005. Climate change and marine plankton. Trends in Ecology and Evolution 20:337–344.

Heal, G., G. C. Daily, P. R. Ehrlich, J. Salzman, C. L. Boggs, J. J. Hellmann, J. Hughes, C. Kremen, and T. Ricketts. 2001. Protecting natural capital through ecosystem service districts. Stanford Environmental Law Journal 20:333-364.

Heino, J., R. Virrkala, and H. Toivonen. 2009. Climate change and freshwater biodiversity: detected patterns, future trends and adaptations in northern regions. Biological Reviews 84:39-54.

Heller, N. E., and E. S. Zavaleta. 2009. Biodiversity management in the face of climate change: A review of 22 years of recommendations. Biological Conservation 142:14-32.

Hillebrand, H., and B. Matthiessen. 2009. Biodiversity in a complex world: consolidation and progress in functional biodiversity research. Ecology Letters 12:1405-1419.

Hoegh-Guldberg, O., P. J. Mumby, A. J. Hooten, R. S. Steneck, P. Greenfield, E. Gomez, C. D. Harvell, P. F. Sale, A. J. Edwards, K. Caldeira, N. Knowlton, C. M. Eakin, R. Iglesias-Prieto, N. Muthiga, R. H. Bradbury, A. Dubi, and M. E. Hatziolos. 2007. Coral Reefs Under Rapid Climate Change and Ocean Acidification. Science 318:1737-1742.

Hölker, F., D. Beare, H. Dorner, A. di Natale, H. Ratz, A. Temming, and J. Casey. 2007. Comment on "Impacts of Biodiversity Loss on Ocean Ecosystem Services". Science 316:1285c.

Holland, M. M., C. M. Bitz, and B. Tremblay. 2006. Future abrupt reductions in the summer Arctic sea ice. Geophysical Research Letters 33: L23503.

Howarth, R., and S. Bringezu. 2008. Biofuels: Environmental Consequences and Interactions with Changing Land Use. SCOPE, Gummersbach, Germany.

Hughes, T. P., A. H. Baird, D. R. Bellwood, M. Card, S. R. Connolly, C. Folke, R. Grosberg, O. Hoegh-Guldberg, J. B. C. Jackson, J. Kleypas, J. M. Lough, P. Marshall, M. Nystrom, S. R. Palumbi, J. M. Pandolfi, B. Rosen, and J. Roughgarden. 2003. Climate Change, Human Impacts, and the Resilience of Coral Reefs. Science 301:929-933.

Hughes, T. P., D. R. Bellwood, C. Folke, R. S. Steneck, and J. Wilson. 2005. New paradigms for supporting the resilience of marine ecosystems. Trends in Ecology and Evolution 20:380–386.

Hutchings, J., and J. Reynolds. 2004. Marine fish population collapses: Consequences for recovery and extinction risk. BioScience 54:297-309.

Ibanez, I., J. Clark, M. Dietze, K. Feeley, M. Hersh, S. LaDeau, A. McBride, N. Welch, and M. Wolosin. 2006. Predicting biodiversity change: Outside the climate envelope, beyond the species-area curve. Ecology 87:1896-1906.

IEEP, Alterra, Ecologic, PBL, and UNEP-WCMC. 2009. Scenarios and models for exploring future trends of biodiversity and ecosystem services changes. Final report to the European Commission, DG Environment on Contract ENV.G.1/ETU/2008/0090r., Institute for European Environmental Policy, Alterra Wageningen UR, Ecologic, Netherlands Environmental Assessment Agency, United Nations Environment Programme World Conservation Monitoring Centre.

IPCC. 2007. Climate Change 2007: Synthesis Report. Contribution of Working Groups I, II and III to the Fourth Assessment Report of the Intergovernmental Panel on Climate Change [Core Writing Team, Pachauri, R.K and Reisinger, A. (eds)]. Page 104 pp. IPCC, Geneva, Switzerland.

Ishidaira, H., Y. Ishikawa, S. Funada, and K. Takeuchi. 2008. Estimating the evolution of vegetation cover and its hydrological impact in the Mekong River basin in the 21st century. Hydrological Processes 22:1395-1405.

Jankowski, T., D. Livingstone, H. Buhrer, R. Forster, and P. Niederhauser. 2006. Consequences of the 2003 European heat wave for lake temperature profiles, thermal stability, and hypolimnetic oxygen depletion: Implications for a warmer world. Limnology and Oceanography 51:815-819.

Jetz, W., D. S. Wilcove, and A. P. Dobson. 2007. Projected impacts of climate and land-use change on the global diversity of birds. PLoS Biology 5:e157.

Johnson, P., J. Olden, and M. vander Zanden. 2008. Dam invaders: impoundments facilitate biological invasions into freshwaters. Frontiers in Ecology and the Environment 6:359-365.

Koch, P. L., and A. D. Barnosky. 2006. Late Quaternary Extinctions: State of the Debate. Annual Review of Ecology, Evolution and Systematics 37:215-250.

Kok, M. T. J., J. A. Bakkes, B. Eickhout, A. J. G. Manders, M. M. P. V. Oorschot, D. V. Vuuren, M. V. Wees, and H. J. Westhoek. 2008. Lessons from global environmental assessments. Netherlands Environmental Assessment Agency, Bilthoven.

Kremen, C., N. M. Williams, M. A. Aizen, B. Gemmill-Herren, G. LeBuhn, R. Minckley, L. Packer, S. G. Potts, T. Roulston, I. Steffan-Dewenter, D. P. Vázquez, R. Winfree, L. Adams, E. E. Crone, S. S. Greenleaf, T. H. Keitt, A. Klein, J. Regetz, and T. H. Ricketts. 2007. Pollination and other ecosystem services produced by mobile organisms: a conceptual framework for the effects of land-use change. Ecology Letters 10:299-314.

Lake, P. S., and N. R. Bond. 2007. Australian futures: Freshwater ecosystems and human water usage. Futures 39:288-305.

Leclerc, M. 2005. The ecohydraulics paradigm shift: IAHR enters a new era. Journal of Hydraulic Research 43:63-64.

Lemke, P., J. Ren, R. B. Alley, I. Allison, J. Carrasco, G. Flato, Y. Fujii, G. Kaser, P. Mote, R. H. Thomas, and T. Zhang. 2007. Observations: changes in snow, ice and frozen ground. Pages 337–383 in S. Solomon, D. Qin, M. Manning, Z. Chen, M. Marquis, K. B. Averyt, M. Tignor, and H. L. Miller, editors. Climate Change 2007: the physical science basis. Contribution of Working Group I to the Fourth Assessment Report of the Intergovernmental Panel on Climate Change. Cambridge University Press, Cambridge, United Kingdom and New York, NY, USA.

Leprieur, F., O. Beauchard, S. Blanchet, T. Oberdorff, and S. Brosse. 2008. Fish invasions in the world's river systems: When natural processes are blurred by human activities. PLoS Biology 6:404-410.

Lindemann-Matthies, P., X. Junge, and M. Dierhart (2010). The influence of plant diversity on people's perception and aesthetic appreciation of grassland vegetation. Biological Conservation, 143, 195-202

Loreau, M., S. Naeem, P. Inchausti, J. Bengtsson, J. P. Grime, A. Hector, D. U. Hooper, M. A. Huston, D. Raffaelli, B. Schmid, D. Tilman, and D. A. Wardle. 2001. Biodiversity and Ecosystem Functioning: Current Knowledge and Future Challenges. Science 294:804-808.

Lucht, W., S. Schaphoff, T. Erbrecht, U. Heyder, and W. Cramer. 2006. Terrestrial vegetation redistribution and carbon balance under climate change. Carbon Balance and Management 1:6.

Ludeke, M. K., G. Petschel-Held, and H. J. Schellnhuber. 2004. Syndromes of global change: the first panoramic view. GAIA-Ecological Perspectives for Science and Society 13:42-49.

MA - Millennium Ecosystem Assessment. 2005. Ecosystems and human well-being: synthesis. Island Press, Washington DC.

Malcolm, J. R., C. Liu, R. P. Neilson, L. Hansen, and L. Hannah. 2006. Global Warming and Extinctions of Endemic Species from Biodiversity Hotspots. Conservation Biology 20:538-548.

Malhi, Y., J. T. Roberts, R. A. Betts, T. J. Killeen, W. H. Li, and C. A. Nobre. 2008a. Climate change, deforestation, and the fate of the Amazon. Science 319:169-172.

Maynard, J., K. Anthony, P. Marshall, and I. Masiri. 2008. Major bleaching events can lead to increased thermal tolerance in corals. Marine Biology 155:173-182.

Mbow, C., O. Mertz, A. Diouf, K. Rasmussen, and A. Reenberg. 2008. The history of environmental change and adaptation in eastern Saloum-Senegal-Driving forces and perceptions. Global and Planetary Change 64:210-221.

McGuire AD, Anderson LG, Christensen TR, Dallimore S, Guo LD, Hayes DJ, Heimann M, Lorenson TD, Macdonald RW, Roulet N. 2009. Sensitivity of the carbon cycle in the Arctic to climate change. Ecological Monographs 79: 523-555.

Mooney, H.A., R.N. Mack, J.A. McNeely, L.E. Neville, P.J. Schei, and J.K. Waage (eds) 2005. Invasive alien species: A new synthesis. Island Press, Washington DC. 368 p.

Moore, S. E., and H. P. Huntington. 2008. Arctic marine mammals and climate change: Impacts and resilience. Ecological Applications 18:S157-S165.

Morris, J. T., P. V. Sundareshwar, C. T. Nietch, B. Kjerfve, and D. R. Cahoon. 2002. Responses of coastal wetlands to rising sea-level. Ecology 83: 2869-2877.

Naidoo, R., A. Balmford, R. Costanza, B. Fisher, R.E. Green, B. Lehner, T. Malcolm, and T. Ricketts. 2008. Global mapping of ecosystem services and conservation priorities. Proceedings of the National Academy of Sciences 105:9495-9500.

Neilson R.P., I.C. Prentice, B. Smith, T.G.F. Kittel, D. Viner. 1998. Simulated changes in vegetation distribution under global warming. p. 439–56 in Watson R.T., M.C. Zinyowera, R.H. Moss, D.J. Dokken (eds) The regional impacts of climate change: an assessment of vulnerability. Cambridge University Press, Cambridge.

Nelson, E., G. Mendoza, J. Regetz, S. Polasky, H. Tallis, D. Cameron, K. M. Chan, G. C. Daily, J. Goldstein, P. M. Kareiva, E. Lonsdorf, R. Naidoo, T. H. Ricketts, and M. Shaw. 2009. Modeling multiple ecosystem services, biodiversity conservation, commodity production, and tradeoffs at landscape scales. Frontiers in Ecology and the Environment 7:4-11.

Nentwig, W. (ed.) 2007. Biological invasions. Ecological Studies series No. 193, Springer, Berlin, 441 p.

Nepstad, D. C., C. M. Stickler, B. Soares, and F. Merry. 2008. Interactions among Amazon land use, forests and climate: prospects for a near-term forest tipping point. Philosophical Transactions of the Royal Society B-Biological Sciences 363:1737-1746.

Newton, K., I. M. Côté, G. M. Pilling, S. Jennings, and N. K. Dulvy. 2007. Current and Future Sustainability of Island Coral Reef Fisheries. Current Biology 17:655-658.

Nielsen, S., E. Bayne, J. Schieck, J. Herbers, and S. Boutin. 2007. A new method to estimate species and biodiversity intactness using empirically derived reference conditions. Biological Conservation 137:403-414.

Nilsson, C., C. A. Reidy, M. Dynesius, and C. Revenga. 2005. Fragmentation and Flow Regulation of the World's Large River Systems. Science 308:405-408.

Nobre, C. A., and L. D. Borma. 2009. 'Tipping points' for the Amazon forest. Current Opinion in Environmental Sustainability 1:28–36.

Oberdorff, T., S. Lek, and J. Guegan. 1999. Patterns of endemism in riverine fish of the Northern Hemisphere. Ecology Letters 2:75-81.

OECD, 2008. Environmental outlook to 2030. Paris, France: Organization for Economic Cooperation and Development

Oelmann, Y., C. Potvin, T. Mark, L. Werther, S. Tapernon, and W. Wilcke. 2010. Tree mixture effects on aboveground nutrient pools of trees in an experimental plantation in Panama. Plant and Soil 326:199-212.

Orr, J. C., V. J. Fabry, O. Aumont, L. Bopp, S. C. Doney, R. A. Feely, A. Gnanadesikan, N. Gruber, A. Ishida, F. Joos, R. M. Key, K. Lindsay, E. Maier-Reimer, R. Matear, P. Monfray, A. Mouchet, R. G. Najjar, G. Plattner, K. B. Rodgers, C. L. Sabine, J. L. Sarmiento, R. Schlitzer, R. D. Slater, I. J. Totterdell, M. Weirig, Y. Yamanaka, and A. Yool. 2005. Anthropogenic ocean acidification over the twenty-first century and its impact on calcifying organisms. Nature 437:681-686.

Overpeck, J., and J. Weiss. 2009. Projections of future sea level becoming more dire. Proceedings of the National Academy of Sciences 106:21461-21462.

Palahi M, R. Mavsar, C. Gracia, Y. Birot. 2008. Mediterranean Forests under focus. International Forestry Review 10: 676-688.

Palmer, M. A., C. A. R. Liermann, C. Nilsson, M. Floerke, J. Alcamo, P. S. Lake, and N. Bond. 2008. Climate change and the world's river basins: anticipating management options. Frontiers in Ecology and the Environment 6:81-89.

Pandolfi, J. M., R. H. Bradbury, E. Sala, T. P. Hughes, K. A. Bjorndal, R. G. Cooke, D. McArdle, L. McClenachan, M. J. H. Newman, G. Paredes, R. B. Aronson, R. R. Warner, J. B. C. Jackson;, T. P. Hughes, A. H. Baird, D. R. Bellwood, S. R. Connolly, C. Folke, R. Grosberg, O. Hoegh-Guldberg, J. B. C. Jackson, J. F. Bruno, J. Kleypas, J. M. Lough, P. Marshall, M. Nystrom, S. R. Palumbi, J. M. Pandolfi, B. Rosen, J. Roughgarden, W. F. Precht, P. W. Glynn, C. D. Harvell, L. Kaufman, C. S. Rogers, E. A. Shinn, and J. F. Valentine;. 2003. Causes of Coral Reef Degradation. Science 302:1502b-1504.

Paterson, J., M. B. Araújo, P. M. Berry, J. M. Piper, and M. Rounsevell. 2008. Mitigation, Adaptation, and the Threat to Biodiversity. Conservation Biology 22:1352-1355.

Pauly, D., and J. Alder. 2005. Marine Fisheries Systems. p. 477-512 in Hassan R., R. Scholes and N. Ash (eds). Ecosystems and Human Well-Being: Current State and Trends, Volume 1. The Millennium Ecosystem Assessment. Island Press, Washington DC.

Pauly, D., J. Alder, E. Bennett, V. Christensen, P. Tyedmers, and R. Watson. 2003. The future for fisheries. Science 302:1359-1361.

Pauly, D., V. Christensen, S. Guénette, T. J. Pitcher, U. R. Sumaila, C. J. Walters, R. Watson, and D. Zeller. 2002. Towards sustainability in world fisheries. Nature 418:689–695.

Pausas, J. G., J. Llovet, A. Rodrigo, and R. Vallejo. 2008. Are wildfires a disaster in the Mediterranean basin? – A review. International Journal of Wildland Fire 17:713-723.

Pejchar, L., and H. Mooney. 2009. Invasive species, ecosystem services and human well-being. Trends in Ecology & Evolution 24:497-504.

Perry, A. L., P. J. Low, J. R. Ellis, and J. D. Reynolds. 2005. Climate Change and Distribution Shifts in Marine Fishes. Science 308:1912-1915.

Poff N.L., M.M. Brinson, and J.W. Day Jr. 2002. Aquatic ecosystems and global climate change: Potential impacts on inland freshwater and coastal wetland ecosystems in the United States. Pew Center on Global Climate Change, Philadelphia and Washington DC.

Pounds, J., M. R. Bustamante, L. A. Coloma, J. A. Consuegra, M. P. L. Fogden, P. N. Foster, E. La Marca, K. L. Masters, A. Merino-Viteri, R. Puschendorf, S. R. Ron, G. A. Sanchez-Azofeifa, C. J. Still, and B. E. Young. 2006. Widespread amphibian extinctions from epidemic disease driven by global warming. Nature 439:161-167.

Prugh, L. R., K. E. Hodges, A. R. E. Sinclair, and J. S. Brashares. 2008. Effect of habitat area and isolation on fragmented animal populations. Proceedings of the National Academy of Sciences 105:20770-20775.

Randall, D.A., R.A. Wood, S. Bony, R. Colman, T. Fichefet, J. Fyfe, V. Kattsov, A. Pitman, J. Shukla, J. Srinivasan, R.J. Stouffer, A. Sumi and K.E. Taylor (2007) Climate models and their evaluation. In Solomon, S., D. Qin, M. Manning, Z. Chen, M. Marquis, K.B. Averyt, M.Tignor and H.L. Miller (eds) Climate Change 2007: The Physical Science Basis. Contribution of Working Group I to the Fourth Assessment Report of the Intergovernmental Panel on Climate Change. Cambridge University Press, Cambridge, UK and New York, NY, USA.

Ranganathan, J., R. Daniels, M. Chandran, P. Ehrlich, and G. Daily. 2008. Sustaining biodiversity in ancient tropical countryside. Proceedings of the National Academy of Sciences 105:17852-17854.

Raven, J., K. Caldeira, H. Elderfield, O. Hoegh-Guldberg, P. Liss, U. Riebesell, J. Shepherd, C. Turley, and A. Watson. 2005. Ocean acidification due to increasing atmospheric carbon dioxide.Policy document 12/05. Policy document, The Royal Society. The Clyvedon Press Ltd, Cardiff.

Reynolds, J. F., D. M. Stafford Smith, E. F. Lambin, B. L. Turner, M. Mortimore, S. P. J. Batterbury, T. E. Downing, H. Dowlatabadi, R. J. Fernandez, J. E. Herrick, E. Huber-Sannwald, H. Jiang, R. Leemans, T. Lynam, F. T. Maestre, M. Ayarza, and B. Walker. 2007. Global Desertification: Building a Science for Dryland Development. Science 316:847-851.

Richardson, A. J., A. Bakun, G. C. Hays, and M. J. Gibbons. 2009. The jellyfish joyride: causes, consequences and management responses to a more gelatinous future. Trends in Ecology and Evolution 24:312-322.

Richardson, D., J. Hellmann, J. McLachlan, D. Sax, M. Schwartz, P. Gonzalez, E. Brennan, A. Camacho, T. Root, O. Sala, S. Schneider, D. Ashe, J. Clark, R. Early, J. Etterson, E. Fielder, J. Gill, B. Minteer, S. Polasky, H. Safford, A. Thompson, and M. Vellend. 2009. Multidimensional evaluation of managed relocation. Proceedings of the National Academy of Sciences of the United States of America 106:9721-9724.

Riebesell, U., A. Kortzinger, and A. Oschlies. 2009. Sensitivities of marine carbon fluxes to ocean change. Proceedings of the National Academy of Sciences 106:20602-20609.

Riebesell, U., I. Zondervan, B. Rost, P. D. Tortell, R. E. Zeebe, and F. M. M. Morel. 2000. Reduced calcification of marine plankton in response to increased atmospheric CO2. Nature 407:364-367.

Roberts, C. M., J. A. Bohnsack, F. Gell, J. P. Hawkins, and R. Goodridge. 2001. Effects of Marine Reserves on Adjacent Fisheries. Science 294:1920-1923.

Rost, B., I. Zondervan, and D. Wolf-Gladrow. 2008. Sensitivity of phytoplankton to future changes in ocean carbonate chemistry: current knowledge, contradictions and research directions. Marine Ecology Progress Series 373:227-237.

Rothman, J. Agard, and J. Alcamo. 2007. The future today. Pages 397-456 in Global Environmental Outlook 4. UNEP, Nairobi.

Roughgarden, J., and F. Smith. 1996. Why fisheries collapse and what to do about it. Proceedings of the National Academy of Sciences of the United States of America 93:5078-5083.

Ruitenbeek, H. J. 1996. The great Canadian fishery collapse: some policy lessons. Ecological Economics 19:103-106.

Sala, O. E., D. P. Van Vuuren, H. M. Pereira, D. Lodge, J. Alder, G. Cumming, A. Dobson, W. Volters, M. Xenopoulos, and A. Zaitsev. 2005. Biodiversity across scenarios. Ecosystems and Human Well-Being: Scenarios. Pages 375-408 in Millennium Ecosystem Assessment. Island Press, Washington DC.

Sala, O.E., F.S.Chapin, J.J. Armesto, E. Berlow, J. Bloomfield, R. Dirzo, E. HuberSanwald, L.F. Huenneke, R.B. Jackson, A. Kinzig, R. Leemans, D.M. Lodge, H.A. Mooney, M. Oesterheld, N.L. Poff, M.T. Sykes, B.H. Walker, M. Walker and D.H. Wall. 2000. Biodiversity: Global biodiversity scenarios for the year 2100. Science, 287, 1770-1774.

Sax, D.F., and S.D. Gaines. 2008. Species invasions and extinction: The future of native biodiversity on islands. Proceedings of the National Academy of Science 105:11490-11497.

Schaphoff, S., W. Lucht, D. Gerten, S. Sitch, W. Cramer, and I. C. Prentice. 2006. Terrestrial biosphere carbon storage under alternative climate projections. Climatic Change 74:97-122.

Scheffer, M., S. H. Hosper, M. L. Meijer, B. Moss, and E. Jeppesen. 1993. Alternative equilibria in shallow lakes. Trends in Ecology and Evolution 8:275–279.

Schmitz, O. J., E. Post, C. E. Burns, and K. M. Johnston. 2003. Ecosystem responses to global climate change: Moving beyond color mapping. BioScience 53:1199-1205.

Scholes, R.J. and R. Biggs (eds). 2004. Ecosystem services in southern Africa: a regional assessment. CSIR, Pretoria.

Schroter, D., W. Cramer, R. Leemans, I. C. Prentice, M. B. Araujo, N. W. Arnell, A. Bondeau, H. Bugmann, T. R. Carter, C. A. Gracia, A. C. de la Vega-Leinert, M. Erhard, F. Ewert, M. Glendining, J. I. House, S. Kankaanpaa, R. J. T. Klein, S. Lavorel, M. Lindner, M. J. Metzger, J. Meyer, T. D. Mitchell, I. Reginster, M. Rounsevell, S. Sabate, S. Sitch, B. Smith, J. Smith, P. Smith, M. T. Sykes, K. Thonicke, W. Thuiller, G. Tuck, S. Zaehle, and B. Zierl. 2005. Ecosystem service supply and vulnerability to global change in Europe. Science 310:1333-1337.

Sitch, S., C. Huntingford, N. Gedney, P. E. Levy, M. Lomas, S. L. Piao, R. Betts, P. Ciais, P. Cox, P. Friedlingstein, C. D. Jones, I. C. Prentice, and F. I. Woodward. 2008. Evaluation of the terrestrial carbon cycle, future plant geography and climate-carbon cycle feedbacks using five Dynamic Global Vegetation Models (DGVMs). Global Change Biology 14:2015-2039.

Smith, V. H., and D. W. Schindler. 2009. Eutrophication science: where do we go from here? Trends in Ecology and Evolution 24: 201-207.

Stehfest, E., L. Bouwman, D. van Vuuren, M. den Elzen, B. Eickhout, and P. Kabat. 2009. Climate benefits of changing diet. Climatic Change 95:83-102.

Stempniewicz, L., K. Blachowlak-Samolyk, and J. M. Weslawski. 2007. Impact of climate change on zooplankton communities, seabird populations and arctic terrestrial ecosystem - A scenario. Deep-sea Research Part II. Topical Studies in Oceanography 54:2934-2945.

Stork, N. E., J. A. Coddington, R. K. Colwell, R. L. Chazdon, C. W. Dick, C. A. Peres, S. Sloan, and K. Willis. 2009. Vulnerability and Resilience of Tropical Forest Species to Land-Use Change. Conservation Biology 23:1438-1447.

ten Brink, B., R. Alkemade, M. Bakkenes, B. Eickhout, M. de Heer, T. Kram, T. Mander, M. van Oorschot, F. Smout, J. Clement, D. P. van Vuuren, H. J. Westhoek, L. Miles, I. Lysenko, L. Fish, C. Nellemann, H. van Meijl, and A. Tabeau. 2007. Cross-roads of Life on Earth – Exploring means to meet the 2010 Biodiversity Target. Solution – oriented scenarios for Global Biodiversity Outlook 2. Secretariate of the Convention on Biological Diversity, Montreal, Technical series no. 31, 90 pages.

Thomas, C. D., A. Cameron, R. E. Green, M. Bakkenes, L. J. Beaumont, Y. C. Collingham, B. F. N. Erasmus, M. F. de Siqueira, A. Grainger, L. Hannah, L. Hughes, B. Huntley, A. S. van Jaarsveld, G. F. Midgley, L. Miles, M. A. Ortega-Huerta, A. Townsend Peterson, O. L. Phillips, and S. E. Williams. 2004. Extinction risk from climate change. Nature 427:145-148.

Thuiller, W., C. Albert, M. B. Araújo, P. M. Berry, M. Cabeza, A. Guisan, T. Hickler, G. F. Midgley, J. Paterson, F. M. Schurr, M. T. Sykes, and N. E. Zimmermann. 2008. Predicting global change impacts on plant species' distributions: Future challenges. Perspectives in Plant Ecology, Evolution and Systematics 9:137-152.

Thuiller, W., S. Lavorel, M. B. Araujo, M. T. Sykes, and I. C. Prentice. 2005. Climate change threats to plant diversity in Europe. Proceedings of the National Academy of Sciences of the United States of America 102:8245-8250.

UNEP. 2002. Global Environment Outlook 3. UNEP.

UNEP. 2007. Global Environment Outlook 4. UNEP, Valleta, Malta.

UNEP-WCMC. 2009. International Expert Workshop on the 2010 Biodiversity Indicators and Post-2010 Indicator Development. UNEP-WCMC, Cambridge.

Vallejo, V. R., J. Aronson, J. Pausas,and J. Cortina. 2006. Restoration of mediterranean woodlands. Chapter 14 in J. Van Andel, and J. Aronson, editors, Restoration ecology. The new frontier. Blackwell Publishing, Oxford.

Van Minnen J.G., K. Klein Goldewijk, E. Stehfest, B. Eickhout, G. Van Drecht, and R. Leemans (2009) The importance of three centuries of land-use change for the global and regional terrestrial carbon cycle. Climatic Change 97:123-144.

van Vuuren, D., O. Sala, and H. M. Pereira. 2006. The Future of Vascular Plant Diversity Under Four Global Scenarios. Ecology and Society 11:25.

Wahren, C. H. A., M. D. Walker, and M. S. Bret-Harte. 2005. Vegetation responses in Alaskan arctic tundra after 8 years of a summer warming and winter snow manipulation experiment. Global Change Biology 11:537-552.

Walker, M., M. McLean, A. Dison, and R. Peppin-Vaughan. 2009. South African universities and human development: Towards a theorisation and operationalisation of professional capabilities for poverty reduction. International Journal of Educational Development 29:565-572.

Whitehead, H., B. McGill, and B. Worm. 2008. Diversity of deep-water cetaceans in relation to temperature: implications for ocean warming. Ecology Letters 11:1198-1207.

Willis, K., and S. Bhagwat. 2009. Biodiversity and Climate Change. Science 326:806-807.

Willis, K., M. Araujo, K. Bennett, B. Figueroa-Rangel, C. Froyd, and N. Myers. 2007. How can a knowledge of the past help to conserve the future? Biodiversity conservation and the relevance of long-term ecological studies. Philosophical Transactions of the Royal Society B-Biological Sciences 362:175-186.

Winton, M. 2006. Does the Arctic sea ice have a tipping point. Geophysical Research Letters 33:L23504.

Wise, M., K. Calvin, A. Thomson, L. Clarke, B. Bond-Lamberty, R. Sands, S. J. Smith, A. Janetos, and J. Edmonds. 2009. Implications of Limiting CO_2 Concentrations for Land Use and Energy. Science 324:1183-1186.

Wood, S., S. Ehui, J. Alder, S. Benin, K. Cassman, D. Cooper, T. Johns, J. Gaskell, R. Grainger, S. Kadungure, J. Otte, A. Rola, R. Watson, U. Wijkstrom, and C. Devendra. 2005. Food. Pages 209-241 *in* Ecosystems and Human Well-Being: Current State and Trends. Island Press, Washington DC.

World Bank, Climate Change and Clean Energy Initiative. 2010. Assessment of the Risk of Amazon Dieback. http://www.bicusa.org/en/Document.101982.aspx

Worm, B., E. B. Barbier, N. Beaumont, J. E. Duffy, C. Folke, B. S. Halpern, J. B. C. Jackson, H. K. Lotze, F. Micheli, S. R. Palumbi, E. Sala, K. A. Selkoe, J. J. Stachowicz, and R. Watson. 2006. Impacts of Biodiversity Loss on Ocean Ecosystem Services. Science 314:787-790.

Worm, B., R. Hilborn, J. K. Baum, T. A. Branch, J. S. Collie, C. Costello, M. J. Fogarty, E. A. Fulton, J. A. Hutchings, S. Jennings, O. P. Jensen, H. K. Lotze, P. M. Mace, T. R. McClanahan, C. Minto, S. R. Palumbi, A. M. Parma, D. Ricard, A. A. Rosenberg, R. Watson, and D. Zeller. 2009. Rebuilding Global Fisheries. Science 325:578-585.

WWF. 2008. Living planet report 2008. WWF International, Gland, Switzerland.

Xenopoulos, M. A., D. M. Lodge, J. Alcamo, M. Marker, K. Schulze, and D. P. Van Vuuren. 2005. Scenarios of freshwater fish extinctions from climate change and water withdrawal. Global Change Biology 11:1557-1564.

Xenopoulos, M. A., and D. M. Lodge. 2006. Going with the flow: using species–discharge relationships to forecast losses in fish biodiversity. Ecology 87:1907-1914.

Appendix 1. ARCTIC TUNDRA

Juan F. Fernandez-Manjarrés (Université Paris-Sud 11, juan.fernandez@u-psud.fr)
Paul Leadley (Université Paris-Sud 11, paul.leadley@u-psud.fr)

SUMMARY

▸ Climate warming has been and will be stronger in the Arctic than other parts of the globe with >+4°C warming over the 20th century in some areas of North America and projected increases of 2.8°C to 7.8°C for the arctic region by the end of the 21st century. Due to lags in the earth system, this warming is predicted to persist for several centuries even if greenhouse gas emissions decline substantially.

▸ Experiments, observations and models show that all plausible climate scenarios will lead to continued and widespread increases in dominance of deciduous shrubs in tundra communities and decreases in abundance of herbaceous, bryophyte and lichen species. Most models project that boreal forest will heavily invade tundra over large areas by the end of the century, as has occurred during warm periods in the recent past (e.g., 6000 years BP). The risk of 21st century extinctions is moderate given the large, contiguous ranges of many tundra species.

▸ Inevitable climate warming are projected to increase the rate of widespread melting of permafrost and lead to emissions of very large quantities of greenhouse gases from organic tundra soils. Transformations from tundra to boreal forest are predicted to decrease albedo and change aerosol emissions. These changes in tundra systems substantially increase climate warming in many models.

▸ Permafrost melting and changes in game availability have already heavily impacted some indigenous populations and these impacts are likely to become widespread and severe over the coming decades.

▸ Because of long lags in the earth system, we have probably already passed a tipping point for long-term, widespread permafrost degradation and invasion of tundra by boreal forest, but aggressive climate mitigation would substantially slow these processes. Adaptive management to conserve tundra systems is not feasible outside of very small areas. Relocation of indigenous populations is currently a viable adaptation strategy for preserving traditional livelihoods, but long-term adaptation will require substantial cultural adjustments.

DESCRIPTION

Status

Tundras are the northernmost treeless vegetation that grows between the boreal forest and barren or glaciated arctic land areas. The presence of permafrost is considered the main limitation for tree establishment. Tundra vegetation can be subdivided in several categories, ranging from communities dominated by tall shrubs to very short stature communities dominated by cushion forb, lichen and moss tundra (Bigelow et al. 2003). Present day tundra is generally bounded at the North at 7.5°C to 5.0°C July isotherms and at the South by the boreal forest at the 10°C to 12°C July isotherms (MacDonald et al. 2000). Low and high shrub tundras, being it the southernmost and the closest to boreal forest is the vegetation type susceptible to invasion by boreal forest trees. About one quarter of the tundra vegetation is composed of shrublands while the rest is composed of 18% peaty graminoid tundras, 13% mountain complexes, 12% barrens, 11% mineral graminoid tundras, 11% prostrate-shrub tundras, and 7% wetlands (Walker et al. 2005, Figure 1).

Tipping point mechanisms

We have classified the Tundra as a global biodiversity tipping point for three reasons (see also Foley 2005): First, inertia in socio-economic systems, biogeochemical cycles and the physical climate-ocean system mean that substantial further increases in temperature in the Arctic are inevitable (IPCC 2007). The average projected increase in temperature for arctic land areas between the 1980-1999 and 2080-2099 period is ca. 4.4°C (ca. 1°C warmer than sub-arctic regions of North America and Eurasia), but perhaps more importantly the minimum projected increase for terrestrial arctic systems is ca. 2.8°C for the lowest emissions scenarios used by the IPCC. In addition, climate models suggest that these increased temperatures

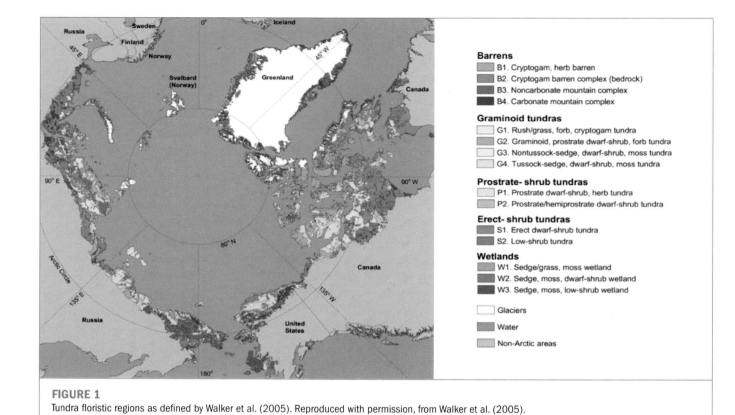

FIGURE 1
Tundra floristic regions as defined by Walker et al. (2005). Reproduced with permission, from Walker et al. (2005).

can be reversed only following many centuries of very low greenhouse gas emissions (IPCC 2007). Second, very high greenhouse gas emissions originating from the thawing of deep organic tundra soils that are currently permanently frozen will lead to a significant exacerbation of climate warming, as may increased albedo due to boreal forest invasion of tundra (i.e., the uniform snow blanket of tundra is highly reflective compared to boreal forests and, therefore, limits heating of the earth by the sun, see detailed description in "Ecosystem Services" section). Third, warming is likely to lead to very large changes in the distribution and abundance of species, including a high likelihood of the replacement of tundra by boreal forest over large areas of the Arctic. A recent analysis of global tipping points by Lenton et al. (2008) did not retain the tundra as an Earth System tipping point, because the changes described above are likely to be "gradual" rather than abrupt. We feel that the essentially irreversible nature of these changes over the next centuries, the potentially strong positive feedback to climate warming and the likely high impacts on global biodiversity and ecosystem functioning clearly qualify this as one of the most critical areas of change for the Earth System.

IMPACTS ON BIODIVERSITY

Biome level shifts

Global-level vegetation models (DGVMs) strongly suggest that boreal forests will permanently replace tundra ecosystems if current trends of greenhouse gas emissions persist. For example, Bigelow al. (2003) using vegetation models and emissions scenarios from the 1992 IPCC (IS92a scenario) found that increases in CO_2 concentrations of 1% annually – i.e., "business as usual" emissions – produce increments in the net production of tundra areas because of the colonization of boreal forest trees. Similarly, Sitch et al. (2008) found that three out of four vegetation models strongly suggest that boreal forest would colonize most present tundra areas under an increased and intensive use of fossil fuel (SRES scenario A1F1) as did Lucht et al. (2006) and Schaphoff et al. (2006). Indeed, recent simulations on an average scenario of 2°C increase suggest that tundra areas would be reduced by the end of the century by 44% while boreal forest would increase 55% from current areas, with tree lines increases up to 400 km, only limited by tree dispersal capabilities (Kaplan and New 2006). Finally, models suggest that boreal forest progression by increased CO_2 and increased temperatures are more significant than changes due to Earth orbital variations as during the mid-Holocene (Kaplan et al. 2003). New areas of tundra, however, could be formed in present areas that are occupied by very sparse vegetation such as the northernmost polar deserts. For example, in northern Canada, new tundra is predicted to be formed on the Arctic fringe that at present is only sparsely or not vegetated (Lucht et al. 2006).

Species and species-group level responses

Experimental and observational data suggest that community structure will change in tundra ecosystems in favor of shrubs and that they will be colonized by boreal forest trees. A recent meta-analysis of 11 experimental sites from the ITEX initiative (international tundra experiment) that uses standardized protocols, show that warming increased height and cover of deciduous shrubs and graminoids, decreased cover of mosses and lichens, and decreased species diversity and evenness. These results suggest that warming will cause a decline in biodiversity across a wide variety of tundra, at least in the short term (Wahren et al. 2005) confirming trends observed in previous independent studies. Observations in Alaska over the past 50 years are concordant with experimental data as warming-related increases in dwarf birch, willow, and white spruce (*Picea glauca*) cover and abundance are observable (Sturm et al. 2001, Tape et al. 2006).

Results from species distribution models using climate projections from 30 coupled atmosphere–ocean general circulation models predict that species will move substantial distances to the North. The long-term projection is for average gains in species richness of 30% or more in the Tundra ecoregion under the lower greenhouse gas emissions scenario (SRES B1) and 57% gains or more under the mid-to-high emissions scenario (Lawler et al. 2009). Differences in these projections and reduced species diversity found in experimental studies are related to the time lag required for dispersal and colonization to provide for specie turnover. Assuming no dispersal constraints, Southern areas of tundra are likely to experience over 90% species turnover, so that faunal distributions in the future may bear little resemblance to those of today. Arctic mammals, although largely spared from human intervention, may have high risks related to the adaptation to new environmental conditions (Cardillo et al. 2006).

It should be noted that most projections of changes in species and biome distributions may be influenced by the substantial projected increase in precipitation in arctic systems with strong agreement across climate models for this trend (on average about +20% by the end of the century).

ECOSYSTEM SERVICES

Tundra systems provide a wide variety of ecosystem services to relatively small populations of indigenous and non-indigenous peoples at local scales, and provide extremely important regulating services to all of humanity through their influence on climate.

Supporting and regulating services (sensu MA 2005)

The invasion of tundra by boreal forests can have a profound impact on global temperatures since low surface albedo from boreal forests during the winter season warms climate compared to tundra. For example, the changes in insulation due to changes in the earth's orbit alone do not appear sufficient to explain the warming during the mid-Holocene (ca. 6000 years bp) and can potentially be explained by albedo changes related to boreal forest invasion of tundra (Foley et al. 1994). Consequently, boreal forests have the greatest biogeophysical effect of all biomes on annual mean global temperature (Snyder et al. 2004). Hence, tundras will unlikely recuperate as decreased albedo of the forested areas will contribute to increase global temperatures that in turn favour the establishment of trees at high latitudes producing a constant feedback permanently detrimental to tundra ecosystems i.e., a tipping point would be reached (Chapin et al. 2005, Foley 2005).

The loss of permafrost in the tundra ecosystem will probably release more Carbon into the atmosphere than the amount stored by new colonizing boreal forest (Schuur et al. 2008). If one considers only carbon in vegetation, aboveground tundra vegetation contains roughly 0.4 kg C per m^2 (Shaver et al. 1992), whereas boreal forest can average approximately 5 kg C per m^2 (Gower et al. 2001) suggesting a gain of about 4.5 kg C per m^2 as treeline advances into tundra. However, a typical tundra permafrost soil can contain up to 10 times that amount i.e., approximately 44 kg C per m^2 in the top meter (Michaelson et al. 1996), compared with approximately 9 kg C per m^2 in the top meter of non permafrost boreal forest soil (Jobbagy and Jackson 2000) resulting in a potential loss of up to approximately 35 kg C per m^2. Moreover, this potential loss can become greater (on the order of 100 kg C per m^2) if soil to the depth of 3 m is considered

(Schuur et al. 2008). Combined losses of CO_2 and methane to the atmosphere from conversion of tundra to boreal forest are, therefore, one of the principal earth system feedbacks that could exacerbate climate warming (Schuur et al. 2008).

Provisioning and cultural services (sensu MA 2005)

Economic activities of people who live in the arctic tundra include hunting, fishing, nomadic herding, and mining. In particular, nomadic herding could be key in the maintenance of open areas by impeding the expansion of trees and shrubs under warmed tundra areas as results tend to suggest for caribou and muskoxen (Post and Pedersen 2008). However, whether global warming would increase or reduce reindeer, caribou or muskoxen populations remains unclear (Forchhammer et al. 2002, Post 2005).

Arctic peoples are already adapting to 20th century climate change. "Inuit hunters are now navigating new travel routes in order to try to avoid areas of decreasing ice stability that is making them less safe. In the future, increased rainfall may trigger additional hazards such as avalanches and rock falls." In addition, "Inuit hunters are also changing their hunting times to coincide with shifts in the migration times and migration routes of caribou, geese as well as new species moving northwards" (http://www.grida.no/polar/news/2395.aspx). The extent to which adaptation is possible remains unknown.

UNCERTAINTIES

▸ Most models of boreal forest invasion of tundra lack migration and soil type limitations on tree colonization and may, therefore, overestimate rates at which boreal forest replaces tundra.
▸ Tree invasion of tundra areas have been documented for the past century but colonizing dynamics may vary greatly from site to site. For example, although the continued advance of white spruce (*Picea alba*) forests is the most likely scenario of future change in Alaska, variability in the rate of forest response to warming may be limited by seed dispersal and early establishment and recent changes in the growth responses of individual trees to temperature (Chapin et al. 2005, Cacciniga and Payette 2006 , Payette et al. 2008). Likewise, colonization by black spruce (*Picea mariana*) into shrub dominated tundra areas although noticeable during the 20th century have been limited by drought on wind exposed sites and difficult to correlate with short-term climate trends (Gamache and Payette 2005).
▸ Paleo-ecological data suggest that tundra has been displaced by boreal forest during recent warmer periods like the mid-Holocene but that this displacement was not homogenous around the circumpolar region. For instance, paleoecological reconstructions based on pollen taxa show that the reconstructed treeline was farther north than present in Fennoscandia (western Europe) and central Siberia (Bigelow et al. 2003). However, the Beringia region shows little or no displacement compared to present, and the treeline was south of its present position in Labrador and Keewatin (Bigelow et al. 2003). These results are consistent with the other studies that infer biomes (Prentice and Dominique 2000), and with reconstructions based on subfossil tree remains (MacDonald et al. 2000). Hence, contrary to other interpretations (Foley et al. 1994), the tree line did not move synchronously northwards during the mid-Holocene. Why the boreal forest tree line was further South under the warmer climate of the mid-Holocene remains controversial, but local glaciers and differences between west and eastern polar ice dynamics (western ice sheets tend to be thicker) may partially explain this paradoxical result (Vavrus and Harrison 2003).

LOCAL TO GLOBAL ACTION AND OPPORTUNITIES

Global actions

▸ Mitigation of climate change is the primary avenue for taking action to conserve tundra systems or at least to slow the rate at which large scale changes in biodiversity and ecosystem services occur. "Dangerous" changes in tundra systems appear to already be underway and to occur at levels well below those fixed by the IPCC for "dangerous" climate change (i.e., keeping radiative forcing below levels that would lead to more than ca. 2°C global warming by the end of the century). This occurs because arctic systems are much more sensitive to increases in radiative forcing than other terrestrial systems and appear to have a relatively linear response to warming. The only reasonable recommendation from the point of view of tundra systems is that greenhouse gas emissions be reduced as rapidly as possible to very low levels.

▶ Little adaptation appears possible in these regions, because of the very large spatial scale at which these changes will occur and the very low impact of human land management on tundra systems. However, as noted above, grazing in some regions and fire could potentially slow the colonization of tundra by trees.

Regional and local action

As stated elsewhere, the tundra tipping point, also known as the greening of the arctic, makes part of a large biome-level transformation that includes the tundra, the permafrost and the neighbouring polar ice cap, as well as terrestrial ice reduction (Greenland). As all these tipping points are externally driven by the increase of global atmospheric temperatures, only global reduction in greenhouse gases can counteract the major driver for this area (see Appendix 8. Arctic Ocean). Hence, global actions that are valid for the polar ice cap or permafrost are also valid for the tundra because of the tight interactions and feedbacks of these three components of the arctic system.

At the regional scale, Arctic countries have begun an important series of inter-government actions. In particular, since 1996, the Ottawa declaration formally established the Arctic Council as a high level inter-governmental forum to provide a means "for promoting cooperation, coordination and interaction among the Arctic States, with the involvement of the Arctic Indigenous communities and other Arctic inhabitants on common Arctic issues, in particular issues of sustainable development and environmental protection in the Arctic". Member States of the Arctic Council are Canada, Denmark (including Greenland and the Faroe Islands), Finland, Iceland, Norway, Russian Federation, Sweden, and the United States of America. Also, indigenous people have been granted the category of "Permanent Participants" regardless of their distribution. There are six Working Groups of the Arctic Council that perform assessments and monitoring of climate, flora, fauna, contaminants and emergencies.

Since 2007, the council launched the Vulnerability and Adaptation to Climate Change in the Arctic (VACCA) project designed to "provide useful knowledge and information-sharing at different governance levels and for different sectors so that this learning can be incorporated into policies and decision-making" tightly related to the SDWG and other working groups. The last report of this project (VACCA 2008) highlighted that that interest and capacity are increasing for, and are being used to deal with, climate change vulnerability and adaptation in the Arctic but that the number of community-based projects remains a minority. Lack of coordination and information exchange regarding initiatives on reducing vulnerability and implementing adaptation to climate change around the Arctic remains, however, the greater weakness of these multinational actions.

Important opportunities have been identified with the VACCA report showing that basing research on community needs and efficient scientific communication of results could be used to build capacity for vulnerability reduction and adaptation to climate change (e.g. W040 Polar Affairs). Overall, the largest constraints that have been identified for the application of policies is the short time available to cope with ecosystem change, the lack of sufficient economic resources to apply policies, and the fact that many projects are trying to do "too much too quickly".

REFERENCES

Bigelow, N. H., L. B. Brubaker, M. E. Edwards, S. P. Harrison, I. C. Prentice, P. M. Anderson, A. A. Andreev, P. J. Bartlein, T. R. Christensen, W. Cramer, J. O. Kaplan, A. V. Lozhkin, N. V. Matveyeva, D. F. Murray, A. D. McGuire, V. Y. Razzhivin, J. C. Ritchie, B. Smith, D. A. Walker, K. Gajewski, V. Wolf, B. H. Holmqvist, Y. Igarashi, K. Kremenetskii, A. Paus, M. F. J. Pisaric, and V. S. Volkova. 2003. Climate change and Arctic ecosystems: 1. Vegetation changes north of 55 degrees N between the last glacial maximum, mid-Holocene, and present. Journal of Geophysical Research-Atmospheres 108.

Caccianiga, M., and S. Payette. 2006. Recent advance of white spruce (*Picea glauca*) in the coastal tundra of the eastern shore of Hudson Bay (Quebec, Canada). Journal of Biogeography 33:2120-2135.

Cardillo, M., G. M. Mace, J. L. Gittleman, and A. Purvis. 2006. Latent extinction risk and the future battlegrounds of mammal conservation. Proceedings of the National Academy of Sciences of the United States of America 103:4157-4161.

Chapin, F. S., III, M. Sturm, M. C. Serreze, J. P. McFadden, J. R. Key, A. H. Lloyd, A. D. McGuire, T. S. Rupp, A. H. Lynch, J. P. Schimel, J. Beringer, W. L. Chapman, H. E. Epstein, E. S. Euskirchen, L. D. Hinzman, G. Jia, C. L. Ping, K. D. Tape, C. D. C. Thompson, D. A. Walker, and J. M. Welker. 2005. Role of land-surface changes in Arctic summer warming. Science 310:657-660.

Foley, J. A., J. E. Kutzbach, M. T. Coe, and S. Levis. 1994. Feedbacks between climate and boreal forests during the Holocene epoch. Nature 371:52-54.

Folley, J. A. 2005. Tipping points in the tundra. Science 310:627-628.

Forchhammer, M. C., E. Post, N. C. Stenseth, and D. M. Boertmann. 2002. Long-term responses in arctic ungulate dynamics to changes in climatic and trophic processes. Population Ecology 44:113-120.

Gamache, I., and S. Payette. 2005. Latitudinal response of subarctic tree lines to recent climate change in eastern Canada. Journal of Biogeography 32:849-862.

Gower, S. T., O. Krankina, R. J. Olson, M. Apps, S. Linder, and C. Wang. 2001. Net primary production and carbon allocation patterns of boreal forest ecosystems. Ecological Applications 11:1395-1411.

IPCC. 2007. Climate Change 2007: Synthesis Report. Contribution of Working Groups I, II and III to the Fourth Assessment Report of the Intergovernmental Panel on Climate Change. Core Writing Team, R.K. Pachauri, and A. Reisinger (eds.). IPCC, Geneva, Switzerland.

Jobbagy, E. G., and R. B. Jackson. 2000. The vertical distribution of soil organic carbon and its relation to climate change and vegetation. Ecological Applications 10:423-436.

Kaplan, J. O., N. H. Bigelow, I. C. Prentice, S. P. Harrison, P. J. Bartlein, T. R. Christensen, W. Cramer, N. V. Matveyeva, A. D. McGuire, D. F. Murray, V. Y. Razzhivin, B. Smith, D. A. Walker, P. M. Anderson, A. A. Andreev, L. B. Brubaker, M. E. Edwards, and A. V. Lozhkin. 2003. Climate change and Arctic ecosystems: 2. Modeling, paleodata-model comparisons, and future projections. Journal of Geophysical Research-Atmospheres 108.

Kaplan, J. O., and M. New. 2006. Arctic climate change with a 2 degrees C global warming: Timing, climate patterns and vegetation change. Climatic Change 79:213-241.

Lawler, J. J., S. L. Shafer, D. White, P. Kareiva, E. P. Maurer, A. R. Blaustein, and P. J. Bartlein. 2009. Projected climate-induced faunal change in the Western Hemisphere. Ecology 90:588-597.

Lenton, T. M., H. Held, E. Kriegler, J. W. Hall, W. Lucht, S. Rahmstorf, and H. J. Schellnhuber. 2008. Tipping elements in the Earth's climate system. Proceedings of the National Academy of Sciences 105:1786-1793.

Lucht, W., S. Schaphoff, T. Erbrecht, U. Heyder, and W. Cramer. 2006. Terrestrial vegetation redistribution and carbon balance under climate change. Carbon Balance and Management 1:6.

MacDonald, G. M., A. A. Velichko, C. V. Kremenetski, O. K. Borisova, A. A. Goleva, A. A. Andreev, L. C. Cwynar, R. T. Riding, S. L. Forman, T. W. D. Edwards, R. Aravena, D. Hammarlund, J. M. Szeicz, and V. N. Gattaulin. 2000. Holocene Treeline History and Climate Change Across Northern Eurasia. Quaternary Research 53:302-311.

Michaelson, G., C.-L. Ping, and J. Kimble. 1996. Carbon storage and distribution in tundra soils of arctic Alaska. U.S.A.. Arctic and Alpine Research 28:414–424.

Payette, S., L. Filion, and A. Delwaide. 2008. Spatially explicit fire-climate history of the boreal forest-tundra (Eastern Canada) over the last 2000 years. Philosophical Transactions of the Royal Society B-Biological Sciences 363:2301-2316.

Post, E. 2005. Large-scale spatial gradients in herbivore population dynamics. Ecology 86:2320-2328.

Post, E., and C. Pedersen. 2008. Opposing plant community responses to warming with and without herbivores. Proceedings of the National Academy of Sciences of the United States of America 105:12353-12358.

Prentice, C. I., and J. Dominique. 2000. Mid-Holocene and glacial-maximum vegetation geography of the northern continents and Africa. Journal of Biogeography 27:507-519.

Schaphoff, S., W. Lucht, D. Gerten, S. Sitch, W. Cramer, and I. C. Prentice. 2006. Terrestrial biosphere carbon storage under alternative climate projections. Climatic Change 74:97-122.

Schuur, E. A. G., J. Bockheim, J. G. Canadell, E. Euskirchen, C. B. Field, S. V. Goryachkin, S. Hagemann, P. Kuhry, P. M. Lafleur, H. Lee, G. Mazhitova, F. E. Nelson, A. Rinke, V. E. Romanovsky, N. Shiklomanov, C. Tarnocai, S. Venevsky, J. G. Vogel, and S. A. Zimov. 2008. Vulnerability of Permafrost Carbon to Climate Change: Implications for the Global Carbon Cycle. Bioscience 58:701-714.

Shaver, G., W. Billings, F. I. Chapin, A. Giblin, K. Nadelhoffer, W. Oechel, and E. Rastetter. 1992. Global change and the carbon balance of arctic ecosystems. Bioscience 42:433–441.

Sitch, S., C. Huntingford, N. Gedney, P. E. Levy, M. Lomas, S. L. Piao, R. Betts, P. Ciais, P. Cox, P. Friedlingstein, C. D. Jones, I. C. Prentice, and F. I. Woodward. 2008. Evaluation of the terrestrial carbon cycle, future plant geography and climate-carbon cycle feedbacks using five Dynamic Global Vegetation Models (DGVMs). Global Change Biology 14:2015-2039.

Snyder, P. K., C. Delire, and J. A. Foley. 2004. Evaluating the influence of different vegetation biomes on the global climate. Climate Dynamics 23:279-302.

Sturm, M., C. Racine, and K. Tape. 2001. Climate change – Increasing shrub abundance in the Arctic. Nature 411:546-547.

Tape, K., M. Sturm, and C. Racine. 2006. The evidence for shrub expansion in Northern Alaska and the Pan-Arctic. Global Change Biology 12:686-702.

Vavrus, S., and S. P. Harrison. 2003. The impact of sea-ice dynamics on the Arctic climate system. Climate Dynamics 20:741-757.

Wahren, C. H. A., M. D. Walker, and M. S. Bret-Harte. 2005. Vegetation responses in Alaskan arctic tundra after 8 years of a summer warming and winter snow manipulation experiment. Global Change Biology 11:537-552.

Walker, D. A., M. K. Raynolds, F. J. A. Daniëls, E. Einarsson, A. Elvebakk, W. A. Gould, A. E. Katenin, S. S. Kholod, C. J. Markon, E. S. Melnikov, N. G. Moskalenko, S. S. Talbot, B. A. Yurtsev, and the other members of the CAVM Team. 2005. The Circumpolar Arctic vegetation map. Journal of Vegetation Science 16:267-282.

Appendix 2. MEDITERRANEAN FOREST

Vânia Proença (University of Lisbon, vaniaproenca@fc.ul.pt)
Henrique M. Pereira (University of Lisbon, hpereira@fc.ul.pt)

SUMMARY

▸ Changes in land use, in the fire regime and in climate are interacting and driving ecosystem dynamics in the Mediterranean Basin towards the dominance of early successional communities, and also slowing natural forests regeneration in abandoned farmland.

▸ Current projections of climate change predict increasing temperatures and decreasing precipitation in the Mediterranean region, which will lead to more frequent periods of drought. In addition, land use scenarios project a decrease in cropland, due to rural abandonment, and an increase of naturally regenerated vegetation and forest plantations. These changes, in climatic conditions and in land cover, will most probably conduce to an increase in fire risk and fire occurrence.

▸ An increase of fire disturbance will drive the expansion of early successional and species-poor communities, such as shrublands, which are more adapted to frequent fires and drought conditions. In addition, shrublands promote the recurrence of fire due to their flammability, thus contributing for a further expansion and difficult to reverse transition to early successional communities, with generalized biodiversity loss.

▸ The expansion of early successional communities will also result in serious drawbacks for human well-being. Consequences for ecosystem services include carbon losses, from vegetation and soil, which may worsen climate change at the global scale, and the failure of a wide range of ecosystem services, which may affect human-well being and result in large economic losses from local to national scales.

▸ Adopting forest management practices that support native broadleaved forest regeneration and promote its expansion is fundamental to progress to a new forest paradigm focused in multifunctional forests managed to deliver multiple ecosystem services and more resistant to fire than fire prone plantations. At the same time, it is important to persist in raising public awareness regarding fire prevention and the holistic value of forests, in particular the delivery of non-marketed services.

DESCRIPTION

Status and trends

The Mediterranean Basin constitutes one of the world's biodiversity hotspots, it supports 25000 native plant species, 10% of the world's flowering plants, and about 13000 endemic species (Myers et al. 2000, Cuttelod et al. 2008). The species diversity found in this region results from (Blondel and Aronson 1999): the geographic location, in the transition of three continents (Europe, Asia and Africa), a complex geography and topography, with mountain ranges, islands and islets, and the geographical and climatic events that punctuated history (e.g., glaciations). In parallel with plants richness, the Mediterranean Basin is also important for its fauna uniqueness: two thirds of amphibian species, nearly half of reptile species and a quarter of mammal species are endemic (Cuttelod et al. 2008). However, and despite the high plant endemism found in the Mediterranean Basin, nearly 70% of the original habitat has been human-modified and only about 5% of the vegetation is in a pristine condition (MA 2005, Palahi et al. 2008).

Tipping point mechanisms

Man and fire have been part of the history of the Mediterranean Basin for millennia. The recurrent use of fire to clear forests and produce pastures (Blondel and Aronson 1999) favoured species with features that increased resistance to fire, such as an insulating bark, or species that that were able to promptly regenerate after fire (Naveh 1975). Therefore, fire has structured plant communities to become more resilient to fire disturbance. Today, changes in the fire regime, namely the increase in the annual number of fires, which has quadrupled since 1960, and the increase in the frequency of large fires (> 500 ha), are again driving ecosystem

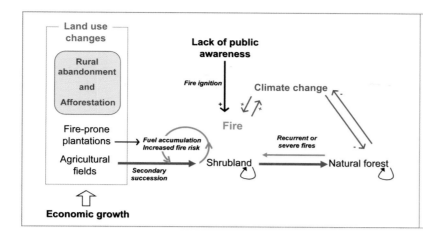

FIGURE 1
Ecosystem change in the northern rim of the Mediterranean Basin: interactions between drivers and simplified successional pathways (adapted from Pereira et al. 2006 and Vallejo et al. 2006). Shrublands and natural forests represent the alternative steady states in Mediterranean landscapes (i.e. points of equilibrium where communities present a high resilience to perturbation).

change in the Mediterranean Basin (Pausas et al. 2004, Bassi et al. 2008). Under these conditions, composition of ecosystems may shift towards early successional and more simplified communities, causing the loss of biodiversity and the breakdown of important ecosystem services.

In the northern (European) rim of the Mediterranean Basin changes in fire regime are due to three main drivers: land use changes, climate change and public behaviour (Lloret et al. 2002, Pausas et al. 2008) (Figure 1)[1].

Land use changes are following two trends: rural abandonment and the expansion of fire prone plantations. Both trends are being driven by the economic growth of the last decades. Rural abandonment was triggered by a reduction of agricultural revenues that was caused by an increase of public and private investment in the industry and in the services sector (Pereira et al 2006, Palahi et al. 2008). In the same way, wood production to provide raw materials to pulp and timber industries became more profitable than agriculture, leading to the forestation of agricultural fields (Pereira et al 2006). Today, Spain, Italy, France and Portugal are among the countries in the world with the highest annual net gain of forest area, with a mean net gain between 2000 and 2005 of 120 000 ha yr^{-1} (FAO 2006a). Most new forests present a high density of trees and are composed of fire-prone species, mainly pines (*Pinus* spp.) but also other species such as the eucalyptus (*Eucalyptus* spp.) (Sedjo 1999, Pausas et al. 2008). Moreover forest plantations, including forests planted before the mid 20th century, often lack an adequate management (e.g. fuel load control) and structure (i.e., dense monocultures with equally spaced even-aged trees) (Rudel et al. 2005, Pausas et al. 2008).

In abandoned fields secondary succession often results in the reestablishment of native forest[2]. However, the accumulation of biomass in unmanaged land increases fire risk. Fires will halt succession and drive communities to early successional stages. Similarly, the large fuel load in continuous and dense fire-prone plantations also increases fire risk and potentiates severe fires (Pausas et al. 2008). Extreme climatic events, such as heat waves and droughts, also contribute to increase fire risk (Lavorel et al. 2007). Additionally, the combustion of organic matter during fires causes the release of CO_2, which contributes to climate change. A tipping-point occurs when frequent or severe fires cause irreversible damages, such as the loss of keystone species or soil degradation (Pausas et al. 2008), and these damages prevent communities to progress to later successional stages. Recurrent and severe fires may also cause the degradation of natural forests causing their permanent replacement by earlier successional communities[3]. The third driver affecting fire disturbance is public behaviour. While land use change and climate change are causing an increase in fire risk and affecting fire behaviour, fire ignition is mostly man induced (both arson and unintentional fires), being the cause of about 95% of fires (Bassi et al.

---

1 This tipping point is focused on the Northern rim of the Mediterranean basin. In southern and eastern regions of the Mediterranean Basin, the main threats for forest conservation are overexploitation and deforestation (Palahi et al 2008). In these regions, forests play a primary role in the provision of fuel and forest goods to rural populations. The rapid population growth in the last decades and the high population density in rural areas are the indirect drivers leading to pressures over forest ecosystems.

2 Forest natural regeneration is a long time process that depends on the existence of adequate soil conditions and on the existence of sources of dispersal of forest species, such as forests remnants.

3 Mediterranean forests comprise two main forest types: oak forests and pine woodlands. Oak trees are resistant to fire and associated plant communities are very resilient (Pausas et al. 2008). Pine woodlands, on the other hand, are vulnerable to wildfires. Pine trees are less resistant to fire and contrary to oaks do not resprout, being therefore vulnerable to frequent or severe fires that could prevent the production of seeds or affect their viability (Pausas et al. 2008).

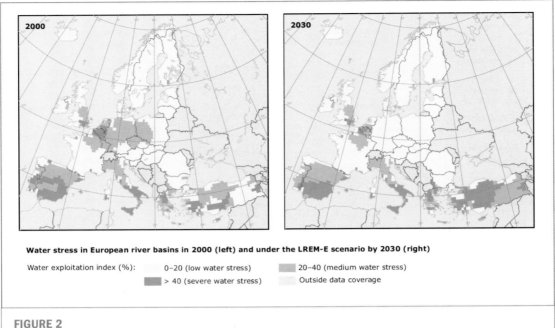

Water stress in European river basins in 2000 (left) and under the LREM-E scenario by 2030 (right)

Water exploitation index (%):   0–20 (low water stress)   20–40 (medium water stress)

                                     > 40 (severe water stress)   Outside data coverage

FIGURE 2

Stress status of European river basins in 2000 and projections to 2030 under a baseline scenario of water use (i.e., assuming that current environmental policies continue), using the WaterGAP model. Water stress is the ratio of withdrawal to water availability. Source: EEA 2007, Center for Environmental System Research (University of Kassel, Germany), 2003-2004.

2008, EC 2007). Fire has been used in the Mediterranean Basin for millennia, for example to renew pastures and clear fields (Blondel and Aronson 1999). These practices are still maintained today, but now fires get easily out of control due to fuel accumulation and also due to people's inability to manage fire. There are less people in rural areas and the ones remaining are usually elderly people (FAO 2006b). Also, many fires are caused by negligence (e.g., barbecues in campsites) and others are criminal, for example as a way of retaliation against restrictions to human activities in protected areas (FAO 2006b).

Besides its effect on fire risk, climate change also has a negative direct effect on forests condition, in particular on the physiology of trees (Pereira et al. 2002, Palahi et al. 2008). Field data and analysis have shown that under warmer and dry conditions trees present an increase in respiration rates but not in the photosynthetic response, i.e., water stress is acting as a limiting factor to primary production (Palahi et al. 2008). If these conditions are maintained for three or four consecutive years, the reserves of carbohydrates may become depleted, which will weaken the trees and increase their vulnerability to pests and diseases, and may eventually cause their death (Palahi et al. 2008, Pereira et al. 2002). On the other hand, forest may contribute to limit climate change because it sequesters carbon and regulates local climate.

Climate models predict a temperature increase between 2.1°C and 4.4°C by 2080 in Europe (Schroeter et al 2005). In the Mediterranean countries, the raise of temperature could be more accentuated with increases between 2.5°C and 3.5°C by 2050 (Palahi et al. 2008) and values over 6°C after 2080 (IPCC 2007). In addition, precipitation is expected to decrease in up to 30%-45% in the Mediterranean Basin (IPCC 2007). Water availability will be further aggravated by increasing water demand. Therefore, in the next decades the major water basins in the Mediterranean will likely be affected by increased water stress levels (Schroeter et al. 2005, EEA 2005, 2007) (Figure 2).

Under this conjunction of factors the Mediterranean region will likely be the most affected by climate change in Europe (Schroeter et al. 2005). Fire risk and the length of fire season will increase and large and severe fires will be more frequent (Zaehle et al. 2007). This will cause ecosystem dynamics to run towards the dominance of early successional communities, namely shrublands, which are more adapted to frequent fires and to water stress conditions (Moreira et al. 2001, Lloret et al. 2002, Mouillot et al. 2003, Baeza et al. 2007). Large-scale transitions to shrubland will cause landscape homogenization, biodiversity loss and breakdown of the services provided by forests, such as air purification, water retention or regulation of the local climate. Moreover, shrublands, especially when occurring in continuous formations, are highly flammable and contribute for fire occurrence and, consequently, for the perpetuation of warm and dry conditions (Mouillot et al. 2003, Alcamo et al. 2007).

IMPACTS ON BIODIVERSITY

Land use changes scenarios for Europe agree in predicting a reduction of cropland area and an increase in forest cover in the next century, with the Mediterranean region experiencing the greater changes (Schroeter et al. 2005, Rounsevell et al. 2005). Rural abandonment is expected to have a negative effect on species that depend on agricultural ecosystems, such as farmland birds (Moreira and Russo 2007). On the other hand, forest regeneration is expected to have a positive effect on forest species, such as the wolf (*Canis lupus*), and on several ecosystem services, in particular regulating and supporting services (*sensu* MA 2005) (Rudell et al. 2005, Vallejo et al. 2006, Benayas et al. 2008, Chazdon 2008). Because forest regeneration is a long term process it will not be fully experienced before 2050 (ten Brink et al. 2007). Forest expansion through plantation can also be positive for ecosystem services and biodiversity, in particular if forests are planted in degraded land (Chazdon 2008). However, the usual composition and setting of plantations (monotonous stands of fire-prone species) does not potentiates biodiversity and increases fire risk (Rudel et al. 2005, Vallejo et al. 2006, Pausas et al. 2008).

The increase of burnt area in the Mediterranean is consensual in land use scenarios, independently of the base socio-economic storyline (Schroter et al. 2005). Fires may cause the decline of several native species, such as cork oak (*Quercus suber*), holm oak (*Quercus ilex*), allepo pine (*Pinus halepensis*) and maritime pine (*Pinus pinaster*) and conduce to the expansion of shrublands (Pereira et al. 2002, Schroter et al. 2005, Peñuelas et al. 2008).

Estimations of species loss for different taxa agree in considering the Mediterranean Basin as the region most vulnerable to climate change in Europe. Thuiller et al. (2005) predicted that under a severe climate scenario (A1 - SRES) up to 62% of plant diversity in the Mediterranean mountains could be lost by 2080. Bakkenes et al. (2006) worked with a least severe climate scenario and estimated that up to 25% of plant species could disappear from Southern Europe by 2100. Regarding fauna, estimates of species loss also predict a greater loss of herptile species (Araújo et al. 2006) and mammals (Levinsky et al. 2007) in the Mediterranean region in comparison with the rest of Europe. Amphibians will likely be affected by water stress, and mammals, despite being more mobile will probably have difficulty to move northwards due to the barrier effect of East-West oriented mountain ranges (e.g., Pyrenees).

ECOSYSTEM SERVICES

The Mediterranean Basin is home to 455 million people, and is a touristic destination par excellence, being visited by a large number of tourists every year (e.g., 211 million tourists in 2006) (Cuttelod et al. 2008, EC 2008). Mediterranean forests provide several benefits to society, which have effects on people's health (e.g., air purification), economy (e.g., timber) and social relationships (e.g., clean water). The current trend of increased fire disturbance and ecosystem shift towards early-successional communities could result in serious drawbacks for human well-being in the Mediterranean Basin.

Economically, as the number and extent of fires increase, governments will have to ascribe more money to fire prevention and combat, for example, more than €475 million were spent in Portugal between 2000 and 2004 (DGRF 2007). Moreover, burning will cause damages to infrastructures and affect people's health, including injuries, respiratory problems or even death, accruing large costs for economic and public health.

Additionally to the costs of fire prevention and fire combat and the costs of direct damages caused by fire, there are also the costs associated with the breakdown of forest ecosystem services. Merlo and Croitoru (2005) estimated the economic value of services provided by the Mediterranean forests

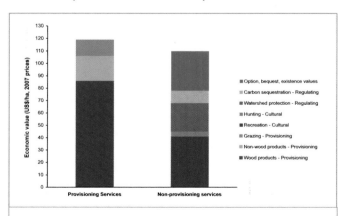

FIGURE 3

Economic value of forest ecosystem services in the northern rim of the Mediterranean Basin. Ecosystem services are classified *sensu* MA (2005) in provisioning, cultural and regulating services. Based on data from Croitoru (2008).

(Figure 3). In average, for the northern rim of the basin, provisioning services (*sensu* MA 2005) accounted for 52% of the total economic value (TEV). The remaining value is accounted for non-provisioning services such as cultural services, regulating services, option values (i.e., values with a potential utility in the future, such as medicines) and existence values (biodiversity conservation). The economic value ascribed to each type of service varies across countries, for example timber production may reach annual values of US$206 ha^{-1} in Slovenia be as low as US$37 ha^{-1} in Spain, in Portugal non-wood forest products reach US$183 ha^{-1} per year due to cork production, and in Italy watershed protection accounts for more the 50% of the TEV (US$ 133 ha^{-1}) (Croitoru 2008). Moreover, non-provisioning services are certainly underestimated. Contrary to services with a direct use value, such as timber production or revenues from recreational activities, services with an indirect use value, such as soil formation and nutrient cycling (supporting services) or soil protection from erosion and climate regulation (regulation services), are non-marketed values which makes difficult (if possible) to assess of their economic value.

At the global level, Mediterranean forests may assume a relevant role in climate regulation through carbon sequestration. Presently, European forests act as a carbon sink (Schroter et al. 2005), i.e. primary production exceeds carbon losses. Forests in Mediterranean countries sequester annually between 0.01-1.08 t C ha^{-1} according to countries' use of forest resources, i.e., more carbon is sequestered in countries were forests are preserved (Merlo and Croitoru 2005). Carbon may be stored in the form of forest biomass or retained in the soil. While afforestation and land abandonment have a positive effect on carbon sequestration, climate change and fire will likely counteract this effect and conduce to carbon releases by the end of the 21st century (Schroter et al.2005, Zaehle et al. 2007). Warmer temperatures and reduced precipitation will lead to an increase in heterotrophic respiration (carbon uptake from soil) but not in photosynthesis (biomass production) and consequently in litterfall (carbon input into soil), and fire will cause the loss of carbon stored in soil and in forest biomass. (Schroter et al. 2005, Zaehle et al. 2007, Chazdon 2008).

UNCERTAINTIES

- Projections of species loss tend to have high levels of uncertainty, because it is difficult to predict factors such as species ability to disperse and successfully colonize new areas, effects of climate change on species physiologic responses and biotic interactions in changed communities (Thuiller et al. 2005, Thuiller et al. 2008). In the case of the Mediterranean Basin, estimates of species loss may be particularly uncertain due to the geographical location of the Basin, in the transition of different climatic regions, and its topography, with high mountains (shifts in altitude). Both are factors that potentiate species transitions and biotic interactions with unpredictable results.
- Scenarios of land use change have a large level of uncertainty, because land use changes are mainly dependent on the social, political and economic developments at the European and global levels (Rounsevell et al. 2005, Schroeter et al. 2005).
- Scenarios of changes in fire regime have moderate to large uncertainty because fire ignition depends on human behavior.
- The occurrence of extreme events, such as wildfires and droughts, and their consequences for forest condition and for the land-atmosphere carbon flux constitute a source of uncertainty in scenarios of land cover change and climate change due to the unpredictable nature of disturbance events (Zahele et al. 2007).
- Scenarios of climate change and of ecosystem functioning (e.g., cabon sequestration) show a large variability depending on the socio-economic storylines and models used (Schroeter et al. 2005, Zaehle et al. 2007, Pereira et al. 2009).

LOCAL TO GLOBAL ACTION AND OPPORTUNITIES

Land use changes in the Mediterranean Basin may be regarded as a threat to biodiversity and ecosystems condition or, as an opportunity to restore natural forest, with a high biodiversity value, and forest services. However, forest regeneration in abandoned land is a slow process that not only will take several decades (Benayas et al. 2008) but will also involve the development of flammable biomass, which in conjunction with climate change will increase fire risk and may jeopardize secondary succession. Moreover, natural regeneration will be limited by the presence of dispersion sources and/or dispersal agents (e.g., seeds dispersed by jays) and most of all, by the existence of adequate soil conditions (Chazdon 2008).

For the above reasons a passive attitude regarding forest regeneration will not be the right option, action is needed. Actions at the local and regional levels include:

▸ Increase legal protection over areas of natural forest that may act as sources of forest species, and reservoirs of biodiversity, and may also preserve ecosystem function.
▸ Work with shepherds and local communities towards a more careful use of fire in the management of pastures and scrubland.
▸ Invest in the transition towards a multifunctional forestry and sustainable forest management. The relevance of this option is already recognized at the inter-governmental level (MCPFE 2007) but the prevailing paradigm of forest management is still centred in wood production (Palahi et al. 2008).
▸ Promote the expansion of broadleaved species. Multifunctional and sustainable forests of broadleaved species are more stable in face of fire disturbance and therefore more reliable when it comes to the provision of ecosystem services, therefore presenting a twofold economic advantage: less economic losses (e.g. fire combat, human injuries) and more steady gains.
▸ Raise public awareness about the economic value of non-marketed ecosystem services and their contribution for human-well being. Multifunctional forests will only gain true relevance in forestry when society not only acknowledges the value of non-marketed services but is also willing to subsidize efforts that promote the provision of those services (Patterson and Coelho 2009).
▸ Opt for intermediate solutions between natural regeneration and reforestation with native species. This will contribute for a faster development of natural forest in abandoned land, while still considering the restoration of biodiversity and ecosystem services (Benayas et al. 2008). Management options that join efforts with natural succession may be the best and less expensive way to make the transition towards multifunctional forests (Vallejo et al. 2006, Benayas et al. 2008, Chazdon 2008).
▸ Increase countries adaptive capacity (i.e., the potential to implement planned adaptation measures) in order to reduce countries vulnerability to fire disturbance (Metzger and Schroeter 2006, Alcamo et al. 2007).
▸ Reduce populations vulnerability to fire disturbance, namely through land planning and the establishment of land buffers in the urban-wildland interface for fire protection. Buffer zones could be converted in agricultural areas or in open space parks (Keeley 2002).

At the global level, it is crucial to pursue international efforts to limit climate change. Analysis of supply of ecosystem services under different socio-economic scenarios sugest the importance of keeping climate change to a minimum, preferably with CO_2 concentrations below 550 ppm. (Schroeter et al. 2005, Pereira et al. 2009).

REFERENCES

Alcamo, J., J. M. Moreno, B. Nováky, M. Bindi, R. Corobov, R. J. N. Devoy, C. Giannakopoulos, E. Martin, J. E. Olesen, and A. Shvidenko. 2007. Europe. Climate Change 2007: impacts, adaptation and vulnerability. Contribution of Working group II to the Fourth Assessment Report of the Intergovernmental Panel on Climate Change. Fourth Assessment Report of the Intergovernmental Panel on Climate Change. Cambridge: Cambridge University Press, S:541–580.

Araújo, M. B., W. Thuiller, and R. G. Pearson. 2006. Climate warming and the decline of amphibians and reptiles in Europe. Journal of Biogeography 33:1712-1728.

Baeza, M., A. Valdecantos, J. Alloza, and V. Vallejo. 2007. Human disturbance and environmental factors as drivers of long-term post-fire regeneration patterns in Mediterranean forests. Journal of Vegetation Science 18:243-252.

Bakkenes, M., B. Eickhout, and R. Alkemade. 2006. Impacts of different climate stabilisation scenarios on plant species in Europe. Global environmental change 16:19-28.

Bassi, S., M. Kettunen, E. Kampa, and S. Cavalieri. 2008. Forest fires: causes and contributing factors to forest fire events in Europe. Study for the European parliament committee on environment, public health and food safety under contract IP/A/ENVI/FWC/2006-172/LOT1/C1/SC10.

Benayas, J. M. R., J. M. Bullock, and A. C. Newton. 2008. Creating woodland islets to reconcile ecological restoration, conservation, and agricultural land use. Frontiers in Ecology and the Environment 6:329-336.

Blondel, J., and J. Aronson. 1999. Biology and wildlife of the Mediterranean region. Oxford University Press, Oxford.

Chazdon, R. L. 2008. Beyond deforestation: restoring forests and ecosystem services on degraded lands. Science 320:1458-1460.

Appendix 3. AMAZONIAN FOREST

Carlos Nobre (Instituto Nacional de Pesquisas Espaciais, nobre@cptec.inpe.br)
Paul Leadley (Université Paris-Sud 11, paul.leadley@u-psud.fr)
Juan F. Fernandez-Manjarrés (Université Paris-Sud 11, juan.fernandez@u-psud.fr)

SUMMARY

▸ There is a growing scientific consensus based on models, observations and experiments that complex interactions between deforestation, fire, regional climate change and global climate change could lead to widespread Amazonian forest dieback over the coming decades, in particular in the Southeastern areas of the Amazon basin.

▸ If current trends in land use and climate change continue, some models project that deforestation and dieback will leave less than 50% of original Amazonian forest by 2030 and less than 10% of original forest by 2080.

▸ Widespread dieback of humid tropical forest would lead to reductions in species abundance and extinctions of plants and animals at levels unprecedented in human history due to the exceptionally high diversity of these systems combined with very small ranges of many species.

▸ Deforestation, fires and widespread dieback would lead to losses of stored Carbon in vegetation and soils that are large enough to significantly influence atmospheric CO_2 concentrations and global climate. Regional effects include significant reductions in rainfall over large areas of Latin America and beyond. Mass extinctions and reductions in species abundance will have large cultural impacts and eliminate many of the tremendous provisioning values provided by primary forests.

▸ There is need for further long-term monitoring at the ecosystem level in Amazonia as the effects of alternate severe droughts and extreme flooding, coupled with CO_2 fertilization, may provide some resilience to the system.

▸ Keeping deforestation below 20% of original forest area and investing in forest restoration, substantially reducing the use of fire, and limiting climate warming to well below 2°C is predicted to significantly reduce the risk of widespread dieback.

DESCRIPTION

Status and Trends

The Amazon forest is the largest and most species-rich continuous broad-leaved tropical rain forest in the world. It is estimated to harbour more than 30000 species of vascular plants with 5000 to 10000 species of trees alone (Henderson et al. 1991, Myers et al. 2000). The Amazon forest covers almost 40% of South America and includes most of the Amazon River basin beginning east of the Andes and extending to the Atlantic coast. The watershed comprises more than 7000 square-km and the longest dimension of the basin is more than 6800 km long (Hubbell et al. 2008). Different rainforest within this large basin occur in nine countries: Brazil, Peru, Colombia, Venezuela, Ecuador, Bolivia, Guyana, Suriname and French Guyana, but Brazil alone contains 60% of the estimated Amazon forest area. Climatically, it is characterized by a total absence of frosts and abundant rains all year round with relatively short dry periods no longer than four months. Rainfall varies between 2000 mm and > 4000 mm per year. Far from being a homogenous vegetation type, the Amazon forest includes different forest types ranging from flooded forests to areas of sandy soils subject to water stress and includes ecotones towards surrounding seasonal dry forests or savanna vegetation, like in South Eastern Amazonia. Soils are extremely poor and most of the available nutrients exist in the uppermost layers of organic matter.

Amazonian forests have exceptionally high species diversity and have been estimated to harbour roughly a quarter of the earth's terrestrial species (Dirzo and Raven 2003). For example, it has been estimated

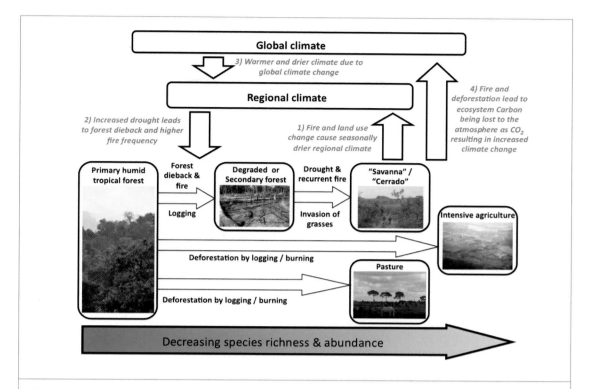

FIGURE 1

Interactions between global climate, regional climate, fire and deforestation that lead to loss and degradation of Amazonian primary tropical forest. Adapted from Nepstad et al. (2008) and the Crossroads of Life (CoL 2007). The vegetation that will result from repeated drought and fire over many decades remains somewhat speculative ("Savanna" box). For clarity, several key land use types, especially forest plantations and mixed land use systems have been omitted, as have several key transitions, including the transition back to secondary forest following land abandonment. Image credits from left to right: CNRS Photothèque / C. Delhaye, CNRS Photothèque / H. Thery , P. Leadley, CNRS Photothèque / F.-M. Le Tourneau, CNRS Photothèque / H. Thery

that there are more than 10000 tree species in the Amazonian forests of Brazil with local species richness that frequently exceed 200 tree species per hectare in primary humid tropical forest (Hubbell et al. 2008). Human activities have already impacted biodiversity in Amazonian forests especially through large-scale deforestation over the last several decades that have reduced its extent by about 13-16%.

Tipping point mechanisms

There is increasing evidence that humid tropical forest in the Amazon could suffer from widespread and severe dieback due to interactions between global climate change, deforestation and fire over the next few decades (Figure 1) (Betts et al. 2008, Huntingford et al. 2008, Malhi et al. 2008a, Nepstad et al. 2008, Nobre 2008). Deforestation and conversion to pastures or crops combined with widespread burning of forests have been shown to reduce regional rainfall and increase drought (Figure 1, arrow 1). A key tipping-point appears to occur at 30-50% deforestation, beyond which these regional climate impacts will become strong. Changes in forest structure caused by drought, fire and fragmentation substantially increase the susceptibility of tropical forests to fire, thus creating a positive feedback loop that leads to widespread forest degradation and dieback (Figure 1, arrow 2). On longer time scales, substantial warming and drying of the Amazon due to global climate change are projected by a majority of climate models amplifying drought caused by the regional effects of deforestation and burning (Figure 1, arrow 3). Massive ecosystem carbon losses from deforestation, fire and dieback will turn the Amazonian forest from a large net sink of Carbon to a large net source, amplifying global warming and regional drought (Figure 1, arrow 4). New simulations of the combined effects of land use change, fire and climate change undertaken under various climate and deforestation assumptions for the 21st Century indicated the tipping point may occur at around 20% deforestation (World Bank, 2010). Separate studies indicate that the Amazonian ecosystems can be committed to long-term change well before any response is observable, finding that the risk of significant loss of forest cover rises rapidly for a global mean temperature rise above 2 degrees (Jones et al 2009). In summary, a tipping-point occurs because the combined effects of deforestation, fire and global climate change permanently switch the Amazon to a drier climate regime that does not support humid tropical forest. This view of Amazonian forest dynamics is gaining support based on a wide range of experiments, observations and modeling studies (Barlow and Peres 2008, Huntingford et al. 2008, Malhi et al. 2008a, Phillips et al. 2009). Rainfall suppression experiments (Fisher et al. 2007, Nepstad et al. 2007, Brando et al. 2008, Meir et al. 2008) suggest that Western Amazon forests whose natural dry seasons are short are more prone to tree mortality because of droughts compared to eastern Amazon forest.

If this tipping-point scenario is correct, recent model projections suggest that more than half of Amazonian forest may be cleared or suffering from serious degradation in the next few decades (Nepstad et al. 2008) and reduced to small fragments by the end of the century (Betts et al. 2008). This tipping-point scenario is viewed with broadly varying degrees of caution by scientists because of large uncertainties in projections of climate change, land-use change and sensitivity of tropical forest to drought (Malhi et al. 2008a). Even in the absence of widespread forest dieback, the interactive effects of global climate change, deforestation and fire are viewed as major threat to biodiversity and ecosystem services in the Amazon over the coming century by the vast majority of the scientific community.

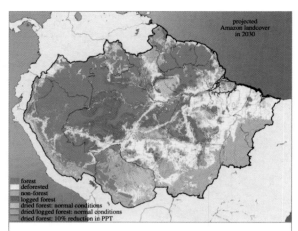

FIGURE 2

Near-term (2030) projections of Amazonian forest loss due to deforestation (yellow) and forest degradation due to logging and climate change (brown is for logging impacts only, pink is for climate impacts using "normal" climate over the previous decade which has been warm and punctuated by drought, red is for climate assuming a 10% reduction in precipitation due to global climate change and land cover changes on regional climate). Reproduced from Nepstad et al. (2008). Copyright © 2008 The Royal Society.

IMPACTS ON BIODIVERSITY

Amazonian forests have exceptionally high species diversity and have been estimated to harbour roughly a quarter of the earth's terrestrial species (Dirzo and Raven 2003). For example, it has been estimated that there are more than 10000 tree species in the Amazonian forests of Brazil with local species richness that frequently exceed 200 tree species per hectare in primary humid tropical forest (Hubbell et al. 2008). Human activities have already impacted biodiversity in Amazonian forests especially through large-scale deforestation over the last several decades that have reduced its extent by about 13-16%.

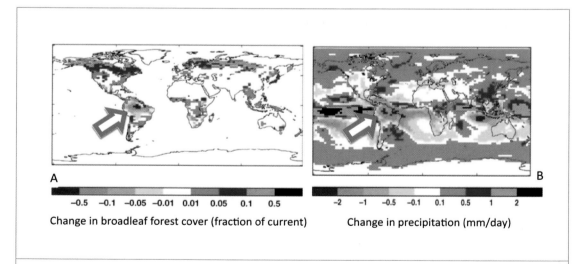

FIGURE 3

Long-term (2080) projections of the impacts of global climate change on A) broadleaf forest cover and B) precipitation in 2080 compared to 2000. Large red arrows point to Amazon region. Projections were made using the HadCM3LC coupled climate-vegetation model and the IPCC IS92a greenhouse gas emissions scenario. Figures reproduced from Betts et al. (2004). British Crown Copyright, reproduced with permission of the Met Office.

Future loss and shifts in biomes and habitats

No current models account for the full set of global climate, regional climate, deforestation and fire interactions that could lead to an Amazonian forest tipping point, but a few models account for several of the key interactions. Nepstad et al. (2008) have estimated the near term impacts of this tipping-point using a number of simple assumptions about future climate and land use and predict a 55% loss or degradation of Amazonian forest by 2030 (Figure 2). Longer-term, widespread Amazonian forest dieback due to climate change is projected by some global vegetation models for scenarios of moderate to high greenhouse gas emissions (White et al. 1999, Cox et al. 2004, Oyama and Nobre 2004). In these model projections, nearly all Amazonian forest is replaced by savanna or desert by the end of the 21st century with the exception of small areas of Western Amazonia and the Andes (Figure 3A). There appears to be very limited opportunity for large-scale shifts of this biome to adjoining areas (Figure 3A).

Future species loss, reductions in abundance and shifts in ranges

The risk of massive species extinctions and reductions in species abundance in Amazonian forest has been underestimated in previous model-based projections of species loss, since a scenarios of widespread Amazonian forest dieback have not yet been studied. In particular, estimates of diversity impacts of global change across a broad range of species in the Millennium Assessment (MA 2005), GLOBIO3 model assessments (Crossroads of Life 2007, Alkemade et al. 2009) the Global Environmental Outlook 4 (GEO4), or for species groups like birds (Jetz et al. 2007) have not included this tipping point. If widespread forest dieback does occur, the vegetation that will replace humid tropical forest in the near term is projected to be degraded seasonally dry forest and grasses that have substantially lower abundance of a wide range of plant and animals species than primary forest (Barlow et al. 2003, Barlow et al. 2006, Barlow and Peres 2008). Widespread dieback would also greatly increase the number of projected species extinctions above previous estimates, particularly since the risk of extinctions increases greatly as habitat area declines. Hubbell et al. (2008) have recently estimated the impacts of land use change on tree diversity that include scenarios of severe forest loss (75% of Brazilian forest is heavily or moderately impacted by deforestation, Laurance et al. 2002). Under these scenarios, 33% of the roughly 10000 tree species are predicted to go extinct over the next several decades. Hubbell et al. (2008), however, predict that roughly 3000 tree species are sufficiently abundant and widespread that the risk of extinction is low. Deforestation in the Western arc of Amazonian forest is particularly critical because diversity of plants and animals with very restricted ranges is exceptionally high and because land conversion and infrastructure could substantially reduce the capacity of species to migrate to climate "refugia" in the Andes (Killeen and Solorzano 2008).

ECOSYSTEM SERVICES

Amazonian forests provide a broad range of ecosystem services at local to global scales that will be seriously degraded as a result of widespread deforestation and dieback.

Supporting and regulating services

Supporting and regulating services (*sensu* MA 2005) can be directly and quantitatively coupled to the changes in ecosystem functioning due to the loss or degradation of Amazonian primary forest ecosystems. The most important of these services at global and regional scales are Carbon sequestration and control of regional climate. Amazonian forests contain a substantial fraction of terrestrial carbon (ca. 120 Pg C) and currently appear to be a large sink for Carbon (ca. 0.6 Pg C year^{-1}), except in years of extreme drought when they become a large net Carbon source (Phillips et al. 2009). Model estimates that include deforestation and forest dieback show that Amazonian forest can become a large, near-term global source of Carbon, for example emitting 15-26 Pg C over the 20 years in the scenario of (Figure 2) (Nepstad et al. 2008) which equals roughly 2 years of current global carbon emissions due to human activities. Global climate change may lead to the loss of between roughly half and three quarters of vegetation and soil carbon in the Amazon by the end of the century (Huntingford et al. 2008) (Figure 3C), substantially contributing to global warming. At regional scales, large-scale forest loss and burning have been demonstrated to reduce rainfall, primarily through the modification of water transfer by plants to the atmosphere and changes in aerosol production (Betts et al. 2008, Malhi et al. 2008a). Models that couple climate and vegetation dynamics suggest that the removal of 30% to 40% of Amazonian forest could lead to a tipping-point in which the regional climate becomes permanently drier (Figures 1 and 3B). Secondary forests and forest plantations could serve some of the ecosystem function roles of primary forests, but the soil degradation, repeated fires, dieback due to drought and the long time lags to recover lost Carbon stocks following deforestation make these options best reserved for restoration of areas in which primary forest has already been lost (Chazdon 2008).

Provisioning and cultural services

Provisioning and cultural services (*sensu* MA 2005) will be substantially altered by widespread dieback, but many are more difficult to quantify, especially cultural ecosystem services. We focus here on provisioning services. The timber sector in Brazil accounts for ca. 3.5% of GDP, but the capacity of this sector to adapt to widespread dieback is difficult to forecast. Loss of "option" value due to species extinctions includes the loss of novel genes and species for new drug development especially. Species of Amazonian primary forest have received considerable attention for treatments of cancer and infectious diseases because of their exceptionally high diversity of organic compounds (Suffredini et al. 2007a, Suffredini et al. 2007b, Younes et al. 2007). Widespread forest dieback would have a large economic impact on indigenous people and subsistence farmers since the economic value of biodiversity in primary and old secondary forests for extractive use of wood, food, medicines, etc. are non-negligible (Coomes and Ban 2004, Gavin 2004, Borner and Wunder 2008) and communities may rely on the use of several hundred species (Gavin 2004). There is potentially substantial room for adaptation, because extractive use of plants and animals from Amazonian forests varies greatly in its contribution to livelihoods of indigenous people and subsistence farmers even at local scales (Coomes and Ban 2004) and is typically combined with other land uses, especially cultivation (Gavin 2004, Salisbury and Schmink 2007, Borner and Wunder 2008).

UNCERTAINTIES

▸ Many climate models underestimate current rainfall in the Amazon, so they may also exaggerate future drought (Malhi et al. 2008a). In addition, a minority of climate models do not project reductions in rainfall and there is considerable debate about the ability of climate models to correctly simulate rainfall in the Amazonian basin (Huntingford et al. 2008, Malhi et al. 2008a).

▸ Global vegetation models used in predicting Amazonian forest response to climate have only been infrequently tested against observations and, therefore, may over – or underestimate the sensitivity of these forests to warming and drought. Paleontological data from dry periods several thousand years ago suggest that the tropical forest may be more resilient than models predict (Bush et al. 2007, Mayle and Power 2008, but see Cowling et al. 2001) as do some experiments and satellite observations (Malhi et al. 2008a).

▸ Most models of Amazonian forest response to climate change assume that rising atmospheric CO_2 concentrations will partially alleviate drought stress. This effect of CO_2 on tropical trees has not been demonstrated experimentally and if it does not occur forests may be much more senstive to climate change than most models predict.

▸ Land cover and land use scenarios have very high levels of uncertainty and, therefore, must always be interpreted as providing storylines of possible futures.

▸ Estimates of percent species loss and species extinctions in the Amazon are and will remain controversial, in part due to the problems inherent in species-area methods often used for these estimates and the high level of undescribed biodiversity and weak predictive understanding of extinctions (Ibanez et al. 2008). Estimates of species extinctions will also need to explicitly account for the heterogeneous nature of diversity within the Amazon, especially the very high number of species that are restricted to the Western edge of the Amazon.

▸ Current climate change may entail alternate events of extreme droughts and extreme flooding that may give resilience to many tree species if excess of water accumulated in flooding events may compensate longer dry seasons (Nobre and Borma, 2009). For example, the severe drought of 2005 was followed by floods only six months later. Similarly, the first five months of 2009 have shown above normal precipitation producing record flood levels. Hence, multiyear monitoring is urgently needed at the ecosystem level to asses the impact of increased climate variability on the long term survival of present vegetation types.

LOCAL TO GLOBAL ACTION AND OPPORTUNITIES

Global Action

▸ Pressure to convert forests to pastures must be reduced. Recent evidence suggests that deforestation should be kept below 20%. Cumulatative deforestation is already over 17%, and current trends will likely take cumulative deforestation to 20% of the Brazilian Amazon at or near 2020. Therefore it is urgent to halt deforestation, and a program of significant forest restoration would be a prudent measure to build in a margin of safety. Controlling the demand for meat production from Amazonian pastures or from feed grown in Brazil must also be dealt with internationally since a large fraction of deforestation is related to cattle grazing and much of the meat is exported. If international demands for biofuels indirectly drive deforestation in the Amazon (Fargione et al. 2008), then this pressure must also be reduced.

▸ International action must minimize climate change in order to reduce the probability of drying and warming of Amazonia. Clear thresholds are difficult to define, but climate warming should be kept well below 4°C (Nobre 2008), and recent evidence suggests that this should be below 2°C. Implementation of the "Reducing Emissions from Deforestation and Degradation" (REDD) mechanism in the UNFCCC, if done wisely, has the potential for mitigating climate change and substantially reducing deforestation, the two main direct drivers of biodiversity loss.

▸ Even though most of the Amazon is contained in Brazil and most of the deforestation occurs within that country, no large multinational initiatives exist among the other eight countries that harbour the periphery of the Amazon basin forests. Considering that climate change may 'push' species towards the Andean zone, a clear opportunity exists of maintaining the Eastern Andean lowland forest as a refuge for the Amazon basin as a whole.

Regional and local action

▸ National programs should aim to keep deforestation well below thresholds that have significant effects on regional climate (ca. 20-40% deforestation).

▸ Projects to reduce burning of forests and other ecosystems can minimize land use impacts on regional climate.

▸ Protection of large areas of intact forest can preserve both ecosystem function and biodiversity. Biodiversity will be particularly sensitive to protection of areas the Western edge of the Amazon.

▸ Rethinking road construction projects is a high priority, since roads have been and are projected to remain a key element in opening up primary forest to degradation and deforestation (Soares et al. 2006).

▸ National biofuel programs should avoid placing direct and indirect pressure on forests.

Tremendous efforts have been made in Brazil to develop a scientifically and socially sound program of protected areas and to develop real-time capacity to detect deforestation using remote sensing. These efforts and changes in commodity prices have reduced deforestation over the last decade, but large hurdles remain. Details of these actions and barriers and opportunities for implementing them are discussed in more depth in Lahsen and Nobre (2007), Betts et al. (2008), Boyd (2008), Killeen and Solozano (2008), Malhi et al. (2008b) and Nepstad et al. (2008).

REFERENCES

Alkemade, R., M. van Oorschot, L. Miles, C. Nellemann, M. Bakkenes, and B. ten Brink. 2009. GLOBIO3: A Framework to Investigate Options for Reducing Global Terrestrial Biodiversity Loss. Ecosystems 12:374-390.

Barlow, J., and C. A. Peres. 2008. Fire-mediated dieback and compositional cascade in an Amazonian forest. Philosophical Transactions of the Royal Society B-Biological Sciences 363:1787-1794.

Barlow, J., C. A. Peres, L. M. P. Henriques, P. C. Stouffer, and J. M. Wunderle. 2006. The responses of understorey birds to forest fragmentation, logging and wildfires: an Amazonian synthesis. Biological Conservation 128:182-192.

Barlow, J., C. A. Peres, B. O. Lagan, and T. Haugaasen. 2003. Large tree mortality and the decline of forest biomass following Amazonian wildfires. Ecology Letters 6: 6-8.

Betts, R. A., P. M. Cox, M. Collins, P. P. Harris, C. Huntingford, and C. D. Jones. 2004. The role of ecosystem-atmosphere interactions in simulated Amazonian precipitation decrease and forest dieback under global climate warming. Theoretical and Applied Climatology 78:157–175.

Betts, R. A., Y. Malhi, and J. T. Roberts. 2008. The future of the Amazon: new perspectives from climate, ecosystem and social sciences. Philosophical Transactions of the Royal Society B-Biological Sciences 363:1729-1735.

Borner, J., and S. Wunder. 2008. Paying for avoided deforestation in the Brazilian Amazon: from cost assessment to scheme design. International Forestry Review 10:496-511.

Boyd, E. 2008. Navigating Amazonia under uncertainty: past, present and future environmental governance. Philosophical Transactions of the Royal Society B-Biological Sciences 363:1911-1916.

Brando, P. M., D. C. Nepstad, E. A. Davidson, S. E. Trumbore, D. Ray, and P. Camargo. 2008. Drought effects on litterfall, wood production and belowground carbon cycling in an Amazon forest: results of a throughfall reduction experiment. Philosophical Transactions of the Royal Society B-Biological Sciences 363:1839-1848.

Bush, M. B., M. R. Silman, and C. M. C. S. Listopad. 2007. A regional study of Holocene climate change and human occupation in Peruvian Amazonia. Journal of Biogeography 34:1342-1356.

Chazdon, R. L. 2008. Beyond deforestation: restoring forests and ecosystem services on degraded lands. Science 320:1458-1460.

Coomes, O. T., and N. Ban. 2004. Cultivated plant species diversity in home gardens of an Amazonian peasant village in northeastern Peru. Economic Botany 58:420-434.

Cowling, S. A., M. A. Maslin, and M. T. Sykes. 2001. Paleovegetation simulations of lowland Amazonia and implications for neotropical allopatry and speciation. Quaternary Research 55:140-149.

Cox, P. M., R. A. Betts, M. Collins, P. P. Harris, C. Huntingford, and C. D. Jones. 2004. Amazonian forest dieback under climate-carbon cycle projections for the 21st century. Theoretical and Applied Climatology 78:137-156.

Dirzo, R., and P. H. Raven. 2003. Global state of biodiversity and loss. Annual Review of Environment and Resources 28:137-167.

Fargione, J., J. Hill, D. Tilman, S. Polasky, and P. Hawthorne. 2008. Land clearing and the biofuel carbon debt. Science. 319: 1235-1238.

Fisher, R. A., M. Williams, A. L. Da Costa, Y. Malhi, R. F. Da Costa, S. Almeida, and P. Meir. 2007. The response of an Eastern Amazonian rain forest to drought stress: results and modelling analyses from a throughfall exclusion experiment. Global Change Biology 13:2361-2378.

Gavin, M. C. 2004. Changes in forest use value through ecological succession and their implications for land management in the Peruvian Amazon. Conservation Biology 18:1562-1570.

Henderson, A., S. P. Churchill, and J. L. Luteyn. 1991. Neotropical plant diversity. Nature 351:21-22.

Hubbell, S. P., F. L. He, R. Condit, L. Borda-de-Agua, J. Kellner, and H. ter Steege. 2008. How many tree species and how many of them are there in the Amazon will go extinct? Proceedings of the National Academy of Sciences of the United States of America 105:11498-11504.

Huntingford, C., R. A. Fisher, L. Mercado, B. B. B. Booth, S. Sitch, P. P. Harris, P. M. Cox, C. D. Jones, R. A. Betts, Y. Malhi, G. R. Harris, M. Collins, and P. Moorcroft. 2008. Towards quantifying uncertainty in predictions of Amazon 'dieback'. Philosophical Transactions of the Royal Society B-Biological Sciences 363:1857-1864.

Ibanez, I., J. S. Clark, and M. C. Dietze. 2008. Evaluating the sources of potential migrant species: Implications under climate change. Ecological Applications 18:1664-1678.

Jetz, W., D. S. Wilcove, and A. P. Dobson. 2007. Projected impacts of climate and land-use change on the global diversity of birds. Plos Biology 5:1211-1219.

Jones, C., J. Lowe, S. Liddicoat, and R. Betts. 2009. Committed terrestrial ecosystem changes due to climate change. Nature Geoscience 2: 484-487.

Killeen, T. J., and L. A. Solorzano. 2008. Conservation strategies to mitigate impacts from climate change in Amazonia. Philosophical Transactions of the Royal Society B-Biological Sciences 363:1881-1888.

Lahsen, M., and C. A. Nobre. 2007. Challenges of connecting international science and local level sustainability efforts: the case of the large-scale biosphere-atmosphere experiment in Amazonia. Environmental Science and Policy 10:62-74.

Laurance, W. F., A. K. M. Albernaz, G. Schroth, P. M. Fearnside, S. Bergen, E. M. Venticinque, and C. Da Costa. 2002. Predictors of deforestation in the Brazilian Amazon. Journal of Biogeography 29:737-748.

Malhi, Y., J. T. Roberts, R. A. Betts, T. J. Killeen, W. H. Li, and C. A. Nobre. 2008a. Climate change, deforestation, and the fate of the Amazon. Science 319:169-172.

Malhi, Y., T. Roberts, and R. A. Betts. 2008b. Climate change and the fate of the Amazon – Preface. Philosophical Transactions of the Royal Society B-Biological Sciences 363:1727-1727.

Mayle, F. E., and M. J. Power. 2008. Impact of a drier Early-Mid-Holocene climate upon Amazonian forests. Philosophical Transactions of the Royal Society B-Biological Sciences 363:1829-1838.

Meir, P., D. B. Metcalfe, A. C. L. Costa, and R. A. Fisher. 2008. The fate of assimilated carbon during drought: impacts on respiration in Amazon rainforests. Philosophical Transactions of the Royal Society B-Biological Sciences 363:1849-1855.

Myers, N., R. A. Mittermeier, C. G. Mittermeier, G. A. B. da Fonseca, and J. Kent. 2000. Biodiversity hotspots for conservation priorities. Nature 403:853-858.

Moorcroft, P. 2003. Recent advances in ecosystem-atmosphere interactions: an ecological perspective. Proceedings Royal Society of London. Biological sciences 270:1215–1227.

Nepstad, D. C., C. M. Stickler, B. Soares, and F. Merry. 2008. Interactions among Amazon land use, forests and climate: prospects for a near-term forest tipping point. Philosophical Transactions of the Royal Society B-Biological Sciences 363:1737-1746.

Nepstad, D. C., I. M. Tohver, D. Ray, P. Moutinho, and G. Cardinot. 2007. Mortality of large trees and lianas following experimental drought in an amazon forest. Ecology 88:2259-2269.

Nobre, C. A. 2008. A scientific and technological revolution for the Brazilian Amazon. Journal of the Brazilian Chemical Society 19:Iv-Iv.

Nobre, C. A., and L. D. Borma. 2009. 'Tipping points' for the Amazon forest. Current Opinion in Environmental Sustainability 1:28–36.

Oyama, M. D., and C. A. Nobre. 2004. Climatic consequences of a large-scale desertification in northeast Brazil: A GCM simulation study. Journal of Climate 17:3203-3213.

Phillips, O. L., L. E. O. C. Aragao, S. L. Lewis, J. B. Fisher, J. Lloyd, G. Lopez-Gonzalez, Y. Malhi, A. Monteagudo, J. Peacock, C. A. Quesada, G. van der Heijden, S. Almeida, I. Amaral, L. Arroyo, G. Aymard, T. R. Baker, O. Banki, L. Blanc, D. Bonal, P. Brando, J. Chave, A. C. A. de Oliveira, N. D. Cardozo, C. I. Czimczik, T. R. Feldpausch, M. A. Freitas, E. Gloor, N. Higuchi, E. Jimenez, G. Lloyd, P. Meir, C. Mendoza, A. Morel, D. A. Neill, D. Nepstad, S. Patino, M. C. Penuela, A. Prieto, F. Ramirez, M. Schwarz, J. Silva, M. Silveira, A. S. Thomas, H. ter Steege, J. Stropp, R. Vasquez, P. Zelazowski, E. A. Davila, S. Andelman, A. Andrade, K. J. Chao, T. Erwin, A. Di Fiore, E. Honorio, H. Keeling, T. J. Killeen, W. F. Laurance, A. P. Cruz, N. C. A. Pitman, P. N. Vargas, H. Ramirez-Angulo, A. Rudas, R. Salamao, N. Silva, J. Terborgh, and A. Torres-Lezama. 2009. Drought Sensitivity of the Amazon Rainforest. Science 323:1344-1347.

Salisbury, D. S., and M. Schmink. 2007. Cows versus rubber: Changing livelihoods among Amazonian extractivists. Geoforum 38:1233-1249.

Soares, B. S., D. C. Nepstad, L. M. Curran, G. C. Cerqueira, R. A. Garcia, C. A. Ramos, E. Voll, A. McDonald, P. Lefebvre, and P. Schlesinger. 2006. Modelling conservation in the Amazon basin. Nature 440:520-523.

Suffredini, I. B., M. L. B. Paciencia, S. A. Frana, A. D. Varella, and R. N. Younes. 2007a. In vitro breast cancer cell lethality of Brazilian plant extracts. Pharmazie 62:798-800.

Suffredini, I. B., M. L. B. Paciencia, A. D. Varella, and R. N. Younes. 2007b. In vitro cytotoxic activity of Brazilian plant extracts against human lung, colon and CNS solid cancers and leukemia. Fitoterapia 78:223-226.

White, A., M. G. R. Cannell, and A. D. Friend. 1999. Climate change impacts on ecosystems and the terrestrial carbon sink: a new assessment. Global Environmental Change-Human and Policy Dimensions 9:S21-S30.

World Bank – Climate Change and Clean Energy Initiative. 2010. Assessment of the Risk of Amazon Dieback. http://www.bicusa.org/en/Document.101982.aspx

Younes, R. N., A. D. Varella, and I. B. Suffredini. 2007. Discovery of new antitumoral and antibacterial drugs from Brazilian plant extracts using high throughput screening. Clinics 62:763-768.

Appendix 4. WEST AFRICA: THE SAHARA, SAHEL AND GUINEAN REGION

Cheikh Mbow (Ecole Supérieure Polytechnique ESP, Université Cheikh Anta Diop de Dakar-Sénégal, Dakar, Senegal, cmbow@ucad.sn)
Mark Stafford Smith (CSIRO Sustainable Ecosystems, Canberra, Australia, mark.StaffordSmith@csiro.au)
Paul Leadley (Université Paris-Sud 11, paul.leadley@u-psud.fr)

SUMMARY

▸ Coupled human-environment interactions in West Africa, extending from the southern Sahara down through the Sahel and into the Guinean Forest, are highly vulnerable to climate, land use and land management changes that can cause ecosystems to shift to alternate states with high impacts on biodiversity, ecosystem services and human well-being. Poverty, lack of governance, conflict and resulting human migrations leave this region with little margin for adaptive responses.

▸ Tipping-points in West Africa are complex due to the multiplicity of drivers and their interactions. We focused on four interacting tipping-points that influence this region:
Climate regime shifts: Future climate regime shifts are highly uncertain, especially for precipitation for which projections range from a persistent increase, to increased variability, to long-term reductions in rainfall.
Overuse of marginal resources: Marginal resources coupled with overuse result in a downward spiral of productivity, poverty and biodiversity impoverishment. Accompanying land degradation makes it difficult to restore biodiversity and ecosystem services even when socio-economic and climatic conditions improve.
Globalisation and overexploitation: Agricultural development and market globalization drive exploitation in areas of more abundant natural resources, with forest clearing having the most serious impact. Improvements in access and increasing local wealth in these areas of the region drive improved access and further increases in exploitation.
Instability and limited resources: Ineffectual governance caused by instability and conflict permits unregulated use of natural resources including those in protected areas. This also drives refugee movements to other regions, increasing stress on natural resources in those areas and triggering further social and political disruption.

▸ Combinations of drought, overuse of natural capital and political instability have led to widespread biodiversity loss, land degradation and famine in the recent past, clearly illustrating the region's high potential vulnerability to future global changes. Current trends in biodiversity responses indicate a strong decline in bird and mammal populations and range shifts due to land use and climate change. At the other extreme, the Sahara/Sahel has been much "greener" during wetter climate regimes over the last several thousand years and the Sahel is currently "greening".

▸ Global biodiversity projections suggest that this region will be one of the most highly impacted regions of the world in terms of destruction of natural habitat, decreasing species abundance and species extinctions. Models of habitats and birds suggest that land use will be the dominant driver of biodiversity change in the 21st century. Climate change is often projected to be a positive factor for biodiversity due to regime shifts to a wetter climate and rising CO_2 concentrations, but these projections have typically overlooked the importance of climate variability and uncertainty in their analyses.

▸ Ecosystems in this region are a major source of environmental capital for ecosystem goods and services used by local populations, but globalization and marketing of these resources is projected to continue to lead to a degradation of services provided by natural and semi-natural ecosystems.

▸ Local, national and international efforts to reduce impacts on biodiversity and improve human well-being have often been hindered by rapid population growth, lack of consistent governance and conflict. Resolving these human development issues is the key to protecting biodiversity in this region.

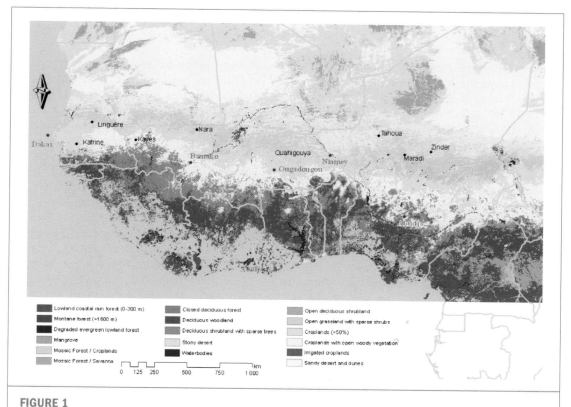

FIGURE 1

Vegetation cover of West Africa. Source: Global Land Cover 2000 database. European Commission, Joint Research Centre, 2003, http://www-gem.jrc.it/glc2000.

DESCRIPTION

Status and Trends

West Africa is characterized by a north-south bands of vegetation types ranging from the Sahara desert, southward trough the Sahel and savanna and into the to moist forests of the Guinean forests of West Africa and on to the Congo basin of Central Africa (Fig.1). North-south trends in rainfall are the primary driver of these natural and semi-natural vegetation types. West Africa ecosystems have very high levels of local species endemism, mostly concentrated in the forests. A comprehensive survey by Conservation International indicates that 20% of endemic plants, 38% of amphibians, 24% of reptiles and 21% of endemic mammals worldwide are found in West Africa. (http://www.biodiversityhotspots.org/xp/hotspots/west_africa/Pages/biodiversity.aspx).

▸ *Sahara* – The present-day Sahara occupies an area of slightly over 8 million km² between latitudes 16 and 32 degrees N, circumscribed within the isohyetss of 100 ± 50 mm mean annual rainfall (grey areas in Fig. 1). The Sahara is dominated by rocky and sandy deserts with sparse vegetation. Most large mammals present in the desert until the second half of the 19th century are now extinct or are on the verge of local extinction in the Sahara. The situation is far less dramatic for the flora, which still includes ca. 3000 species of vascular plants (Le Houerou 1997).

▸ *Sahel* – The Sahel region lies between the isohyets of ca. 150 and 700mm of mean annual rainfall (tan and northern edges of pink areas in Fig 1). It is characterized by strong seasonality in rainfall, with a rainy season extending from July until September. The vegetation is a mix of herbaceous species and short stature woody species, many of the Acacia family. Large herds of grazing ungulates have been reduced to much smaller populations over the last century. Land degradation in the West African Sahel has become a central aspect of environment dynamics in that sub region. This process came to the world's attention during the drought catastrophes of the 1970s and 80s, and is associated with the image of rolling sand dunes and vegetation shifts devastating otherwise productive land. This vision of a moving front of land degradation is not accurate, with recent investigations providing very different perceptions of the direction, magnitude and impact of environmental change (Reynolds et al. 2007; Mortimore 2009).

▸ *West African Savanna* – Savannas are plant communities dominated by continuous stratum of grass, with trees of variable density (Kellman 1997, yellow and brown areas in Fig 1, much of which has been converted to croplands along a northern band indicated by pink areas in Fig 1). Savanna ecosystems are one of the most productive zones of West Africa, supporting several intertwined activities such as agriculture, grazing and an extensive use of wildlife and forest resources for subsistence livelihoods. This ecosystem is usually burnt during the dry season as a management tool (Ayoub et al. 1998, Mbow et al. 2000, Nielsen et al. 2003). Bush fires are seen as unavoidable, but acknowledged as having both positive and negative impacts on biodiversity, for example by maintaining the tree-grass balance by inhibiting regeneration of trees, but also possibly degrading soil quality or aggravating soil erosion (Ahlgren et al. 1960, Afolayan,1978, Brookman-Amissah et al., 1980, Sabiiti et al. 1988).

▸ *Guinean forests* – The Guinean forests consist of a range of distinct vegetation zones varying from moist forests along the coast, freshwater swamp forests, and semi-deciduous forests inland with prolonged dry seasons. The Guinean Forests of West Africa include two main subregions, the first are forests ranging from southern Guinea into eastern Sierra Leone and through Liberia, Côte d'Ivoire and Ghana into western Togo and the second, separated from the first by the Dahomey Gap, is forest that extends along the coast from western Nigeria to south-western Cameroon (green areas in Fig 1). Guinean forests include mangrove ecosystems that have been highly degraded with several ecological (destruction of fish nurseries, soil erosion, salinization of soils and freshwater supplies, etc.) and human impacts (loss of natural resources, increased vulnerability of local populations, etc.) (Conchedda et al. 2009).

Tipping point mechanisms

West Africa is confronted with a wide variety of tipping points that are related to complex interactions in coupled human-environment (H-E) systems. We have divided the drivers and responses in this region into four tipping points outlined below. These tipping-points are highly inter-related and, therefore, the system is even more complex than our analysis suggests. In addition to a climate tipping point, we focus on three sets of regional H-E feedbacks that can lead to runaway degradation of the H-E system. Most of these tipping points focus on changes related to dryland biodiversity and ecosystem services which are (i) long-term and hard to reverse, and (ii) have significance at a scale that has global ramifications. We conceptualize drylands as coupled human-environment (H-E) systems in which changes in either subsystem can trigger tipping points and push the system beyond thresholds (Liu et al. 2007, Reynolds et al. 2007, Stafford Smith et al. 2009). Drylands are renowned for this behavior at all scales, and have been the source of significant original thinking about states and transitions (Westoby et al. 1989, Friedel 1991, Reynolds et al. 2007, Stafford Smith et al. 2009), and disequilibrium theory (Ellis 1994, Vetter 2005).

▸ *Climate regime shifts* – Lenton et al. (2008) identified the Sahara/Sahel region as one of the most important Earth System tipping points in which global warming may drive climate regime shifts that fundamentally alter ecosystem productivity, biogeochemical cycles and human well-being. Despite large variability in model projections of climate regimes in this region, Lenton et al. gave the most weight to models projecting increased in rainfall in this region with subsequent increases in plant productivity. They concluded that "such greening of the Sahara/Sahel is a rare example of a beneficial potential tipping element" due to climate change. Our interpretation of climate scenarios is substantially less optimistic.

The climate regime that controls rainfall in West Africa is complex and potentially bi-stable (Cook & Vizy 2006, Nicholson 2009). Because of this complexity, there is little agreement among the broad range of climate models that were used for the IPCC (2007) projections concerning precipitation changes as illustrated in Figure 2. The mean IPCC projection shows an increase in rainfall over most of this region, but this masks

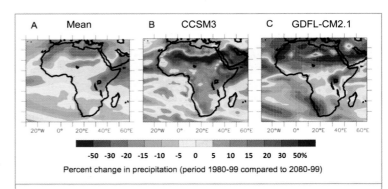

FIGURE 2

A) Mean of 21 model General Circulation Models for precipitation change in Africa due to 21st century climate change showing projected reductions in Northern and Southern African and increases in parts of Western and Central Africa. B) The CCSM3 climate model projection of substantial increases in rainfall over the entire Sahara / Sahel / Guinean forest transect. C) The GDFL climate model projection of substantial decreases in rainfall over this same region. (Source IPCC 2007)

very high variability across models (Fig 2). A review of three climate models considered to be among the most reliable for this region because of their ability to reproduce currently weather patterns came to a similar conclusion. One model projects a climate regime shift to persistent increased rainfall, a second projects a climate regime shift to a less stable state where moderate decreases in rainfall are associated with an increase in periods of drought, and a third projects a regime shift to a persistently drier climate (Cook & Vizy 2006). Despite major advances in understanding the factors controlling the climate of West Africa there is a strong feeling in the climate community that future climate patterns for this region are highly uncertain (Cook & Vizy 2006, IPCC 2007, Giannini et al. 2008, Nicolson 2009). In addition, future projections of vegetation shift must take into account interactions with land use. Because of these uncertainties we suggest that adaptive management strategies must take into account a wide range of potential future climates.

▸ *Overuse of marginal resources* – The 'Sahel' syndrome, which occurs in various forms in other dryland systems, is characterized by situations in which marginal resources coupled with overuse result in a downward spiral of productivity, poverty and biodiversity impoverishment (Ludeke et al. 2004). This downward spiral is driven by feedbacks in between and within the human and environment subsystems, which in West Africa occur at a spatial scale that is large enough to affect regional climate and population movements, both with global ramifications.

Underlying this syndrome are population growth and poverty. At current growth rates, populations in West Africa are expected to double by 2025. Population growth, particularly in rural areas, has and will continue to increase the extent and intensity of land use. Poverty combined with population growth has often led to situations where urgent short-term needs over-ride long-term considerations. For example, traditional slash-and-burn agriculture was associated with rotation techniques for forest, which allowed a swift recovery of soil and vegetation (Tschakert et al. 2004, Wood et al. 2004, Vagen et al. 2005). Higher population density, combined with the promotion of commercial crops (Burgess 1991) has led to shorter, or nonexistent, fallow durations and widespread soil degradation. This situation is further aggravated by the influx of farmers from arid and less productive lands, because better rainfall and soils exert a strong attraction (Mbow et al. 2008, Mertz et al. 2008).

The overuse of fire is an additional hindrance to good management of biodiversity and ecosystem services. In West Africa, annual burning early in the dry season has several goals, such as preventing later fires that can damage natural resources, forest resource extraction (e.g., hunting, honey), and the maintenance of rangelands (Mbow et al. 2000). The process of gradually burning off the driest vegetation creates a seasonal mosaic of habitat patches that increases the potential of the landscape for a variety of dry season land uses, including hunting, gathering of savanna products, and grazing (Laris 2002). Grazing can rapidly turn into overgrazing with excessive use of fire. This creates irreversible changes locally which, accumulated over large areas, can change land cover at a regional scale.

▸ *Globalization and overexploitation* – This syndrome is driven principally by agricultural development and globalization of markets for natural resources; it parallels the 'Overexploitation' global syndrome of Ludeke et al. (2004). Its feedbacks are mostly through the social system, where access and increasing (but low) local wealth leads to increased clearing of natural systems, and is triggered or exacerbated by overseas and domestic urban market demands.

Global markets and the commercialization of production in West Africa are driving many biodiversity impacts. First, forest clearing for commercial crops is now cutting into the remaining islands of dryland forests and woodlands, including in protected areas. A more recent trend in the Sudan and Guinean regions is deforestation in biodiversity hotspots of dense forest ecosystems for subsequent activities such as animal breeding or intensive agriculture (Reenberg et al. 2003, Ba et al. 2004). A second direct impact of globalization on biodiversity is wood extraction. West Africa has become Europe's source of wood, increasing commercial extraction through large-scale logging. Illegal logging due to lack of control (see the "Instability" tipping point below) plays an important role in deforestation processes for several countries. Irregular forest extraction is known in almost all West African countries and usually exceeds the annual allowed sustainable harvest level (Sambou et al. 2004). A third globalization pressure with individually local but widespread effects comes from mining. Large and small scale mining for various minerals such as iron, diamonds, gold, and bauxite, particularly in mountains and along rivers, is a major threat to many important biodiversity areas. Miners additionally stress forest resources through hunting of wild animals, particularly antelope and primates. With improved international regulations and reduced stocks of the targets species, these types of activity have been substantially reduced.

Land use dynamics in West Africa, as elsewhere, are very much linked with the development of infrastructure such as roads and railways. The steady improvement in these networks has made access to forests easier and raised incentives for business development based on forest resources. This process induces a positive feedback, because better road networks increases development, which in turn creates wealth that allows further development of the network.

▸ *Instability and limited resources* – This syndrome is mediated principally by ineffectual governance caused by instability and conflict, which permits unregulated use of natural resources (including biodiversity reserves), but also drives refugee movements to other regions where resources are further stressed, thus often triggering further social and political disruption. The net effect of these feedbacks is that persistent degradation gradually spreads and intensifies over large regions with potential global significance in social and natural domains. This parallels, to some extent, the 'scorched earth' syndrome of Ludeke et al. (2004).

Political instability and conflicts, complicated by weak and inefficient governance, exacerbate the threats to intact forests in West Africa. For example, more than a million refugees from civil wars and persecution in Liberia and Sierra Leone have fled to forests in neighboring countries, increasing the pressures on the forests for food, fuel wood, building materials, and water. This number has increased significantly in recent years with the outbreak of conflicts in Côte d'Ivoire and Liberia, and there are some add-on effects through Chad from Darfur in Sudan.

▸ *Interactions between tipping points* – All of the H-E syndromes strongly interact with climate as was clearly demonstrated when West Africa experienced severe drought during the 1970s and 1980s. There is increasing evidence that regional changes in land cover associated with land degradation can feed back to the regional climate, particularly in semi-arid regions where formation of rain-bearing clouds is highly sensitive to land surface hydrological fluxes (Giannini et al. 2008). Given that such drought periods place further pressure on local people to over-exploit the land, this is likely to be powerful regional feedback effect, until conditions become so extreme that migration occurs. Recent "greening" of the Sahel may be partially attributable to increased rainfall over the last two decades, but detailed analyses of this trend suggest that land management practices have also played an important role (Herrmann et al. 2005, Olssen et al. 2005).

IMPACTS ON BIODIVERSITY

▸ *Future loss and shifts in biomes and habitats* – A relatively broad range of global models have been used to project changes in biomes or habitats in West Africa. However, these models account, at best, for only one or two of the tipping point mechanisms outlined above. None of these models has been run for a wide range of climate scenarios. Because of these shortcomings and the high uncertainty in both climate projections and socio-economic scenarios for this region, we feel that the future of biodiversity in this region is considerably more uncertain than one of these analyses taken alone would suggest. The majority of global vegetation models project an increase in primary productivity in natural and semi-natural ecosystems in this region due to climate change because of increased rainfall and/or rising CO_2 concentrations (e.g., MA 2005, Sitch et al. 2008). This is accompanied by a greening of the southern Sahara in some cases and an increase in woody vegetation in the Sahel in most cases.

Land use scenarios for this region indicate very large to extremely large rates of land use conversion in this region, with particularly heavy impacts on Guinean forests (and forests of the Congo basin) driven by population increase, globalization and increased access (Millennium Assessment MA 2005, African Environmental Outlook-2 AEO2 2006, Global Environmental Outlook GEO4 2007, Alkemade 2009). These analyses agree that, of all regions of the globe, the sub-Saharan region will experience among the highest projected rates of natural and semi-natural habitat destruction over the next several decades. Land use scenarios suggest that the worst prospects for West Africa involve development pathways that focus

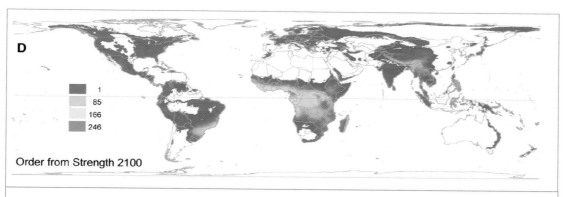

FIGURE 3

Combined impacts of projected habitat conversion and climate change on bird species for 2100 using the MA (2005) "Order from Strength" socio-economic scenario (from Jetz et al. 2008). Colors indicate the number of bird species undergoing large declines (> 50%) in habitat area.

either on market-driven globalization, or on continued regional patterns of rapid population growth, increasing social inequity, weak governance and continued conflict. Globalization scenarios foresee extensive land degradation, with more than 40% of currently cultivated land modeled as degraded by 2025 (AEO2 2006), and massive deforestation across Guinean forests by mid- to late-century (MA 2005, GEO4 2007, although not in AEO2 2006). Scenarios of high population growth and increasing inequity also lead to very high rates of land degradation and deforestation. At the opposite extreme, a scenario of "great transitions" that includes declining population growth rates, aggressive poverty reduction and greatly improved governance suggests that less than 10% of cropped land might be degraded by 2025 and that forest area could actually increase due to improved land management (AEO2 2006). These strong contrasts in scenarios highlight the overwhelming importance of development pathways in determining the fate of biodiversity in this region.

▸ *Future species loss, reductions in abundance and shifts in ranges* - Birds are by far the most intensely studied species group concerning recent trends and future projections for West Africa. Studies of recent trends of both resident and migratory bird populations show disquieting declines in many populations, with the most sensitive species being migratory birds and those primarily restricted to forest areas (e.g., Cresswell et al. 2004, Sanderson et al. 2006, Moller et al. 2008). Most studies attribute these population declines to a variety of human impacts including land use change, hunting, etc. These studies generally conclude that climate change has played a minor role in driving 20th century declines, but a recent study suggest that some migratory birds may lack the capacity to adapt to future climate change (Moller et al. 2008).

In an analysis of climate change impacts on turnover of bird species in protected areas, Hole et al. (2009) concluded that the Western African region was much less exposed to bird species turnover than Southern Africa. An analysis of a broad range of migratory birds using niche based models suggests that sub-Saharan Africa may actually increase in bird species richness due to northward shifts in the range of many Central and Southern African species (Barbet-Massin et al. 2009). In contrast to climate change, land use change is projected to have a large, negative impact on bird populations. An analysis of climate and land use change scenarios, Jetz et al. (2008) found that that projected land use change will contribute the most to the future decline in bird populations globally, with West Africa being the among areas of greatest concern for the future. In the most negative land use scenario, extremely large declines are predicted for the birds in the Guinean forests (Fig. 3). However, these studies did not include climate models with strong reductions or increases in rainfall (see "Climate regime tipping point" discussion), and may therefore underestimate the role of climate change in driving biodiversity change.

Declines in mammal populations are also of great concern especially due to habitat conversion, bushmeat hunting and poaching (Brashares et al. 2004). Trends over the last several decades indicate that mammal declines are well correlated with population growth and the size of protected areas (Brashares et al. 2001). However, we know of no model-based scenarios that have examined possible future trends in mammal populations that include hunting and poaching.

ECOSYSTEM SERVICES

Increasing human appropriation of natural resources is often accompanied by declining species richness, species abundance and destruction of natural habitats, but historically this loss of biodiversity has been accompanied by an increase in provisioning services such as food and fiber production in many region (MA 2005). It has been repeatedly suggested, however, that this relationship will not hold if ecosystems are pushed beyond certain thresholds (MA 2005). Land degradation in drylands of West Africa is among the most powerful examples of how overuse of natural resources can lead to rapid and difficult-to-reverse losses of biodiversity and degradation of a broad range of ecosystem services, including provisioning services. Added to this will be additional challenges posed by climate change since most projections suggest that farm revenues and the ability to feed a growing population will decrease for most climate scenarios (Butt et al. 2005; Sivakumar et al. 2005; Kurukulasuriya et al. 2006).

Local populations are aware that biological diversity is a crucial factor in generating the ecosystem services on which they depend. Some indigenous groups manipulate the local landscape to augment its heterogeneity, and some have been found to be motivated to restore biodiversity in degraded landscapes. It is vital, however, that the value of the knowledge-practice-belief complex of indigenous peoples relating to conservation of biodiversity is fully recognized if ecosystems and biodiversity are to be managed sustainably. Conserving this knowledge could be accomplished by promoting the community-based resource-management systems at local scale (Gadgil et al. 1993, AEO2 2006). Conservation of genetic resources is also a high priority for this region since it is the source of a number of economically important species and wild relatives of cultivated species. For example, the oil palm (*Elaeis guineensis*) is widely planted throughout the tropics for oil production; other species are valuable timber species including *Diospyros gracilis* (African ebony), *Entandophragma* and *Khaya*, *Milicia excelsa* and are widely exploited. Many species are used as medicines, foods, energy, religion, etc., with high gender sensitivity (Kristensen et al. 2003).

UNCERTAINTIES

▸ Land use change dominates projections of biodiversity loss in this region and therefore projections of biodiversity largely depend on regional socio-economic scenarios. Tremendous variability in regional socio-economic scenarios means that this is an area of the world where the future of biodiversity is most uncertain. This uncertainty should not, however, be interpreted as meaning that differences in development scenarios are unimportant for biodiversity: "business-as-usual" development pathways result in very large losses of biodiversity in the vast majority of published studies.

▸ Climate change impacts on biodiversity are difficult to predict due to large remaining uncertainties in climate change projections. However, this region appears to have gone through rapid climate and vegetations shifts over the last several tens of thousands of years. Past greening of the Sahara occurred in the mid-Holocene and may have happened rapidly in the earlier Bolling-Allerod warming. Collapse of vegetation in the Sahara ca. 5,000 years ago occurred more rapidly than orbital forcing suggesting that the system can flip between bistable states that are maintained by vegetation–climate feedback (Lenton et al. 2008).

▸ Species and species distributions are poorly documented for this region hampering scenarios development and validation.

▸ There is a lack of understanding of key thresholds for social and ecological systems. Many of these thresholds are only recognised and understood after they have been passed.

LOCAL TO GLOBAL ACTIONS AND OPPORTUNITIES

Gobal action

▸ Linking human development goals and biodiversity conservation – A wide range of international conventions and programs, e.g., the UN Convention to Combat Desertification (UNCCD) and the UN Millennium Development Goals (MDG), as well as NGOs have recognized that treating environmental issues, including the protection of biodiversity, is intimately related to achieving human development goals in West Africa. There many possibilities for strong synergies between these targets, as illustrated by the "Policy reform" and "Great Transitions" scenarios in the African Environmental Outlook 2. However, the multidimensional nature of the problem requires substantial improvements in governance, eliminating conflicts, correcting perverse elements of local and global market forces, reducing population growth rates, etc., and this complexity has so far stymied many global and African efforts to make significant progress in reaching human development targets or to adequately protect biodiversity (AEO2 2006, Mbow et al. 2008).

- ▸ Linking climate change and biodiversity agendas – Recent agreements on Reducing Emissions from Deforestation and Forest Degradation (REDD+) at the COP-15 of the UNFCCC in Copenhagen potentially provide a mechanism for protecting both biodiversity and carbon stocks in tropical forests. If appropriately funded and managed, this mechanism could substantially reduce rates of deforestation especially in highly biodiverse biomes like the Guinean forests. It has also been suggested that agriculture in sub-Saharan Africa could contribute to climate mitigation by storing C through improved agricultural practices. A recent modeling study covering a wide range of development pathways in Senegal suggests that the opportunities for C sequestration in agro-ecosystems are relatively modest and that the main climate related benefits of agricultural development will be on limiting deforestation (Ballensen et al. 2010).

The National Adaptation Programme of Action (NAPA) was established by the UNFCCC to address the needs for adaptation to adverse impacts of climate change at the national level in Least Developed Countries. The NAPA provides international funds managed by the Global Environment Facility (GEF) to undertake urgent actions for climate change adaptation in developing countries. This could be an important means for increasing environmental protection in West Africa, but given the possibilities for both conflicts and synergies between climate change adaptation and biodiversity protection, great care must be taken when implementing NAPA adaptation strategies. In addition, these adaptation strategies must remain flexible and be revised over time, as climate impacts and vulnerabilities change.

Regional and local action

- ▸ *Linking human development goals and biodiversity conservation* – The "New Partnership for Africa's Development" (NEPAD) and its "Environmental Action Plan" (NEPAD-EAP) and the West African plan for combating desertification have developed regional development strategies that explicitly acknowledge the strong, but complex links between improving human well-being and environmental protection. In particular, agricultural development pathways will be one of the most important determinants of human well-being and biodiversity in West Africa. Sustainable intensification of agriculture combining local knowledge and science-based best practice opens up opportunities for improving rural livelihoods, reducing malnourishment and protecting biodiversity at the regional scale by reducing pressures that contribute to overgrazing, conversion of forests to croplands and bushmeat hunting (Brashares et al. 2004, AEO2 2006, Reynolds et al. 2007, Bellansen et al. 2010). At the same time, moderate levels of grazing are an essential component of maintaining grassland and savanna vegetation, and grazing is likely to remain an important basis of rural livelihoods. Given the diverse demands on ecosystems and large environmental gradients in this region, good spatial planning, i.e., doing the right thing in the right places at local, national and regional levels will be a vital component of managing the synergies and tradeoffs between biodiversity protection and agricultural development.

- ▸ *Combatting desertification* – In addition to agricultural development, several national and regional initiatives have focused on tree planting in semi-arid zones as a means of restoring degraded lands. Some of these have been very successful at pushing back "desertification" at local scales (e.g., the bioreclamation initiative of ICRISAT), but difficulties in tree establishment and long-term care of replanted areas make success rates highly variable (Anonymous 2008). One of the most ambitious initiatives is the "Great Green Wall" project in which a ca. 7000 km long by 15 km wide band stretching from Dakar to Djibouti is to be planted with trees with the objectives of restoring dryland ecosystems, developing infrastructure and improving local living conditions (Anonymous 2008).

- ▸ *Protected areas* – For decades, conservation efforts in West Africa have focused on a network of forest reserves throughout the region. Although these reserves were mostly designed to protect watersheds and timber supplies rather than biodiversity, they are vital for conserving the remaining forest fragments and other ecosystems in West Africa. Nonetheless, many critical forested habitats have not yet been included within the national systems of protected areas. Most protected areas in this region lie in the most populated zones of Africa where land degradation is strongest. This raises the issue of the effectiveness of protected areas in these regions as a means of conserving habitats and species. Since the late 1960s, all countries in the region have made efforts to establish more effectively managed and controlled protected areas. Most of protected forest is currently being encroached by farmlands. One of the greatest conservation challenges in West Africa is finding alternative ways to accommodate human needs, in order to decrease the pressure from rural communities living adjacent to protected areas. Development of economic alternatives such as ecotourism, handicrafts and agro forestry have shown promise. An important way to enhance the effectiveness of protected areas in West Africa will be through the establishment of conservation corridors comprising biodiversity-friendly land uses to link protected areas together. The region has several transboundary national parks and rivers that require improved regional coordination and action for sustainable management.

At a time where much of the discussion about major issues in nature conservation is necessarily being undertaken at a global level, it is important to keep in mind the needs of the smaller organizations that do much of the grass roots work in the protection of biodiversity (Garrod & Willis 1994). International donors and private citizens have invested billions of dollars to protect biodiversity in developing nations. Investments often aim to encourage economic activities that indirectly protect ecosystems and species. An alternative form of investment is to pay directly for conservation outcomes, as is commonly done in high-income nations. Direct approaches may, in many cases, be more effective and efficient than indirect ones, and thus merit greater attention in developing nations (Ferraro et al. 2002, 2003).

REFERENCES

AEO2 – African Environmental Outlook 2: Our Environment, Our Wealth. 2006. United Nations Environment Programme, Nairobi, Kenya, (www.unep.org/dewa/Africa)

Afolayan, T.A. 1978. The effect of fires on the vegetation in Kainji Lake National Park, Nigeria. Oikos. 31 :376-382

Ahlgren, I.F. Ahlgren, C.E. 1960. Ecological effects of forest fires. Botanical Review, 26:483-533.

Alkemade, R., M. van Oorschot, et al. 2009. "GLOBIO3: A Framework to Investigate Options for Reducing Global Terrestrial Biodiversity Loss." Ecosystems 12:374-390.

Anonymous. 2008. The Great Green Wall Initiative for the Sahara and the Sahel \ OSS; CEN-SAD. Introductory Note Number 3. OSS: Tunis. 44pp.

Ayoub A.T. 1998. Extent, severity and causative factors of land degradation in the Sudan. Journal of Arid Environments 38:397-409.

Ba, Magatte, M., Touré, A., Reenberg A. 2004. Mapping land use dynamics in Senegal. Case studies from Kaffrine Departments. SEREIN (Sahel-Sudan Environmental Research Initiative) working paper (45):33.

Balmford, A., Bruner, A., Cooper, P., Costanza, R., Farber, S., Green, R.E., Jenkins, M., Jefferiss, P., Jessamy, V., Madden, J., Munro, K., Myers, N., Naeem, S., Paavola, J., Rayment, M., Rosendo, S., Roughgarden, J., Trumper, K. Turner, R.K. 2002. Economic reasons for conserving wild nature. Science, 297:950-953.

Balmford, A., Green, R.E. Jenkins, M. 2003. Measuring the changing state of nature. Trends in Ecology & Evolution, 18:326-330.

Barbet-Massin, M., B. A. Walther, et al. 2009. Potential impacts of climate change on the winter distribution of Afro-Palaearctic migrant passerines. Biology Letters 5:248-251.

Bellassen, V., R. J. Manlay, et al. 2010. Multi-criteria spatialization of soil organic carbon sequestration potential from agricultural intensification in Senegal. Climatic Change 98: 213-243.

Brashares, J. S., Arcese P., et al. 2001. Human demography and reserve size predict wildlife extinction in West Africa. Proceedings of the Royal Society of London Series B-Biological Sciences. 268:2473-2478.

Brashares, J. S., Arcese P., et al. 2004. Bushmeat hunting, wildlife declines, and fish supply in West Africa. Science 306:1180-1183.

Brookman-Amissah, J., Hall, J.B., Swaine, M.D. Attakorah, J.Y. 1980. A re-assesment of a fire protection experiment in north-eastern Ghana savanna. Journal of Applied ecology, 17:85-99.

Brown S., 1997. Estimating Biomass and Biomass Change of Tropical Forests: a Primer. (FAO Forestry Paper – 134). FAO – Food and Agriculture Organization of the United Nations, Roma, 48 p.

Burgess, M.A. 1991. Cultural responsibility in the preservation of local economic plant resources. Biodiversity and conservation, 3:126-136.

Butt T.A., Mccarl B.A., Angerer J., Dyke P.T., Stuth J.W. 2005. The economic and food security implications of climate change in Mali. Climatic Change. 68:355–378

Chatelain, C., Gautier, L. Spicheger, R. 1996. A recent history of forest fragmentation in southwestern Ivory Coast. Biodiversity and conservation, 5:37-53.

Coley, P.D., 1993. The role of plant/animal interactions in preserving biodiversity. In: O.T. Sandlund and P.J. Schei (Editor). Directorate for Nature Management/Norwegian institute for nature research, Trondheim, Norway, pp. 34-40.

Conchedda G., 2009. Human-environment interactions in two mangrove ecosystems of Senegal., Université Catholique de Louvain.

Cook, K. H., Vizy, E. K.. 2006. Coupled model simulations of the west African monsoon system: Twentieth - and Twenty-First-century simulations. Journal of Climate 19(15): 3681-3703.

Cresswell, W., J. M. Wilson, et al. 2007. "Changes in densities of Sahelian bird species in response to recent habitat degradation." Ostrich 78:247-253.

Cunningham, A.B., 1992. Botanists, brokers and biodiversity. pp. 1-19.

du Toit, J.T., Walker, B.H. Campbell, B.M. 2004. Conserving tropical nature: current challenges for ecologists. Trends in Ecology & Evolution. 19:12-17.

Ellis, J. 1994. Climate variability and complex ecosystem dynamics: Implications for pastoral development. In: 'Living with Uncertainty'. I. Scoones (ed.). pp. 37–46. (Intermediate Technology Publ.: London.)

Etkin, N.L. 2002. Local knowledge of biotic diversity and its conservation in rural Hausaland, northern Nigeria. Economic Botany. 56:73-88.

FAO, 1996. Influences forestières, Organisation des Nations Unies pour l'alimentation et l'agriculture. Rome.

Ferraro, P.J. Kiss, A. 2002. Direct payments to conserve biodiversity. Science, 298:1718-1719.

Ferraro, P.J. Kiss, A. 2003. Will direct payments help biodiversity? Response. Science. 299:1981-1982.

Friedel, M. H. 1991. Range Condition Assessment and the Concept of Thresholds – a Viewpoint. Journal of Range Management. 44:422-426.

Gadgil, M., Berkes, F. Folke, C. 1993. Indigenous knowledge for biodiversity conservation. Ambio. 22:151-156.

Garrod, G.D. Willis, K.G. 1994. Valuing biodiversity and nature conservation at a local level. Biodiversity and Conservation, 3:555-565.

GEO4 – Global Environmental Outlook 4. 2007. UNEP, Nairobi, Kenya.

Giannini, A., Biasutti, M. et al. 2008. A climate model-based review of drought in the Sahel: Desertification, the re-greening and climate change. Global and Planetary Change 64: 119-128.

Gonzalez, P. 2001. Desertification and a shift of forest species in the West African Sahel. Climate Research. 17:217-228.

IPCC. 2007. Climate Change 2007: Synthesis Report. Contribution of Working Groups I, II and III to the Fourth Assessment Report of the Intergovernmental Panel on Climate Change [Core Writing Team, Pachauri, R.K and Reisinger, A. (eds.)]. Page 104 pp. IPCC, Geneva, Switzerland.

James, C. D., Landsberg, J., and Morton, S. R. 1999. Provision of watering points in the Australian arid zone: a review of effects on biota. Journal of Arid Environments. 41, 87-121.

Janzen, D.H. 1991. How to save tropical biodiversity. American Entomologist. 159-171.

Jetz, W., Wilcove, D. S., et al. 2007. Projected impacts of climate and land-use change on the global diversity of birds. PLoS Biology. 5:1211-1219.

Kellman, M., Tackaberry, R., 1997. Tropical environments. The function and management of tropical ecosystems. Routledge, London and New York, 380 p.

Kristensen, M. Balslev, H. 2003. Perceptions, use and availability of woody plants among the Gourounsi in Burkina Faso. Biodiversity and conservation. 12:1715-1739.

Kurukulasuriya P., Mendelsohn R., et al. 2006. Will African agriculture survive climate change? World Bank Economic Review 20:367–388

Laris, P. 2002. Burning the seasonal mosaic: preventative burning strategies in the wooded savanna of southern Mali. Human Ecology. 30:155-186.

Le Houerou, H.N. 1997. Climate, flora and fauna changes in the Sahara over the past 500 million years. Journal of Arid Environments. 37:619-647.

Lebrun, J.-P.S., A.L., 1991. Enumeration des plantes à fleurs d'Afrique tropicale. Conservatoire et Jardin Botanique Genève, Geneva.

Liu, J. G., Dietz, T., Carpenter, S. R., Alberti, M., Folke, C., Moran, E., Pell, A. N., Deadman, P., Kratz, T., Lubchenco, J., Ostrom, E., Ouyang, Z., Provencher, W., Redman, C. L., Schneider, S. H., and Taylor, W. W. 2007. Complexity of coupled human and natural systems. Science. 317:1513-1516.

Ludeke, M. K. B., Petschel-Held, G., and Schellnhuber, H. J. 2004. Syndromes of global change: the first panoramic view. GAIA. 13:42-49.

MA – Millennium Ecosystem Assessment. 2005. Ecosystems and human well-being: synthesis. Island Press, Washington, D.C.

Mbow, C., Mertz, O., Diouf, A., Rasmussen, K., Reenberg A. 2008. The history of environmental change and adaptation in eastern Saloum–Senegal. Driving forces and perceptions. Global and Planetary Change. 64:210–221.

Mbow, C., Nielsen, T.T., Rasmussen K. 2000. Savanna Fires in East-Central Senegal: Distribution Patterns, Resource Management and Perceptions. Human Ecology. 28 4:561-583.

McAlpine, C. A., Syktus, J., Deo, R. C., Lawrence, P. J., McGowan, H. A., Watterson, I. G., and Phinn, S. R. 2007. Modeling the impact of historical land cover change on Australia's regional climate. Geophysical Research Letters 34, 6.

Mertz, O., Mbow, C., Reenberg, A., Diouf A. 2009. Farmers' perceptions of climate change and agricultural adaptation strategies in rural Sahel. Environmental Management. 43:804-816.

Moller, A. P., D. Rubolini, et al. 2008. Populations of migratory bird species that did not show a phenological response to climate change are declining. PNAS. 105:16195-16200.

Mortimore, M. 2009. 'Dryland opportunities: a new paradigm for people, ecosystems and development.' (IUCN; IIED; UNDP/DDC: Gland, Switzerland; London UF; Nairobi, Kenya. (www.iucn.org/publications)

Nielsen, T.T., Rasmussen, K., Mbow, C., Touré A. 2003. The fire regime of Senegal and its determinants. Danish Journal of Geography. 103:43-53.

Nicholson, S. E. 2009. A revised picture of the structure of the "monsoon" and land ITCZ over West Africa. Climate Dynamics 32:1155-1171.

Reenberg, A., Mbow, C., Diallo B., 2003. Temporal and spatial diversity of Sudano-Sahelian landscapes: Land use and land cover dynamics in forest reserves and their margins. In: Negotiated frontiers in Sudano-Sahelian landscapes Implication for natural resource management strategies. D.A. Wardell, A. Reenberg and H.O.R. Harpøth (Eds.), Sahel-Sudan Environmental Research Initiative (SEREIN), Denmark, pp. 137-161.

Reynolds, J. F., Stafford Smith, D. M., Lambin, E. F., Turner, B. L., II, Mortimore, M., Batterbury, S. P. J., Downing, T. E., Dowlatabadi, H., Fernandez, R. J., Herrick, J. E., Huber-Sannwald, E., Jiang, H., Leemans, R., Lynam, T., Maestre, F. T., Ayarza, M., and Walker, B. 2007. Global desertification: building a science for dryland development. Science. 316:847-851

Sabiiti, E.N. Wein, R.W. 1988. Fire behavior and the invasion of *Acacia sieberiana* into savanna grassland openings. Afr. J. Ecol. 26:301-313.

Sambou B., 2004. Evaluation de l'état, de la dynamique et des tendances évolutives de la flore et de la végétation ligneuse dans les domaines soudanien et sub-guinéen au Sénégal. Doctorat D'Etat, Université Cheikh Anta Diop de Dakar (UCAD), Dakar.

Sanderson, F. J., P. F. Donald, et al. 2006. Long-term population declines in Afro-Palearctic migrant birds. Biological Conservation 131:93-105.

Sankhayan, P.L., Hofstad O. 2001. A village-level economic model of land clearing, grazing, and wood harvesting for sub-Saharan Africa: with a case study in southern Senegal. Ecological Economics. 38:423-440.

Stafford Smith, D. M., Abel, N. O., Walker, B. H., and Chapin, F. S., III. 2009. Drylands: coping with uncertainty, thresholds, and changes in state. In: 'Principles of Ecosystem Stewardship: Resilience-Based Natural Resource Management in a Changing World.' F. S. Chapin, III, G. P. Kofinas and C. Folke. (eds) pp. 171-195. Springer-Verlag, New York.

Sivakumar M.V.K., Das H.P., Brunini O. 2005. Impacts of present and future climate variability and change on agriculture and forestry in the arid and semi-arid tropics. Climatic Change 70:31-72

Sitch, S., Huntingford C., et al. 2008. Evaluation of the terrestrial carbon cycle, future plant geography and climate-carbon cycle feedbacks using five Dynamic Global Vegetation Models (DGVMs). Global Change Biology 14:2015-2039.

Tschakert, P., Khouma, M., Sène M. 2004. Biophysical potential for soil carbon sequestration in agricultural systems of the Old Peanut Basin of Senegal. Journal of Arid Environments 59:511-533.

Vagen, T-G., Lal, R., Singh B.R. 2005. Soil carbon sequestration in sub-saharan Africa: A review. Land Degradation and Development. 16:53-71.

Vetter, S. 2005. Rangelands at equilibrium and non-equilibrium: recent developments in the debate. Journal of Arid Environments 62, 321-341.

Westoby, M., Walker, B., and Noy-Meir, I. 1989. Opportunistic management for rangelands not at equilibrium. Journal of Range Management . 42:266-274.

Wood, E.C, Tappan, G.G, Hadj A. 2004. Understanding the drivers of agricultural land use change in south-central Senegal. Journal of Arid Environments. 59:565-582.

Appendix 5. MIOMBO WOODLANDS

Robert J Scholes (Council for Scientific and Industrial Research, bscholes@csir.co.za)
Reinette Biggs (Stockholm Resilience Centre, oonsie.biggs@stockholmresilience.su.se)

SUMMARY

▸ The belt of moist savannas, the 'miombo woodlands', stretching south of the Congo rainforests from Angola to Tanzania, represents one of the largest remaining near-intact ecosystems in the world. It is important as a carbon store and biodiversity habitat, but also represents a largely untapped resource for agriculture and biofuel production.

▸ Large-scale conversion of the miombo to agricultural land is likely over the next three decades. Habitat conversion will have large impacts on biodiversity and associated ecosystem services that will be difficult to reverse. Transformation of the miombo in this way will tend to accelerate climate change.

▸ Climate change may lead to the crossing of additional tipping points in the miombo. Savannas are intrinsically unstable ecosystems, sensitive to elevated carbon dioxide, changing rainfall, rising temperatures and changing fire regimes. Tipping points exist on several of these axes, although they usually trigger negative (i.e., climate-stabilizing), rather than positive feedbacks.

▸ Moderate *intensification* of agriculture in the Miombo zone, within a planned spatial framework, is the best option for preserving as much as possible of the climate and habitat benefits while satisfying demands for food and fuel. Application of REDD (reduced deforestation and degradation) initiatives in the savanna and forest landscape of south central Africa is an important climate-protection strategy.

DESCRIPTION

Between about 3° S and 26° S and virtually from the Atlantic to Indian coast, the continent of Africa is covered by a mosaic of tall, deciduous woodlands and seasonal wetlands, collectively known as the miombo ecosystem (Figure 1). The dominant trees are from a restricted group of the Caesalpinaceae, but the associated flora and fauna is rich and diverse (WWF-US 2003). Historically, the human population has been sparse due to the low soil fertility and presence of diseases such as malaria and trypanosomiasis (which mainly affects cattle). Post-colonial conflicts in Angola, Mozambique and the Democratic Republic of Congo, and slow economic development in Tanzania, Zambia and Malawi have allowed this ecosystem to persist, largely intact, into the current era. However, the cessation or reduction of wars in the region, improving infrastructure and the growing needs for food and fuel in the region make substantial transformation in the coming decades highly probable (Bruinsma 2003, MA 2005, Biggs et al. 2008). The trend is already observable in Malawi, northern Mozambique and Zimbabwe (where it is exacerbated by economic collapse, which has forced the population to draw heavily on natural capital).

While in the other great tropical regions of the world – South-east Asia and South America – the current focus is on the loss of rainforests, this is an emerging issue in the Congo basin

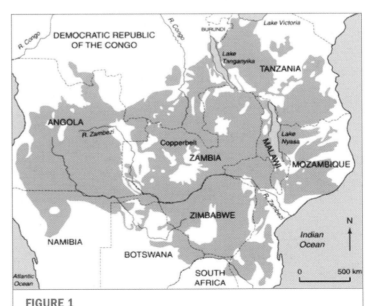

FIGURE 1
Distribution of the Miombo Woodlands in Africa (adapted from Desanker et al 1997)

of Africa. However, what tends to be forgotten is that in those other regions, clearing of the savanna woodlands was much more extensive, and began earlier, than incursions into rainforest. This is because people preferentially settle in savannas: access is easier, the climate is healthier, and the soils, while generally infertile, are usually less infertile than those in the rainforest region, and less prone to flooding. The agronomic constraints imposed by the savanna soils are well-understood, and can be easily ameliorated with additions of lime and fertilizer, particularly phosphates. Thus amended, they are highly productive, given the relatively high rainfall and abundant sunlight, and could easily feed the present and future population of the region.

At present, the growing population is impoverished and food-insecure. The widespread pattern is for small patches of woodland, especially near roads, to be cut and the wood converted to charcoal to supply the energy needs of nearby towns. The

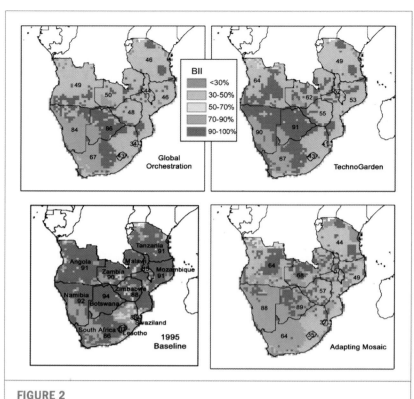

FIGURE 2

Projected changes in BII (Biodiversity Intactness Index) by 2100 according to three of the four MA scenarios (Biggs et al. 2008). Substantial declines in biodiversity are projected in the moister northern and eastern parts of the region. Differences between scenarios are most marked in Angola and Zambia, ranging from modest transformation under the Adapting Mosaic scenario (proactive ecosystem management) to substantial transformation under the Global Orchestration scenario (reactive ecosystem management). In these countries there are still extensive tracts of arable land which have not yet been developed.

cleared area is planted to low-yielding varieties of maize, millet and cassava. Fertilizer is in short supply and unaffordable. After a few years a new patch is cleared due to declining yields. After several cycles of decreasing length, the woodland fails to regenerate, becoming a low-statured, impoverished bushland called *chipya*. The wild birds and mammals are hunted for bushmeat. There are several species of tree with high-value timber, which are usually exploited very early in the process (Desanker et al. 1997).

The miombo ecosystem is vast – over 3 million km^2 – and if only a small fraction was converted to modern agriculture and forestry (with demonstrated yields ten times higher than achieved by subsistence techniques), the food and fuel needs of the countries involved could be satisfied, while leaving intact woodlands and wetlands to supply ecosystem services such as climate regulation and to support biodiversity. Whether this happens, or whether the miombo ecosystem is transformed in an unplanned, unregulated and inefficient way depends on the rate of increase in the demands placed on it for food and timber, and the resources available for landscape planning and agricultural improvement (Biggs et al. 2008). Under a scenario of continued population growth at or above the rate of economic growth, the pattern is likely to be one of ongoing *extensification* of agriculture, with attendant loss of woodlands and wetlands (Figure 2). If capital, expertise and political will can be mobilised to moderately intensify agriculture, using appropriate inputs of fertilizer, mechanization and irrigation, then a productive, multi-purpose landscape could result. This socio-economic-political branch-point will be irrevocably passed in the next two decades (MA 2005, Biggs et al. 2008).

An additional set of tipping points is found on the ecological side of this coupled human-ecological system. Savannas are mixtures of trees and grasses, and the proportions of the mixture are subject to abrupt change, typically in the direction of greater tree dominance. The key factors controlling the mix are the fire regime (less fires lead to more trees; this is in turn controlled by rainfall and its seasonality, and by temperature and humidity) and the concentration of carbon dioxide in the atmosphere (higher CO_2 promotes tree growth more than grass growth) (Desanker et al. 1997).

Invasive species impose a range of severe impacts on island ecosystems, economies and human health, and biological invasions are one of the most important drivers of change to island biotic and abiotic processes (Loope and Mueller-Dombois 1989). Ecologically, introductions of mammals like goats, cats, mongooses, rabbits and rodents have long been threats to native bird, reptile and plant species. Exotic plants, whether trees, shrubs, vines or grasses, are key invaders in habitats already disturbed by human activities or the grazing and rooting of cattle, goats and wild pigs. The list of biological invaders on islands also extends to snails, reptiles, fish, ants, wasps and other pathogens. Such introductions have resulted in a high proportion of species extinctions globally as well as a corresponding reduction in species abundance. Invasive species have also dramatically altered habitats and ecosystem services, which can also provide suitable conditions for additional biological invasions.

Aside from environmental damage, invasive species have direct and indirect economic impacts, not all of which can be measured in monetary terms. Invasive pests can affect agricultural yields for both subsistence and export markets, and animal diseases such as swine fever have had serious repercussions as export markets close their borders to potentially infected products. The destruction of native terrestrial and marine flora and fauna can also adversely impact tourism, which is a major industry for islands. Finally, invasive species can threaten human health. The rooting of wild pigs can create depressions of standing water, which serve as breeding grounds for mosquitoes and facilitate the spread of malaria and other diseases. Rats and other rodents are also renowned vectors carrying a range of viral diseases, which can be spread to humans or native biota (Burgiel et al. 2004).

Tipping point mechanisms

A key question with regard to island biodiversity and invasive species is how to define the criteria or measure the tipping point. In retrospect one can look at a particular case and recognize where impacts have progressed to the point where there is little hope of restoring the "native" ecosystem. Even in cases of eradication and/or effective control, local biotic and abiotic factors can be changed to such a degree that reversion to a previous state is virtually impossible. As David Norton (2009) states:

> reversing biotic thresholds that have been crossed as a result of invasive species is very difficult. This occurs because of legacies resulting from invasions (such as species extinctions); because even when controlled to low levels, invasive species still exert substantial pressure on native biodiversity; and because most invasive species cannot be eliminated with current technology and resources. In these situations, the future ecosystem condition even with restorative management will be different from that which would have occurred at the site had biological invasions not occurred.

Within the process of invasion biology, this would suggest that the initial point of introduction through to the establishment of a viable population is the key action leading to potentially severe and irreversible impacts in the longer term. Yet there is significant uncertainty as not every exotic species can establish or will have adverse impacts. Early detection and rapid response actions (including eradication and control) are certainly options in theory, but in reality are the exception and not the rule. Prevention of introductions in the first place is the preferred option, which is widely accepted by practitioners and even embedded in international agreements addressing the issue (Convention on Biological Diversity 2002).

The tipping point for actual biological impact is thereby after an invasive species establishes and spreads, whereas the critical tipping point for where action can be most effective is just prior to or after an introduction. That said, some of the facets that make islands so vulnerable, particularly their size and relative isolation, also makes them candidates for more successful invasive species eradication and environmental restoration.

IMPACTS ON BIODIVERSITY

While islands hold a disproportionate share of the world's biodiversity relative to their landmass, they have also suffered disproportionately as extinction rates are significantly higher on islands with 95% of the world's bird extinctions, 90% of reptile extinctions, 69% of mammal extinctions and 68% of plant extinctions. Most (55-67%) of these extinctions have either been directly caused or facilitated by invasive species (IUCN 2009, Island Conservation n.d., Donlan and Wilcox 2008). Additionally, while discussion continues as to whether islands are more susceptible invasions, the relative impact and extend of invasions may be more pressing given their limited size (Reaser et al. 2008).

Scenarios of invasive species have largely focused on improving modeling of the potential spread of invasive species using a range of biological, climatic and geographic data. Currently, niche modeling of invasive species is generally performed on a species by species basis under a particular set of bio-climatic parameters. Such models have been used to predict the potential range or spread of an invasive species under present conditions and increasingly under future climate change scenarios. Modeling has largely been done for continental geographies and related species, such as cheatgrass (*bromus tectorum*), rubber vine (*Cryptostegia grandiflora*), sudden oak death (*Phytophthera ramorum*), and silver and bighead carp (*Cyprinidae*) (Bradley 2009, Chen et al. 2003, Kritikos et al. 2003, Meentemeyer et al., Sutherst et al. 2007). For islands, particularly in the Pacific, this type of modeling has been done for major weeds and invasive plants, such as *M. calvescens*, as well as for avian malaria and Oriental fruit fly (Ahumada et al. 2009, Atkinson and LaPointe 2009, Daehler 2006, Fujikawa 2009, Kritikos et al. 2007). Little attention has been devoted to addressing multiple species interactions under a range of future scenarios. Given the complexity of modeling such phenomena combined with the inherent uncertainties around the introduction, establishment and spread of invasive species, development of compelling scenarios for island ecosystems is quite difficult at present.

Rough approximations of future pressures from the introduction of invasive species can be made using trade statistics and pathways as general surrogates to measure rates of biological invasion. Studies have shown that numbers of introduced invasive species are loosely correlated to trade flows, and therefore increases in trade are likely to increase the number of potential introductions. While such trends can be complicated by the level and sophistication of both monitoring efforts and quarantine systems, the broad connections between trade and invasive are assumed to be that:

▸ more introductions lead to a greater probability that an invasive species will become established;
▸ an increasing variety of goods and means of transport increases both the potential array of species that may be moved and their pathways for transfer;
▸ more frequent delivery of goods from and to a wider range of countries and habitats increases the rate and variety of potential introductions; and
▸ faster modes of transport may improve an organism's chance of survival while in transit (Ruiz and Carlton 2003, Burgiel et al. 2006, Jenkins 1996).

Analysis of trade data on island countries in the Caribbean, Indian Ocean and the Pacific show overall increases in both imports and exports over the period from 1950 to 2009. Aggregate data for Caribbean countries show a doubling in the value of commercial and agricultural imports from 1990 to 2009. For Pacific islands in the ACP category (developing countries from Africa, Caribbean, Pacific), there is roughly a tenfold increase across the region, although data is incomplete for all countries. Increases for islands countries in the Indian Ocean are even higher although more varied from country to country (World Trade Organization 2010).

Despite the global economic downturn of 2009, this data suggests increasing pressure on islands to intercept and address invasive species being introduced through trade. Awareness and management efforts are also improving both at the national and regional levels, particularly in the Caribbean, Indian Ocean and the Pacific. These activities include both the identification and management of existing invasive species, as well as increased attention to priority pathways contributing to new introductions. Capacity to effectively shut down these pathways is currently limited in most island regions thereby raising the question as to whether new biosecurity efforts will be able to offset the assumed rate of new introductions from increased trade and transport.

There are numerous examples of how invasive species can alter ecosystem structures and trigger trophic cascades. Introduced sheep on Santa Cruz Island of the coast of California and rabbits on Macquarie Island, a World Heritage Site south of Australia and New Zealand, stripped grasslands and remaining vegetative cover reducing significant portions of the island to bare ground resulting in erosion and negative impacts on native herbaceous and scrubland plant communities and avian diversity (Klinger et al. 2002, Bergstrom et al. 2009, Dowding et al.2009). Research in the Aleutian Islands of Alaska has also shown how predation of introduced rats on seabirds that forage in intertidal areas has shifted those marine communities from algal to invertebrate-dominated systems (Kurle, et al. 2008).

Trophic impacts are also important in considering eradication or control efforts in systems dominated by multiple invasive species. Removal or suppression of one invasive species can have unintended impacts on others by virtue of predation pressures (cats and rodents), vegetation (goats and sheep) and other ecological functions (Zavaleta et al. 2001). From 1998-2000, eradication efforts were undertaken on Sarigan Island in the Pacific's Northern Mariana Islands to remove introduced pigs and goats, which had severely reduced the native tropical forests, shifting it towards grassland habitat thereby endangering a number of native species (e.g., Micronesian megapode – *Megapodius laperouse*, Mariana fruit bat – *Pteropus mariannus*, and coconut crab – *Birgus latro*). While this eradication proved beneficial for tree seedlings and overall plant richness, there was also a rapid expansion of the invasive vine, *Operculina ventricosa*, through the native forest and surrounding grasslands (Kessler 2002).

Despite significant impacts on biodiversity and ecosystems, in many cases ongoing invasive species control and eradication efforts were able to reach a point where natural restoration could take hold. Such efforts are generally costly in terms of time, resources and scientific effort to document impacts, and furthermore are generally the exception rather than common practice. Estimates by Island Conservation place the total number of eradication attempts on islands at 949, which is likely far lower than the number of invaded islands throughout the world (Keitt 2010). This further reinforces the prevailing wisdom that prevention of invasive species introductions in the first instance is far more preferable and cost effective than subsequent efforts for eradication, control and restoration.

ECOSYSTEM SERVICES

Invasive species can have a range of compounding impacts across ecosystem services, thereby impacting their ability to provide their supporting, regulating, provisioning and cultural functions. The discussion below uses a few representative examples to illustrate these impacts.

In Tahiti and other parts of Polynesia, the introduction and establishment of *Miconia calvescens* have played a dramatic role in transforming native habitats. Native to parts of Central and South America, *M. calvescens* is a tree with large leaves that can grow up to 15 meters. Originally, introduced as an ornamental plant into Tahiti in 1937 and in the 1960s to Hawaii, *M. calvescens* thrives in wet tropical forests. By 1996, the plant had spread to 65% of Tahiti with monospecific stands on approximately 25% of the island (Meyer 1996). Such stands generally block sunlight from penetrating the canopy creating conditions that native species cannot tolerate. In Tahiti, experts calculate that 40-50 of the islands 107 endemic species could be at risk (Meyer and Florence 1996). The plant grows in shade and sun conditions and its superficial root structure can destabilize soils, particularly with substantial rainfall, thereby giving rise to landslides and erosion on steep slopes. *M. calvescens* has had significant impacts on the supporting and regulating services that the native ecosystems had provided, first and foremost by exacerbating erosion and thereby hampering the role of native forests in water filtration. Additionally, loss of plant diversity and the creation of closed canopies will also likely alter nutrient cycling and the formation of soils.

In the Caribbean, red palm mite (*Raoiella indica*) is a pest of fruit-producing palm trees and other ornamental plants, which was first identified in Martinique in 2004. The mite has since spread, mostly likely on infested plant products, seeds or by major storms/hurricanes, to: Dominica and St. Lucia (2005); Dominican Republic, Guadeloupe, Puerto Rico, St. Martin and Trinidad and Tobago (2006); and Granada, Haiti, Jamaica and southern Florida (2007). In addition to impacts on coconut palms, the mite has also been feeding on over 20 other species of palm, banana, ginger and heliconia (Welbourn 2009). Economic impacts have been significant with reports of damage on up to 50% of coconut crops in Trinidad, and has also raised a number of trade restrictions on products from countries where the pest is now present (Red Palm Mite Explosion 2007). This invasive pest has the potential to spread throughout the Americas (across the southern US, California, Hawaii as well as to Central and South America). Red palm mite thereby can play a significant role in impacting the provisioning services of the Caribbean agricultural systems, while also wreaking havoc on ornamental and other plants that are important for the regions identity particularly in the tourism industry.

Looking at intersections with other global drivers, invasive species and climate change are likely to have compounded impacts of ecosystems and their services. Climate change impacts, including warming temperatures and changes in CO_2 concentrations, may increase opportunities for invasive species because of their adaptability to disturbance and to a broader range of biogeographic conditions. The impacts of those invasive species may be more severe as they increase both in numbers and extent, and as they compete for diminishing resources such as freshwater. Warmer air and water temperatures may also facilitate species movement along previously inaccessible pathways.

As with invasive species, islands are likely to experience a full range of adverse effects from climate change, including sea level rise, extreme weather events and consequent impacts on their fragile ecosystems. Climate change and invasive species could combine to impact:

- Fisheries: sea level rise may favor salt-tolerant invasive plant species in brackish water systems and estuaries, which are an important habitat and spawning ground for fish and other species. Warming waters could also contribute to range expansion of marine invasive species, such as the lionfish (*Pterois volitans*) from the Caribbean north into the Atlantic as well as the mitten crab (*Eriocheir sinensis*) in Ireland and along both U.S. coasts, that significantly impact aquatic communities and reef fisheries.
- Erosion control and storm surge abatement: natural dune, mangrove and other coastal ecosystems play a key role in buffering the effects of storm surges and other extreme weather events. The establishment of invasive plant species, such as beach vitex (*Vitex rotundifolia*), has exacerbated erosion on island off the southeastern coast of the U.S. thereby increasing the vulnerability of inland ecosystems and coastal communities. Introduced nutria (*Myocaster coypus*) on the barrier islands of the U.S. state of Mississippi have also had major impacts on wetland and dune ecosystems, by destroying plant communities and creating stretches of open water.
- Food security: healthy ecosystems play a critical role in providing pollination services and seasonal climate variability, particularly temperature and precipitation, and mitigate against the spread of pests and disease. Longer and warmer growing seasons could support multiple life cycles of agricultural pests impacting crops and favor early emergence of weeds and other pests.
- Freshwater availability: temperature rise could spur the incursion and spread of species with detrimental impacts on local water tables and species composition, which could be further exacerbated by climate induced declines in precipitation.
- Biodiversity impacts: range expansion of invasive species is one of the most highly referenced consequences of climate change with corresponding effects on biodiversity. For example, the spread of White Syndrome across coral reefs and the Chytrid fungus besetting amphibian populations are two major threats to global biodiversity that have been linked to climatic warming. Retreating glaciers are also providing newfound habitat for invasive plants, such as the spread of winter grass on deglaciated slopes of Australia's Heard Island. (BDAC, GISP 2009, Hellman et al. 2008, World Bank 2008).

UNCERTAINTIES

The establishment and effective management of invasive species is wrought with uncertainties. From the biological point of view, there are still major gaps in knowledge about which species will be introduced and with what propagule pressure (particularly regarding unintentional introductions), the chance that such individuals will survive and establish viable populations and the chance that those populations will then expand and cause harm. This single species perspective is further complicated by the complex relations that develop with the introduction of multiple alien species. In certain cases they can exacerbate each other (e.g., invasive mammals may disturb vegetation or spread seeds thereby facilitating the introduction of invasive plants), and in others they may have some counteracting behaviors (e.g., feral goats that keep invasive plants in check through grazing, or feral cats that prey on introduced rodents) (Veitch and Clout 2002, CBB and IUCN ISSG 2010).

There are similarly uncertainties with the regulation and management of invasive species. While tools and knowledge for complete eradications are improving there are still open questions about the effectiveness of techniques and the ability to establish that the last individual of a particular species has been removed. Most regulators also recognize that there is no practicable system that could establish zero-risk (100% prevention) from the introduction of alien species as this would likely entail complete curtailment of the movement of people, vehicles and goods into a particular country or region. Practitioners are thereby encouraged to identify the level of risk that they are willing to tolerate based on environmental, economic and other social factors and then to establish the necessary mechanisms to reach that level of protection. This is inherently a process of managing uncertainties (Burgiel et al. 2006).

LOCAL TO GLOBAL ACTION AND OPPORTUNITIES

Global Action

▶ Support efforts related to invasive species and islands within the Convention on Biological Diversity and other U.N. processes such as the Commission on Sustainable Development and the Programme of Action for the Sustainable Development of Small Island Developing States.

▶ Develop synergies and leverage support across efforts to fund regional invasive species activities on islands (e.g., the Global Environment Facility, European Community support for work in over-seas territories, the Critical Ecosystem Partnership Fund, and other multilateral and bilateral funding programs).

▶ Promote opportunities for capacity building across relevant international agreements and institutions (e.g., sectors covering biodiversity, animal and plant health, trade and transport).

▶ Facilitate the development of an integrated knowledge management system to improve access to existing tools, best practices and case studies regarding islands and invasive species and to link to or build national and regional datasets on extant invasive species.

▶ Identify and create linkages across initiatives and processes involving island states and those involving continental countries with islands, including overseas territories.

Regional and Local Action

▶ Facilitate development of national invasive species strategies and actions plans along with steps for their implementation and integration into national biodiversity and development plans.

▶ Develop national biosecurity systems oriented toward prevention of future introductions and the prioritization of eradication and control for existing invasive species

▶ Identify capacity needs and knowledge gaps on the regulation and management of invasive species (e.g., risk assessments, niche modeling, multi-species interactions) to inform broader discussions about resource mobilization.

▶ Improve niche modeling methodologies, particularly for multiple invasive species interactions.

▶ Use islands as an opportunity to develop and improve invasive species policy and management practices, particularly in relation to other drivers of global change (climate change).

▶ Support participation in and cooperation with regional invasive species initiatives and relevant intergovernmental processes, particularly in the area of developing early detection/rapid response capacity through regional biosecurity networks.

REFERENCES

Ahumada, J.A., M.D. Samuel, D.C. Duffy, and A. Dobson. 2009. Modeling the Epidemiology of Avian Malaria and Pox. *in* T.K. Pratt, C.T. Atkinson, P.C. Banko, J. Jacobi, and B.L. Woodworth (eds.). The Conservation Biology of Hawaiian Forest Birds: Implications for Island Avifauna. Yale University Press: 331-355.

Atkinson, C.T., and D.A. LaPointe. 2009. Introduced avian diseases, climate change, and the future of Hawaiian honeycreepers. Journal of Avian Medicine and Surgery. 23:53-63.

Bergstrom, D.M., A. Lucieer, K. Kiefer, J. Wasley, L. Belbin, T.K. Pederson, and S.L. Chown. 2009. Indirect effects of invasive species removal devastate World Heritage Island. Journal of Applied Ecology. 46: 73-81.

Bradley, B.A. 2009. Regional analysis of the impacts of climate change on cheatgrass invasion shows potential risk and opportunity. Global Change Biology 15: 196–208.

Burgiel, S.B, A. Perrault, and C. Williams. 2004. Invasive Alien Species and Small Island Developing States: A Briefing Series. Center for International Environmental Law, Defenders of Wildlife and the Nature Conservancy.

Burgiel, S.B, G. Foote, M. Orellana, and A. Perrault. 2006. Invasive Alien Species and Trade: Integrating Prevention Measures and International Trade Rules. Center for International Environmental Law, Defenders of Wildlife, Global Invasive Species Programme, IUCN-Invasive Species Specialist Group and the Nature Conservancy.

Center for Biodiversity and Biosecurity, CBB, and IUCN-Invasive Species Specialist Group. 2010. Island Invasives: Eradication and Management, Presentations and Abstracts (Auckland, New Zealand; 8-12 February 2010).

Convention on Biological Diversity. 2002. Guiding principles for the prevention, introduction and mitigation of impacts of alien species that threaten ecosystems, habitats or species. Decision VI/23 Alien species that threaten ecosystems, habitats or species. Sixth Conference of the Parties (The Hague, 7-9 April 2002).

Daehler, C. C. 2006. Invasibility of tropical islands by introduced plants: Partitioning the influence of isolation and propagule pressure. Preslia 78.361-374.

Donlan, C.J., and C. Wilcox. 2008. Diversity, invasive species and extinctions in insular ecosystems. Journal of Applied Ecology 45: 1113-1123.

Dowding, J.E., E.C. Murphy, K. Springer, A.J. Peacock, and C.J. Krebs. 2009. Cats, rabbits, Myxoma virus, and vegetation on Macquarie Island: a comment on Bergstrom et al. 2009. Journal of Applied Ecology. 46: 1129-32.

Fujikawa, J.Y. 2009. Predicting the Spread of Miconia on O'ahu. 2009 Hawaii Congress of Planning Officials/Hawaii Geographic Information Coordinating Council Congress (23-25 September 2009, Oahu).

GISP - Global Invasive Species Programme. 2009. Turning the tide: Invasive species management, ecosystembased adaptation and responses to climate change (Draft white paper).

Hellman, J.J., J.E. Byers, B.G. Bierwagen, and J.S. Dukes. 2008. Five Potential Consequences of Climate Change for Invasive Species. Conservation Biology 22 (3): 534-43.

Island Conservation/Conservacion de Islas (No date a). Why? (http://islandconservation.org/why/# and http://islandconservation.org/slideshow/).

IUCN. 2009. IUCN Red List of Threatened Species. (Available at http://www.iucnredlist.org).

Jenkins, P. 1996. Free trade and exotic species introductions. Conservation Biology 10(1): 300-2.

Keitt, B. 2010. Global review of vertebrate eradications from islands. Presentation at Island Invasives: Eradication and Management (Auckland, New Zealand; 8-12 February 2010).

Kessler, C.C. 2002. Eradication of feral goats and pigs and consequences for other biota on Sarigan Island, Commonwealth of the Northern Mariana Islands in Veitch, C.R., and Clout, M.N. (eds.) Turning the Tide: The Eradication of Invasive Species. IUCN ISSG.

Klinger, R.C., P. Schuyler, and J.D. Sterner. 2002. The response of herbaceous vegetation and endemic plant species to the removal of feral sheep from Santa Cruz Island, California in Veitch, C.R. and Clout, M.N. (eds.) Turning the Tide: The Eradication of Invasive Species. IUCN ISSG.

Kriticos, D. J., A. E. A. Stephens, and A. Leriche. 2007. Effect of climate change on Oriental fruit fly in New Zealand and the Pacific. New Zealand Plant Protection 60: 271-278.

Kriticos, D. J., R. W. Sutherst, J. R. Brown, S. A. Adkins, and G. F. Maywald. 2003. Climate change and biotic invasions: A case history of a tropical woody vine. Biological Invasions, 5: 145-165.

Kurle, C.M., D.A. Croll, and B.R. Tershy. 2008. Introduced rats indirectly change marine rocky intertidal communities from algae- to invertebrate-dominated. PNAS 105: 3800-4.

Loope, L.L., and D. Mueller-Dombois. 1989. Characteristics of invaded islands, with special reference to Hawaii. in Drake, J.A., Mooney, H.A., di Castri, F., Groves, R.H., Kruger, F.J., Rejmanek, M. and Williamson, M. (eds.) Biological Invasions: A Global Perspective. SCOPE, John Wiley and Sons: 257-80.

Meyer, J.Y. 1996. Status of Miconia calvescens (Melastomataceae), a dominant invasive tree in the Society Islands (French Polynesia). Pacific Science 50: 66-76.

Meyer, J.Y, and J. Florence. 1996. Tahiti's native flora endangered by the invasion of Miconia calvescens D.C. (Melastomataceae). Journal of Biogeography 23: 775-81.

Myers, N. 2003. Biodiversity hotspots revisited. BioScience 53: 916-917.

Myers, N. 1990. The biodiversity challenge: Expanded hot-spots analysis. The Environmentalist. 10: 243–256.

Myers, N., R.A. Mittermeier, C.G. Mittermeier, G.A.B. da Fonseca, and J. Kent. 2000. Biodiversity hotspots for conservation priorities. Nature 403: 853–858.

Norton, D.A. 2009. Species invasions and the limits to restoration: learning from the New Zealand experience. Science 325: 569-70.

Reaser, J.K., L.A. Meyerson, Q. Cronk, M. de poorter, L.G. Eldrege, E. Green, M. Kairo, P. Latasi, R.N. Mack, J. Mauremootoo, D. O'dowd, W. Orapa, S. Sastroutomo, A. Saunders, C. Shine, S. Thrainsson, and L. Vaiutu. 2007. Ecological and socioeconomic impacts of invasive alien species in island ecosystems. Environmental Conservation 34: 98–111.

Red Palm Mite Explosion Causing Caribbean Fruit Losses (21 May 2007) Wallaces Farmer (http://wallacesfarmer.com/story.aspx/red/palm/mite/explosion/causing/caribbean/fruit/losses/8/11967)

Ruiz, G.M., and J.T. Carlton. 2003. Invasion vectors: a conceptual framework for management. In Ruiz, G.M. and Carlton, J.T. (eds.) Invasive Species: Vectors and Management Strategies. Island Press: 459-504.

Sutherst, R. W., R. H. A. Baker, S. M. Coakley, R. Harrington, D. J. Kriticos, and H. Scherm. 2007. Pests Under Global Change, Meeting Your Future Landlords? in Canadell, J.G., D.E. Pataki, and L.F. Pitelka (eds.) Terrestrial Ecosystems in a Changing World. Springer: 211-223.

Veitch, C.R., and M.N. Clout (eds.). 2002. Turning the Tide: The Eradication of Invasive Species. IUCN ISSG.

UNESCO World Heritage (No date). Islands and Protected Areas of the Gulf of California (http://whc.unesco.org/en/list/1182).

Welbourn, C. 2009. Pest Alert: Red Palm Mite Raoiella Indica. Florida Department of Agriculture and Consumer Services (http://www.doacs.state.fl.us/pi/enpp/ento/r.indica.html).

World Bank .2008. Biodiversity, Climate Change and Adaptation: Nature-based Solutions from the World Bank Portfolio. World Bank.

World Trade Organization. 2010. Analysis of CARICOM and ACP Country Imports and Exports from 1950-2009. Downloaded from http://stat.wto.org/Home/WSDBHome.aspx (31 March 2010).

Zavaleta, E.S., R.J. Hobbs, and H.A. Mooney. 2001. Viewing invasive species removal in a whole-ecosystem context. Trends in Ecology and Evolution. 16: 454-9.

Appendix 7. COASTAL TERRESTRIAL SYSTEMS AND SEA-LEVEL RISE

Eric Gilman (Global Biodiversity Information Facility Secretariat, egilman@gbif.org)
Joanna C. Ellison (University of Tasmania, joanna.ellison@utas.edu.au)

SUMMARY

▸ Based on limited monitoring, experiments and modelling of climate change outcomes, relative sea-level rise may be the greatest future threat to tidal wetlands and beaches. Reduced coastal ecosystem area and condition will increase coastal hazards to human settlements, reduce coastal water quality, release large quantities of stored carbon, and eliminate nesting, nursery and forage habitat for numerous species groups, including fish, shellfish, seabirds, waterbirds, sea turtles, crocodiles, manatees and dugongs.

▸ Rising seas will likely have the greatest impact on coastal wetlands experiencing net relative lowering in sediment elevation, and where there is limited area for landward migration due to the physiographic setting or obstacles from development. The majority of mangrove sites studied have not been keeping pace with current rates of relative sea-level rise, this exceeding the observed mean change in mangrove sediment surface elevation of +1 mm a^{-1}. As a result, 0.2% annual reductions in Pacific Islands region mangroves are predicted over this century, contributing about 10 to 20% of total estimated losses.

▸ Longer-term monitoring of coastal ecosystem changes from a larger number of regions is needed for evaluation of ecosystem resistance. There is a need for reliable predictive sediment elevation models and models of coastal ecosystem erosion. There is also a need for improved understanding of the synergistic effects of multiple climate change and other anthropogenic and natural stressors on coastal ecosystems.

▸ Adaptation options, to offset anticipated coastal ecosystem losses and improve resistance and resilience to rising seas, include: coastal planning to facilitate landward migration; 'no regrets' reduction of stressors, including catchment management to minimize disturbance to sedimentation processes; rehabilitation of degraded areas; and increases in protected areas that include functionally linked coastal ecosystems. Establishing coastal ecosystem monitoring through regional networks using standardized techniques enables the separation of site-based influences from global changes, improving the understanding of coastal ecosystem responses to sea level and global climate change, and alternatives to mitigate adverse effects.

DESCRIPTION

Until now, relative sea-level rise has likely been a smaller threat to coastal ecosystems than non-climate related anthropogenic stressors (Duke et al. 2007). However, relative sea-level rise may cause a substantial proportion of predicted future losses of sedimentary tidal wetlands (mangroves, salt marshes, seagrass meadows, mudflats) and beaches.

A tipping-point occurs when a coastal ecosystem does not keep pace with the rise in sea-level relative to a site's surface elevation (inadequate resistance), and due to the physiographic setting, suitable hydrology and sediment composition, competition with species from other ecosystem types, and availability of waterborne seedlings, the coastal ecosystem is gradually reduced in area to a point where it reverts to a narrow fringe or is extirpated (low resilience). A number of interacting factors determine a coastal habitat's resistance and resilience to relative sea-level rise, including the geomorphic and physiographic setting, surface and subsurface controls on sediment surface elevation, and other stressors (Woodroffe 2002, Cahoon et al. 2006). Resistance is a coastal ecosystem's ability to keep pace with a change in relative sea-level without alteration to its functions, processes and structure (Odum 1989, Bennett et al. 2005). Resilience refers to an ecosystem's capacity to absorb and reorganize with change in relative sea-level to maintain its functions, processes and structure (Carpenter et al. 2001, Nystrom and Folke 2001). For coastal sites experiencing sea-level rise relative to the elevation of the surface, the depth, frequency and duration of flooding (hydroperiod) will increase, and the ecosystem may transgress landward, where unobstructed. Coastal species were able to persist through the Quaternary through substantial disruptions from sea-level fluctuations (Woodroffe 1987, 1992), but their organisation into ecosystems has been shown to be less resilient (Ellison and Stoddart 1991, Bird 2008). Over the coming decades, coastal ecosystems will be influenced increasingly by sea-level, as well as by direct anthropogenic impacts.

Coastal wetlands do not keep pace with changing sea-level when the rate of change in elevation of the sediment surface is exceeded by the rate of change in relative sea-level (Figures 1 and 2) (Cahoon et al. 2006, Cahoon and Hensel 2006, Gilman et al. 2008). Coastal wetland resistance and resilience to relative sea-level rise over human time scales are also a result of species composition, as rates of change in sediment elevation is affected in part by the mangrove species composition (Krauss et al. 2003, Rogers et al. 2005, McKee et al. 2007). Speed in colonizing new habitat also varies by species (Lovelock and Ellison 2007). The physiographic setting is a third significant factor

FIGURE 1
Seaward margin of a mangrove retreating landward in response to relative sea-level rise (Photo: E. Gilman, American Samoa).

FIGURE 2
Seaward edge of a mangrove area retreating landward in response to relative sea-level rise (Photo: J. Ellison, Bermuda).

affecting mangrove responses to sea-level rise, including the slope of terrain landward, and presence of obstacles to landward migration (Gilman et al. 2007a). The cumulative effect of all stressors is a fourth factor influencing coastal wetland resistance and resilience to sea-level rise. For instance, stressors such as pollutants can reduce mangrove productivity, reducing belowground root production, causing a reduction in the rate of change in elevation of the sediment surface, compromising the system's resistance and resilience to relative sea-level rise.

Monitoring of mangroves primarily from the western Pacific and Wider Caribbean regions have found that the majority are not keeping pace with current rates of regional relative sea-level rise (Cahoon et al. 2006, Cahoon and Hensel 2006, Gilman et al. 2007b, McKee et al. 2007). Based on this limited, ad hoc monitoring network, the mean net mangrove sediment elevation change was +1 mm a^{-1}, suggesting, as a first-order estimate, that a relative sea-level rise rate > 1 mm a^{-1} constitutes a tipping point for mangroves (Cahoon and Hensel 2006). Relative sea-level rise could be a substantial cause of future reductions in Pacific regional mangrove area, contributing about 10 to 20% of total estimated losses (Gilman et al. 2006).

While relative sea-level rise is small over years and decades, it can result in substantial shoreline erosion in beach ecosystems, of 50-100 times larger than the sea-level rise rate (Figure 3) (Bruun 1962, 1988, Komar 1998).[1] When there are obstacles to landward migration, such as seawalls, coastal ecosystems can be lost and converted to open water habitat (Figure 4). Beach erosion, including from relative sea-level rise, is one threat to sea turtle nesting habitat and seabird colonies, primarily at colonies that are limited by nesting habitat availability (e.g., Congden et al. 2007, Hitipeuw et al. 2007, Tapilatu and Tiwari 2007).

With compromised resistance and resilience, some coastal ecosystems revert to a narrow fringe or are locally extirpated (Ellison and Stoddart 1991, Ellison 1993, 2000, 2001, 2006, Woodroffe 1995, Gilman

---

1   Bruun (1962, 1988) provides a simplistic model of change to beach profile with sea-level rise. The Bruun model can result in large error when applied to coastal systems other than beaches, when used for site-specific estimates of beach erosion even when model assumptions are met, and when used over short time periods (e.g., Pilkey and Cooper 2004). However, the general concept described by the Bruun model, where with increased sea-level, the equilibrium beach profile and shallow offshore migrates upward and landward, is well accepted (SCOR Working Group 1991).

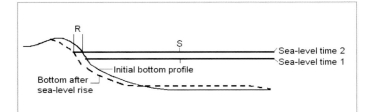

FIGURE 3

The Bruun model net change in beach profile due to a rise in sea-level (S), resulting in offshore deposition and erosion of the upper beach, and landward recession (R) (adapted from Komar 1998). R can be 50-100 times the size of S.

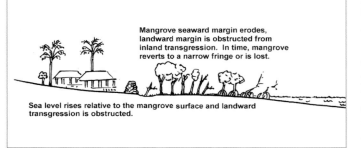

FIGURE 4

Natural mangrove landward migration in response to relative sea-level rise is obstructed by a seawall (adapted from Gilman et al. 2006).

et al. 2008). This occurs where: the slope of land upslope from the wetland is steeper than that of the land the wetland currently occupies; there are obstacles (e.g., seawalls and other erosion control structures) to landward migration of the wetland landward boundary (Figure 3); and stressors reduce the wetland's ability to keep pace with relative sea-level rise (reduced resistance) and stressors reduce the wetland's ability to colonize land at higher elevations (reduced resilience).

Increased CO_2 concentrations, concomitant ocean acidification and reduced calcification rates of corals, and temperature changes are believed to be much larger threats to coral reefs compared to relative sea-level rise (Birkeland 1997, Brown 1997, Kleypas et al. 1999, 2006). If sea-level rises at a rate that is slower than the reef's ability to produce carbonate, the reef will prograde seaward as well as aggrade vertically. If the relative sea-level rise rate is roughly equal to the reef's rate of carbonate production, then the reef will grow vertically and not grow seaward or landward. If sea-level outpaces the accreting reef, the reef will either backstep to higher ground or drown. Reefs may also survive at deeper depths as they grow upward at a lower rate than the rise of sea-level, and catch up if and when the sea-level rise rate slows (Brown 1997). Most coral reef communities are expected to be able to keep pace with projected rates of sea-level rise (Birkeland 1997, Brown 1997). Reef accretion rates range from 1-10 mm a^{-1}, with a rate of 10 mm a^{-1} accepted as the maximum vertical accretion rate that a reef can sustain (Brown 1997). Reef systems may be able to build upward at faster rates, as high as 20 mm a^{-1}, when growing in water depths of less than 20 m where there is abundant sunlight for photosynthesis (Brown 1997). However, some reef flat communities that undergo accelerated coral growth to keep pace with rising relative sea-level would become susceptible to subaerial exposure and substantial mortality if sea-level rise occurs in episodic pulses with periods of sea-level remaining steady (Brown 1997). Also, deeper reefs may not be able to keep pace with projected sea-level rise scenarios. Anthropogenic stresses on reef communities, including increased sedimentation, nutrient loading, rising temperatures, and indirect stresses resulting from the degradation of adjacent coastal communities, are expected to reduce coral reefs' resistance and resilience to accelerated rates of relative sea-level rise (Birkeland 1997).

Adjacent coastal ecosystems are functionally linked (Mumby et al. 2004) and degradation of one may reduce health of a neighbouring ecosystem. For instance, mangroves of low islands and atolls receive a proportion of sediment supply from productive coral reefs (Hubbard and Miller 1990, Glynn 1996), and may suffer lower sedimentation rates and increased susceptibility to relative sea-level rise if coral reefs are disturbed. Terrigenous sediments and nutrients carried by freshwater runoff are filtered by mangrove wetlands, then seagrass beds to benefit coral reefs. The existence and health of coral reefs are dependent on the buffering capacity of these shoreward ecosystems, which support the oligotrophic conditions needed by coral reefs to limit overgrowth by algae (Ellison 2006, Victor et al. 2004). Coral reefs, in turn, buffer the soft sediment landward ecosystems from wave energy (Ellison 2006). Mangroves supply nutrients to adjacent shore fish and seagrass communities, sustaining these habitats' production and general health (Alongi et al. 1992, Dittmar et al. 2006). As fish grow and become less vulnerable to predators, they move from the protective mangrove environment to mudflats, seagrass beds and coral reefs where foraging efficiency increases due to changes in their diet (Laegdsgaard and Johnson 2001, Mumby et al. 2004). Mangroves also provide a natural sunscreen for coral reefs, reducing exposure to harmful solar radiation and risk of bleaching (Anderson et al. 2001, Obriant 2003).

Global sea-level rise is already taking place (12-22 cm of sea-level rise occurred during the 20th century), one outcome from changes in the atmosphere's composition and alterations to land surfaces, and several climate models, as well as available sea-level data, project an accelerated rate of global sea-level rise over coming decades (Bindoff et al. 2007, Solomon et al. 2007). The observed rate of global sea level rise from 1961-2003, is c. 1.8 ± 0.5 mm a^{-1}, whereas from 1993-2003 is c. 3.1 ± 0.7 mm a^{-1}, indicating a possible acceleration in the rate of rise. Projections for global sea-level rise from 1980-1999 to 2090-2099 are of 0.18 – 0.59 m (Solomon et al. 2007). Recent findings on global acceleration in sea level rise indicate that the upper projections of the Intergovernmental Panel on Climate Change are likely to occur (Church and White 2006).

'Relative sea level change', the change in sea level relative to the local land as measured at a tide gauge, is a combination of the change in eustatic (globally averaged) sea level and regional and local factors. The former is the change in sea level relative to a fixed Earth coordinate system, which, over human time scales, is due primarily to thermal expansion of seawater, changes in terrestrial water storage, and the transfer of ice from glaciers, ice sheets and ice caps to water in the oceans (Church et al. 2001, Bindoff et al. 2007, Solomon et al. 2007). The latter is the result of vertical motion of the land from tectonic movement, the glacio- or hydro-isostatic response of the Earth's crust to changes in the weight of overlying ice or water, coastal subsidence such as due to extraction of subsurface groundwater or oil, geographical variation in thermal expansion, and for shorter time scales over years and shorter, meteorological and oceanographic factors, such as changes in density (from changes in temperature and salinity), winds from a constant direction, ocean circulation, and oceanographic processes such as El Nino phases and changes in offshore currents (Church et al. 2001, Solomon et al. 2007). To determine projections in relative sea-level over coming decades, which is of interest due to its potential impact on coastal ecosystems, as well as coastal development and human populations, there is a need to understand how sea-level is changing relative to the site-specific elevation of the sediment surface of coastal ecosystems.

IMPACTS ON BIODIVERSITY AND ECOSYSTEM SERVICES

Coastal ecosystems of mangroves, seagrasses and salt marshes support specialized groups of highly adapted species that are obligate to their habitats. The primary production of these halophytic plants supports a high diversity of invertebrates, fish and birds in the nearshore environments. Many migratory species depend on tidal wetlands for part of their seasonal migrations: an estimated two million migratory shorebirds of the East Asian-Australasian Flyway, which annually migrate from the Arctic Circle through Southeast Asia to Australia and New Zealand and back, stop to forage at numerous wetlands along this flyway, including the wetlands of Oceania (Environment Australia 2000). Other waterbirds (e.g., wading birds and waterfowl), some of which are widely dispersing, and others, which are more stationary, have population dynamics that make them dependent on coastal wetlands (e.g., Haig et al. 1998). Between 1970-2000, marine wetland-dependent species included in the Living Plant Index declined in abundance by about 30% (MA 2005b). The status of globally threatened coastal seabirds deteriorated faster since 1988 than the status of birds dependent on other (freshwater and terrestrial) ecosystems (MA 2005b). All six species of marine turtles, which require coastal habitats for foraging and/or breeding, are listed as threatened in the IUCN Red List (MA 2005b).

Coastal ecosystems are valued for their provision of numerous ecosystem services (e.g., Lewis 1992, Ewel et al. 1998, Bjork et al. 2008). Considering both marketed and nonmarketed economic factors, the total economic value of relatively undisturbed wetlands exceeds that of converted wetlands (MA 2005b). Reduced area and health of coastal ecosystems will increase the threat to human safety and shoreline development from coastal hazards such as erosion, flooding, storm waves and surges and tsunami. Losses will also reduce coastal water quality, eliminate fish and crustacean nursery habitat, adversely affect adjacent coastal habitats, and eliminate a major resource for human communities that rely on coastal ecosystems for numerous services (Ewel et al. 1998, Mumby et al. 2004, Bjork et al. 2008). For instance, mangroves are nursery habitat for many wildlife species, including commercially important species of fish and crustaceans, and thus contribute to sustaining local abundance of fish and shellfish populations (e.g., Ley et al. 2002). Coastal wetlands are a carbon sink; their destruction releases large quantities of stored carbon and exacerbates global warming and other climate change trends. For example, carbon fixation by seagrasses constitutes an estimated 1% of total carbon fixed in marine ecosystems, while seagrasses store 12% of ocean carbon in deep organic mats (Duarte and Cebrian 1996). Conversely, rehabilitating coastal wetlands increases carbon sequestration (Kauppi et al. 2001, Bjork et al. 2008).

Biodiversity of coastal ecosystems globally have been moderately impacted by climate change over the past 50-100 years, and there will be a very rapid increase in impacts from climate change (MA 2005a). Under the Millennium Ecosystem Assessment's four scenarios of plausible future ecosystems, after 2050, sea-level rise and other climate change impacts will have an increasing effect on the provision of ecosystem services, including by coastal ecosystems (MA 2005b). Mangrove wetlands, one coastal ecosystem known to be vulnerable to relative sea-level rise, are found in the inter-

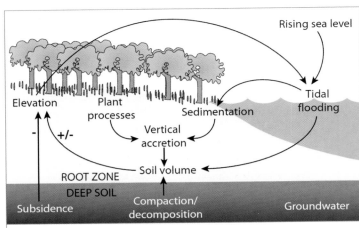

FIGURE 5

Model of the interconnected processes and factors believed to be primary controls on changes in the elevation of the mangrove sediment surface (Lovelock and Ellison 2007: adapted from Cahoon et al. 1999 by Diane Kleine).

tidal zone of tropical and subtropical coastal rivers, estuaries and bays. In general, mangroves are most extensive on macro-tidal coastlines or on low gradient coasts, in areas with a large supply of fine-grained sediment, particularly in large embayments or deltas with strong tidal currents but low wave energy, and are most productive in areas with high rainfall or relatively large freshwater supply from runoff or river discharge (Woodroffe 1992, 2002). The cumulative effects of natural and anthropogenic pressures make mangrove wetlands one of the most threatened natural communities worldwide. Roughly 50% of the global area has been lost since 1900 due primarily to human activities such as conversion for aquaculture and filling (Valiela et al. 2001). To date, relative sea-level rise has likely been a smaller threat to mangroves than non climate-related anthropogenic stressors, such as filling and conversion for agriculture (Valiela et al. 2001, Alongi 2002), which have likely accounted for most of the global average annual rate of mangrove loss, estimated to be 1% to 2%, exceeding the rate of loss of tropical rainforests (0.8%) (Valiela et al. 2001, FAO 2003, Wells et al. 2006, Duke et al. 2007). While the validity of these figures, based on data from the Food and Agriculture Organization of the United Nations (FAO 2003) are questionable, losses during the last quarter century range between 35% and 86% (FAO 2003, Duke et al. 2007). There are roughly 17 million ha of mangroves remaining worldwide (Valiela et al. 2001, FAO 2003).

UNCERTAINTIES

There is a need to develop models for reliable predictions of coastal wetland sediment elevation trends and elevation responses to sea-level rise projections. Reliable predictive sediment elevation models have yet to be developed for coastal ecosystems, and therefore we currently reply upon site-specific monitoring to assess vulnerability and responses to projected changes in sea-level. Existing predictive models of coastal ecosystem erosion produce inaccurate results for small-scale, site-specific estimates (Bruun 1988, List et al. 1997, Komar 1998, Pilkey and Cooper 2004). Predictive elevation models have been developed to estimate salt marsh elevation responses to projected sea-level rise (Allen 1990a, 1992, French 1991, 1993, Morris et al. 2002, Rybczyk and Cahoon 2002). The salt-marsh models developed by Allen (1990a, 1992) and French (1991, 1993) employed an exponentially decreasing rate of inorganic sediment accretion as the elevation of the sediment surface increases, presumably due to decreased tidal inundation frequency and duration. The saltmarsh models assume that the rate of organic accumulation resulting from plant production within the marsh is near-constant and not effected by a change in elevation of the sediment surface, and generally ignore possible effects of change in sediment surface elevation on subsurface processes, which has subsequently been shown to be a poor assumption (Cahoon et al. 1999, Cahoon and Hensel 2006).

The understanding of surface and subsurface processes in affecting mangrove sediment surface elevation, and feedback mechanisms resulting from changes in relative sea-level, is poor (Cahoon et al. 2006) (Figure 5). Relatively short-term observations, over periods of a few years, document positive correlations between relative sea-level rise and mangrove sediment accretion (Cahoon and Hensel 2006), showing mangroves keeping pace with relative sea-level rise. The rate of inorganic sediment accretion may decrease exponentially as the sediment elevation increases due to decreased tidal inundation frequency and duration (Allen 1990, 1992, French 1991, 1993, Woodroffe 2002, Cahoon and Hensel 2006). It is unclear how strong the feedback mechanism is, and is likely site-specific depending on the geomorphic setting and local sedimentation processes. Observations over decades and longer and from numerous sites from a range of settings experiencing rise, lowering and stability in relative sea-level, will improve the understanding of this and other feedback mechanisms.

The understanding of the synergistic effects of multiple climate change and other anthropogenic and natural stressors on coastal ecosystems is also poor. For example, a coastal wetland that is experiencing an elevation deficit to rising sea-level may be located in an area experiencing decreased precipitation, where groundwater extraction for drinking water is predicted to increase. The combined effect of just these three stresses on the coastal wetland could result in an accelerated rate of rise in sea-level relative to the coastal wetland sediment surface, and at the same time decreased productivity, resulting in highly compromised resistance and resilience to stresses from climate change and other sources. Models have not been developed to predict the effects of multiple stresses such as described in this hypothetical example.

LOCAL TO GLOBAL ACTIONS AND OPPORTUNITIES

Global, regional and site-specific adaptation activities can be taken in an attempt to increase the resistance and resilience of ecosystems to climate change stressors, including sea-level rise (Scheffer et al. 2001, Turner et al. 2003, Tompkins and Adger 2004, Julius and West 2007). Alternative options for adaptation for climate-sensitive ecosystems, including coastal ecosystems, are summarized in Table 1.

International efforts need to successfully address the underlying anthropogenic causes of climate change-induced sea-level rise. However, because the effects from climate change are projected to continue for hundreds of years even if greenhouse gas concentrations were immediately stabilized at present concentration levels, we must consider adaption options.

Assessment of coastal ecosystem vulnerability to climate change would allow appropriate adaptation measures, with adequate lead-time to minimize social disruption and cost, and minimize losses of coastal ecosystem services. The selection of adaptation strategies is part a broader coastal site-planning process, where mitigation actions are typically undertaken to address both climate and non-climate threats (Gilman 2002, Adger et al. 2007). This requires balancing multiple and often conflicting objectives of allowing managers and stakeholders to sustain the provision of ecological, economic, and cultural values; address priority threats to natural ecosystem functioning; achieve sustainable development; and fulfil institutional, policy, and legal needs (Gilman 2002).

Given the underdeveloped state of predictive models for coastal ecosystems, systematic and site-specific monitoring is necessary to assess vulnerability and identify responses to change in sea-level. Establishing coastal ecosystem baselines and monitoring gradual changes through regional networks using standardized techniques will enable the separation of site-based influences from global changes to provide a better understanding of coastal ecosystem responses to sea level and global climate change, and alternatives for mitigating adverse effects (CARICOMP 1998, Ellison 2000). For instance, coordinated observations of regional phenomena such as a mass mortality of mangrove trees, or trends in reduced recruitment levels of mangrove seedlings, might be linked to observations of changes in regional climate, such as reduced precipitation. Monitoring networks, while designed to distinguish climate change effects on mangroves, would also therefore show local effects, providing coastal managers with information to abate these sources of degradation. Capacity-building to develop and manage coastal ecosystem monitoring programs has been identified as a priority in some regions (Cahoon et al. 2006, Gilman et al. 2006).

TABLE 1 Adaptation options to augment coastal ecosystem resistance and resilience to climate change (adapted from Gilman et al. 2008).

ADAPTATION OPTION	DESCRIPTION
"No regrets" reduction of stresses	Eliminate non-climate stresses on coastal ecosystems (e.g., filling, conversion for aquaculture) in order to augment overall ecosystem health, in part, to reduce vulnerability to and increase resilience to stresses from climate change. These "no regrets" mitigation actions are justified and beneficial even in the absence of adverse effects on coastal ecosystems from climate change (MA 2005b, Adger et al. 2007, Julius and West 2007).
Manage catchment activities	To attempt to augment coastal ecosystem resistance to sea-level rise, activities within the catchment can be managed to minimize long-term reductions in sediment surface elevation, or enhance sediment elevation.
Managed retreat	Site planning for some sections of shoreline, such as areas that are not highly developed, may facilitate long-term retreat with relative sea level rise (Gilman 2002). Coastal development could remain in use until the eroding coastline becomes a safety hazard or begins to prevent landward migration of coastal ecosystems. Zoning rules for building setbacks and permissible types of new development can reserve zones behind coastal ecosystems for future coastal habitat.
Fortification	For some sections of highly developed coastline, site planning may justify use of shoreline erosion control measures (e.g., groins, seawalls, dune fencing). The structure will prevent natural landward migration and the coastal ecosystem fronting the structure and immediately downstream will eventually be converted to deepwater habitat (e.g., Fletcher et al. 1997).
Protected areas	Protected areas can be established and managed to implement coastal ecosystem representation, replication and refugia. Ensuring representation of all coastal ecosystem community types when establishing a network of protected areas and replication of identical communities to spread risk can increase chances for ecosystems surviving climate change and other stresses (Roberts et al. 2003, Salm et al. 2006, Wells 2006, Julius and West 2007). Protected area selection can include coastal ecosystem areas that act as climate change refugia, communities that are likely to be more resistant to climate change stresses (Palumbi et al. 1997, Bellwood and Hughes 2001, Salm et al. 2006). A system of networks of protected areas can be designed to protect connectivity between coastal ecosystems (Roberts et al. 2003).
Rehabilitation	Enhancement (removing stresses that caused their decline) can augment resistance and resilience to climate change, while restoration (ecological restoration, restoring areas where coastal ecosystem habitat previously existed) (Lewis et al. 2006) can offset anticipated losses from climate change.
Monitoring	Establishing coastal ecosystem baselines and monitoring gradual changes through regional networks using standardized techniques will enable the separation of site-based influences from global changes.
Outreach and education	Outreach and education can augment community support for adaptation actions and a coastal ecosystem conservation ethic.

REFERENCES

Adger, W. N., S. Agrawala, M. M. Q. Mirza, C. Conde, K. O'Brien, J. Pulhin, R. Pulwarty, B. Smit, and K. Takahashi. 2007. Assessment of adaptation practices, options, constraints and capacity *in* M. L. Parry, O. F. Canziani, J. P. Palutikof, P. J. van der Linden, and C. E. Hanson, editors, Climate Change 2007: Impacts, adaptation and vulnerability. Contribution of Working Group II to the Fourth Assessment Report of the Intergovernmental Panel on Climate Change. Cambridge University Press, Cambridge, UK, pp. 717-743.

Allen, J. R. 1990. Constraints on measurement of sea level movements from salt-marsh accretion rates. Journal of the Geological Society 147: 5-7.

Allen, J. R. 1992. Tidally induced marshes in the Severn Estuary, southwest Britain. *In* J. R. Allen and K. Pye, editors, Saltmarshes: morphodynamics, conservation and engineering significance. Cambridge University Press, Cambridge, pp. 123-147.

Alongi, D. M. 1992. Vertical profiles of bacterial abundance, productivity and growth rates in coastal sediments of the central Great Barrier Reef lagoon. Marine Biology 112: 657-663.

Alongi, D. M. 2002. Present state and future of the world's mangrove forests. Environmental Conservation 29: 331-349.

Anderson, S., R. Zepp, J. Machula, D. Santavy, L. Hansen, and F. Mueller. 2001. Indicators of UV exposure in corals and their relevance to global climate change and coral bleaching. Human and Ecological Risk Assessment 7: 1271-1282.

Bellwood, D. R., and T. Hughes. 2001. Regional-scale assembly rules and biodiversity of coral reefs. Science 292: 1532-1534.

Bennett, E.M., G.S. Cumming, and G.D. Peterson. 2005. A systems model approach to determining resilience surrogates for case studies. Ecosystems 8: 945-957.

Bindoff, N. L., J. Willebrand, V. Artale, A. Cazenave, J. Gregory, S. Gulev, K. Hanawa, C. Le Quéré, S. Levitus, Y. Nojiri, C. Shum, L. Talley, and A. Unnikrishnan. 2007. Observations: Oceanic climate change and sea level *in* S. Solomon, D. Qin, M. Manning, Z. Chen, M. Marquis, K. Averyt, M. Tignor, and H. Miller, editors, Climate Change 2007: The Physical science basis. Contribution of Working Group I to the Fourth Assessment Report of the Intergovernmental Panel on Climate Change. Cambridge University Press, Cambridge, United Kingdom and New York, NY, USA.

Bird, E. C. 2008. Coastal geomorphology: an introduction. Chichester, England, Hoboken, NJ John Wiley & Sons, Ltd. (UK). 2nd Edition.

Birkeland, C., editor. 1997. Life and death of coral reefs. New York: Chapman and Hall.

Bjork, M., F. Short, E. Mcleod, and S. Beer. 2008. Managing seagrasses for resilience to climate change. IUCN, Gland, Switzerland, 56pp.

Brown, B.E. 1997. Disturbance to reefs in recent times. Chapter 15 *in* C. Birkeland , editor. Life and Death of Coral Reefs. New York, Chapman and Hall.

Bruun, P. 1962. Sea level rise as a cause of shore erosion. J. Waterways and Harbours Division, Proceedings of the American Society of Civil Engineers 88: 117-130.

Bruun, P. 1988. The Bruun Rule of Erosion by sea-level rise: A discussion of large-scale two and three-dimensional usages. Journal of Coastal Research 4: 627-648.

Cahoon D. R., P. F. Hensel, T. Spencer, D. J. Reed, K. L. McKee, and N. Saintilan. 2006. Coastal wetland vulnerability to relative sea-level rise: wetland elevation trends and process controls. Pages 271-292 *in* J. T. A. Verhoeven, B. Beltman, R. Bobbink, and D. Whigham, editors, Wetlands and Natural Resource Management. Ecological Studies, Volume 190, Springer-Verlag Berlin Heidelberg.

Cahoon, D. R., J. W. Day, and D. J. Reed. 1999. The influence of surface and shallow subsurface soil processes on wetland elevation, a synthesis. Current Topics in Wetland Biogeochemistry 3: 72–88.

Cahoon, D. R., and P. Hensel. 2006. High-resolution global assessment of mangrove responses to sea-level rise: a review. Pages 9-17 *in* E. Gilman, editor, Proceedings of the symposium on mangrove responses to relative sea Level rise and other climate change effects, 13 July 2006, Catchments to Coast, Society of Wetland Scientists 27th International Conference, 9-14 July 2006, Cairns Convention Centre, Cairns, Australia. Western Pacific Regional Fishery Management Council, Honolulu, Hawaii, USA. ISBN 1-934061-03-4.

CARICOMP. 1998. Caribbean Coastal Marine Productivity (CARICOMP): A Cooperative research and monitoring network of marine laboratories, parks, and reserves. CARICOMP methods manual Level 1. Manual of methods for mapping and monitoring of physical and biological parameters in the coastal zone of the Caribbean. CARICOMP Data Management Center, Centre for Marine Sciences, University of the West Indies, Mona, Kingston, Jamaica.

Carpenter, S., B. Walker, J.M. Anderies, N. Abel. 2001. From metaphor to measurement: Resilience of what to what? Ecosystems 4, 765-781.

Church, J., J. Gregory, P. Huybrechts, M. Kuhn, K. Lambeck, M. Nhuan, D. Qin, and P. Woodworth. 2001. Changes in sea level. Chapter 11 *in* J. Houghton, Y. Ding, D. Griggs, M. Noguer, P. van der Linden, X. Dai, K. Maskell, and C. Johnson, editors, Climate Change 2001: the scientific basis. Published for the Intergovernmental Panel on Climate Change. Cambridge University Press, Cambridge, United Kingdom, and New York, NY, USA, 881 pp.

Church, J., and N. White. 2006. A 20th century acceleration in global sea-level rise. Geophysical Research Letters 33: L01602.

Congden, B., C. Erwin, D. Peck, B. Baker, M. Double, and P. O'Neill. 2007. Vulnerability of seabirds on the Great Barrier Reef to climate change. Chapter 14 *in* J. E. Johnson and P. A. Marshall, editor, Climate change and the Great Barrier Reef: a vulnerability assessment. Great Barrier Reef Marine Park Authority and Australian Greenhouse Office, Australia.

Dittmar T, N. Hertkorn, G. Kattner, and R. J. Lara. 2006. Mangroves, a major source of dissolved organic carbon to the oceans. Global Biogeochemical Cycles 20: 1–7.

Duarte, C. M., and J. Cebrian. 1996. The fate of marine autotrophic production. Limnology and Oceanography 41: 1758-1766.

Duke, N. C., J.-O. Meynecke, S. Dittmann, A. M. Ellison, K. Anger, U. Berger, S. Cannicci, K. Diele, K. C. Ewel, C. D. Field, N. Koedam, S. Y. Lee, C. Marchand, I. Nordhaus, and F. Dahdouh-Guebas. 2007. A world without mangroves? Science 317: 41-42.

Ellison, J. C., and D. R. Sroddart. 1991. Mangrove ecosystem collapse with predicted sea-level rise: Holocene analogues and implications. Journal of Coastal Research 7: 151-165.

Ellison, J. 1993. Mangrove retreat with rising sea level, Bermuda. Estuarine, Coastal and Shelf Science 37, 75-87.

Ellison, J. 2000. How South Pacific mangroves may respond to predicted climate change and sea level rise. Chapter 15 *in* A. Gillespie, and W. Burns, editors, Climate change in the South Pacific: impacts and responses in Australia, New Zealand, and small islands States. Kluwer Academic Publishers, Dordrecht, Netherlands, pp. 289-301.

Ellison, J. 2001. Possible impacts of predicted sea-level rise on South Pacific mangroves. Pages 289-301 *in* B. Noye, and M. Grzechnik, editors, Sea-level changes and their effects. World Scientific Publishing Company, Singapore.

Ellison, J. 2006. Mangrove paleoenvironmental response to climate change *in* E. Gilman, editor, Proceedings of the symposium on mangrove responses to relative sea-Level rise and other climate change effects, Society of Wetland Scientists 2006 Conference, 9-14 July 2006, Cairns, Australia. ISBN 1-934061-03-4. Western Pacific Regional Fishery Management Council and United Nations Environment Programme Regional Seas Programme, Honolulu, USA and Nairobi, Kenya. pp. 1-8.

Environment Australia. 2000. Migratory birds, let's ensure their future. Wetlands, Waterways and Waterbirds Unit, Environment Australia, Canberra, Australia.

Ewel, K. C., R. R. Twilley, and J. E. Ong. 1998. Different kinds of mangrove forests provide different goods and services. Global Ecology and Biogeography 7. 83-94.

FAO. 2003. Status and trends in mangrove area extent worldwide. Food and Agriculture Organization of the United Nations, Forest Resources Division, Paris.

Fletcher, C. H., R. A. Mullane, and B. Richmond. 1997. Beach loss along armored shorelines of Oahu, Hawaiian Islands. Journal of Coastal Research 13: 209-215.

French, J. R. 1993. Numerical simulation of vertical marsh growth and adjustment to accelerated sea-level rise, North Norfolk, UK. Earth Surf. Proc. Land. 18: 63-81.

French, J. R. 1991. Eustatic and neotectonic controls on salt marsh sedimentation. *In* N. C. Kraus, K. J. Gingerich, and D. L. Kriebel, editors, Coastal Sediments '91, American Society of Civil Engineers, New York, pp. 1223-1236.

Gilman, E., J. Ellison, N. Duke, and C. Field. 2008. Threats to mangroves from climate change and adaptation options: a review. Aquatic Botany 89: 237-250.

Gilman, E., J. Ellison, V. Jungblat, H. VanLavieren, E. Adler, L. Wilson, F. Areki, G. Brighouse, J. Bungitak, E. Dus, M. Henry, I. Sauni Jr., M. Kilman, E. Matthews, N. Teariki-Ruatu, S. Tukia, and K. Yuknavage. 2006. Adapting to Pacific Island mangrove responses to sea level rise and other climate change effects. Climate Research 32(3): 161-176.

Gilman, E. L. 2002. Guidelines for coastal and marine site-planning and examples of planning and management intervention tools. Ocean and Coastal Management 45: 377-404.

Gilman, E., J. Ellison, and R. Coleman. 2007a. Assessment of mangrove response to projected relative sea-level rise and recent historical reconstruction of shoreline position. Environmental Monitoring and Assessment 124: 112-134.

Gilman, E., J. Ellison, I. Sauni Jr., and S. Tuaumu. 2007b. Trends in surface elevations of American Samoa mangroves. Wetlands Ecology and Management 15: 391-404.

Glynn, P. W. 1996. Coral reef bleaching: facts, hypotheses and implications. Global Change Biology 2: 495-509.

Haig, S. M., D. W. Mehlman, L. W. Oring. 1998. Avian movements and wetland connectivity in landscape conservation. Conservation Biology 12: 749-758.

Hitipeuw, C, P. H. Dutton, S. Benson, J. Thebu, and J. Bakarbessi. 2007. Population status and inter-nesting movement of leatherback turtles, *Dermochelys coriacea*, nesting on the northwest coast of Papua, Indonesia. Chelonian Conservation and Biology 6: 28-36.

Hubbard, D. K., and A. I. Miller. 1990. Production and cycling of calcium carbonate in a shelf-edge reef system (St. Croix, U.S. Virgin Islands): applications to the nature of reef systems in the fossil record. Journal of Sedimentary Research 60.

Julius, S. H., and J. M. West, editors, 2007. Draft. Preliminary review of adaptation options for climate-sensitive ecosystems and resources. Synthesis and assessment product 4.4. U.S. Climate Change Science Program. U.S. Environmental Protection Agency, Washington, D.C., U.S.A.

Kauppi, P., R. Sedjo, M. Apps, C. Cerri, T. Fujimori, H. Janzen, O. Krankina, W. Makundi, G. Marland, O. Masera, G. Nabuurs, W. Razali, and N. Ravindranath. 2001. Technological and economic potential of options to enhance, maintain, and manage biological carbon reservoirs and geo-engineering. Chapter 4 *in* Intergovernmental Panel on Climate Change. Climate Change 2001: Mitigation. A report of Working Group III of the Intergovernmental Panel on Climate Change. Geneva.

Kleypas, J., R. Buddemeir, D. Archer, J. Gattuso, C. Langdon, and B. Opdyke. 1999. Geochemical consequences of increased atmospheric carbon dioxide on coral reefs. Science 284: 118-120.

Kleypas, J., R. Feely, V. Fabry, C. Landgon, C. Sabine, and L. Robbins. 2006. Impacts of ocean acidification on coral reefs and other marine calcifiers: a guide for future research. Workshop report, 18-20 April 2005, St. Petersburg, Floriday. National Science Foundation, NOAA, U.S. Geological Survey, Washington, D.C., USA. 88 p.

Komar, P. 1998. Beach processes and sedimentation. Second Edition. Prentice Hall: Upper Saddle River, NJ, USA.

Krauss, K. W., J. A. Allen, and D. R. Cahoon. 2003. Differential rates of vertical accretion and elevation change among aerial root types in Micronesian mangrove forests. Estuarine, Coastal and Shelf Science 56: 251-259.

Laegdsgaard, P., and C. Johnson. 2001. Why do juvenile fish utilize mangrove habitats? J. Exp. Mar. Biol. Ecol. 257: 229-253.

Lewis III, R. R. 1992. Scientific perspectives on on-site/off-site, in-kind/out-of-kind mitigation *in* J. A. Kusler, and C. Lassonde, editors, Effective mitigation: mitigation banks and joint projects in the context of wetland management plans. Proceedings of the National Wetland Symposium, 24-27 June 1992. Palm Beach Gardens, FL, USA, pp. 101-106.

Lewis III, R. R., P. Erftemeijer, and A. Hodgson. 2006. A novel approach to growing mangroves on the coastal mud flats of Eritrea with the potential for relieving regional poverty and hunger: comment. Wetlands 26: 637-638.

Ley, J. A., I. A. Halliday, A. J. Tobin, R. N. Garrett, and N. A. Gribble. 2002. Ecosystem effects of fishing closures in mangrove estuaries of tropical Australia. Marine Ecology Progress Series 245: 223-238.

List, J., A., Jr. Sallenger, M. Hansen, and B. Jaffe. 1997. Accelerated relative sea-level rise and rapid coastal erosion: testing a causal relationship for the Louisiana barrier islands. Marine Geology 140: 347-365.

Lovelock, C. E., and J. C. Ellison. 2007. Vulnerability of mangroves and tidal wetlands of the Great Barrier Reef to climate change *in* J. E. Johnson, and P. A. Marshall, editors, Climate change and the Great Barrier Reef: a vulnerability assessment. Great Barrier Reef Marine Park Authority and Australian Greenhouse Office, Australia, pp. 237-269.

McKee, K. L., D. R. Cahoon, and I. Feller. 2007. Caribbean mangroves adjust to rising sea level through biotic controls on change in soil elevation. Global Ecology and Biogeography 16: 545-556.

MA – Millennium Ecosystem Assessment. 2005a. Ecosystems and human well-being: biodiversity synthesis. World Resources Institute, Washington, D.C.

MA – Millennium Ecosystem Assessment. 2005b. Ecosystems and human well-being: wetlands and water synthesis. World Resources Institute, Washington, D.C.

Morris, J. T., P. V. Sundareshwar, C. T. Nietch, B. Kjerfve, and D. R. Cahoon. 2002. Responses of coastal wetlands to rising sea-level. Ecology 83: 2869-2877.

Mumby, P., A. Edwards, J. Arlas-Gonzalez, K. Lindeman, P. Blackwell, A. Gall, M. Gorczynska, A. Harbone, C. Pescod, H. Renken, C. Wabnitz, and G. Llewellyn. 2004. Mangroves enhance the biomass of coral reef fish communities in the Caribbean. Nature 427: 533-536.

Nystrom, M., C. Folke. 2001. Spatial resilience of coral reefs. Ecosystems 4, 406-417.

Obriant, M. P. 2003. UV Exposure of Coral Assemblages in the Florida Keys. U.S. Environmental Protection Agency. EIMS Record ID 75671.

Odum, E.P. 1989. Ecology and our Endangered Life-Support Systems. Sinauer Associates Inc, Sunderland, USA.

Palumbi, S. R., G. Grabowsky, T. Duda, L. Geyer, and N. Tachino. 1997. Speciation and population genetic structure in tropical Pacific sea urchins. Evolution 51, 1506-1517.

Pilkey, O. H., and J. A. Cooper. 2004. Society and sea level rise. Science 303: 1781-2.

Roberts, C. M., G. Branch, R. H. Bustamante, J. C. Castilla, J. Dugan, B. S. Halpern, K. D. Lafferty, H. Leslie, J. Lubchenco, D. McArdle, M. Ruckelshaus, and R. R. Warner. 2003. Application of ecological criteria in selecting marine reserves and developing reserve networks. Ecological Applications 13: S215-S228.

Rogers, K., N. Saintilan, and D. R. Cahoon. 2005b. Surface elevation dynamics in a regenerating mangrove forest at Homebush Bay, Australia. Wetlands Ecology and Management 13: 587–598.

Rybczyk, J. M., and D. R. Cahoon. 2002. Estimating the potential for submergence for two subsiding wetlands in the Mississippi River delta. Estuaries 25: 985-998.

Salm, R. V., T. Done, and E. McLeod. 2006. Marine protected area planning in a changing climate *in* J. T. Phinney, O. Hoegh-Guldberg, J. Kleypas, W. Skirving, and A. Strong, editors, Coral reefs and climate change: science and management. American Geophysical Union, Washington, D.C., pp. 207-221.

Scheffer, M., S. Carpenter, J. Foley, C. Folke, and B. Walker. 2001. Catastrophic shifts in ecosystems. Nature 413: 591-596.

SCOR Working Group. 1991. The response of beaches to sea level changes: a review of predictive models. Journal of Coastal Research 7: 895-921.

Solomon, S., D. Qin, M. Manning, R. B. Alley, T. Berntsen, N. L. Bindoff, Z. Chen, A. Chidthaisong, J. M. Gregory, G. C. Hegerl, M. Heimann, B. Hewitson, B. J. Hoskins, F. Joos, J. Jouzel, V. Kattsov, U. Lohmann, T. Matsuno, M. Molina, N. Nicholls, J. Overpeck, G. Raga, V. Ramaswamy, J. Ren, M. Rusticucci, R. Somerville, T. F. Stocker, P. Whetton, R. A. Wood, and D. Wratt. 2007. Technical summary *in* S. Solomon, D. Qin, M. Manning, Z. Chen, M. Marquis, K. B. Averyt, M. Tignor, and H. L. Miller, editors, Climate Change 2007: the physical science basis. Contribution of Working Group I to the Fourth Assessment Report of the Intergovernmental Panel on Climate Change. Cambridge University Press, Cambridge, United Kingdom and New York, NY, USA.

Tapilatu, R., and M. Tiwari. 2007. Leatherback, *Dermochelys coriacea*, hatching success at Jamursba-Medi and Wermon Beaches in Papua, Indonesia. Chelonian Conservation and Biology 6: 154-158.

Tompkins, E. L., and N. W. Adger. 2004. Does adaptive management of natural resources enhance resilience to climate change? Ecology and Society 19: 10.

Turner, B. L., R. Kasperson, P. Matsone, J. McCarthy, R. Corell, L. Christensene, N. Eckley, J. Kasperson, A. Luerse, M. Martello, C. Polsky, A. Pulsipher, A. Schiller. 2003. A framework for vulnerability analysis in sustainability science. Proceedings of the National Academy of Sciences 100: 8074-8079.

Valiela, I., J. Bowen, and J. York. 2001. Mangrove forests: one of the world's threatened major tropical environments. Bioscience 51: 807-815.

Victor, S., Y. Golbuu, E. Wolanski, and R. H. Richmond. 2004. Fine sediment trapping in two mangrove-fringed estuaries exposed to contrasting land-use intensity, Palau, Micronesia. Wetlands Ecology and Management 12: 277-283.

Wells, S., C. Ravilous, and E. Corcoran. 2006. In the front line: shoreline protection and other ecosystem services from mangroves and coral reefs. United Nations Environment Programme World Conservation Monitoring Centre, Cambridge, UK.

Wells, S. 2006. Establishing national and regional systems of MPAs – a review of progress with lessons learned. UNEP World Conservation Monitoring Centre, UNEP Regional Seas Programme, ICRAN, IUCN/WCPA – Marine.

Woodroffe, C. 2002. Coasts: form, process and evolution. Cambridge University Press, Cambridge, UK.

Woodroffe, C. D. 1995. Response of tide-dominated mangrove shorelines in northern Australia to anticipated sea-level rise. Earth Surface Processes and Landforms 20: 65-85.

Woodroffe, C. D. 1992. Mangrove sediments and geomorphology *in* D. Alongi, and A. Robertson, editors, Tropical mangrove ecosystems. Coastal and Estuarine Studies, American Geophysical Union, Washington, D.C., pp. 7-41.

Woodroffe, C. D. 1987. Pacific island mangroves: distributions and environmental settings. Pacific Science 41: 166-185.

Appendix 8. ARCTIC OCEAN

Henry P. Huntington (hph@alaska.net)

SUMMARY

▸ Arctic summer sea ice extent is decreasing rapidly, indeed more quickly than recent models projected, reaching a record low in September 2007, nearly matched in September 2008, and raising the possibility of an ice-free Arctic summer within a few decades.

▸ Sea ice is thinning and most multi-year ice has been lost, setting the stage for further rapid reduction in extent.

▸ Ice-dependent species are thus rapidly losing habitat, creating key mis-matches in timing of seasonal events such as food availability and reproduction or in spatial relationships such as feeding and resting areas for marine mammals.

▸ The arctic marine environment is rapidly becoming a subarctic environment, with consequent threats to arctic species but opportunities for subarctic ones.

▸ Feedbacks to global climate from sea ice loss will lead to still more warming.

▸ Where sea ice is a platform and a provider of ice-associated species, ecosystem services will decline. Where sea ice is a barrier to human activity, development may increase, including perhaps provisioning services such as fisheries, but may also lead to increased conflict among users and potential users.

▸ Conservation action should be taken in advance of major human activities to avoid further stressing the Arctic marine environment.

DESCRIPTION

Status and trends

The Arctic System can be characterized by the presence of three forms of year-round ice: sea ice, permafrost, and glaciers (Overpeck et al. 2005). All of these are deteriorating (e.g. Serreze et al. 2000, Romanovsky et al. 2002., Mote 2007), sea ice most rapidly (Stroeve et al. 2007). Although the minimum (September) extent of Arctic sea ice has been declining for some time, 2007 brought a much sharper decrease, with only 4.3 million km^2 of ice remaining, or 23% lower than the previous record low in 2005. In 2008, despite very extensive sea ice cover in spring, sea ice retreated rapidly in summer, nearly equaling the 2007 record for minimum extent (Richter-Menge et al. 2008) (Figure 1). In the summer of 2008, both the Northwest Passage through the Canadian Arctic Archipelago and the Northern Sea Route across the top of Eurasia were fully navigable for the first time in recorded history. Although atmospheric and oceanic circulation patterns appear to have played a role, the decreasing thickness of the Arctic ice pack left it susceptible to rapid retreat, as predicted by Holland et al. (2006). With little multi-year ice remaining in the Arctic (Nghiem et al. 2006), further rapid retreat appears to be ever more likely. Importantly, many climate models that incorporate sea ice had projected such a rapid decline (but see Holland et al. 2006, Winton 2006), suggesting that Arctic sea ice is more susceptible to climate change that previously known and that a summer ice-free Arctic may occur far sooner than previously thought.

While some areas of ice may persist for many decades, the Arctic may be largely ice free in the summer within few decades, in contrast to recent predictions of perennial ice diminishing but not disappearing before the end of the 21st century (e.g. Walsh 2008). Complete year-round disappearance of the ice cap is indeed predicted by NOAA's Geophysical Fluid Dynamic Laboratory's GFDL CM2.1 coupled model runs (Winton 2006) using the average A1B scenario of 1% year[-1] CO_2 increase (Winton 2006) (Figure 2). Even more conservative measures provided by 10 global circulation models based also on the A1B scenario predict significant reductions in the extent of the ice-cap, and notably those important for the polar bear habitat (Durner et al. 2009). The rapid loss of sea ice leaves even less time for corrective action in the

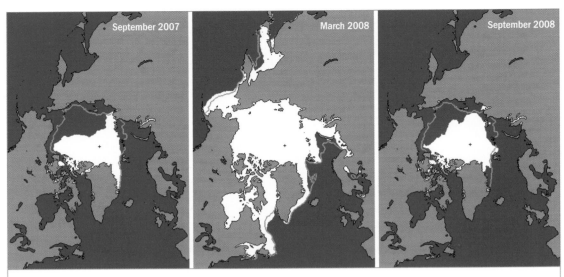

FIGURE 1

Recent sea ice extent in the Arctic, showing the record minimum in September 2007 (left), normal or higher sea ice extent in March 2008 (middle), and the near-record minimum in September 2008, in which both the Northern Sea Route and the Northwest Passage were ice-free. The magenta line indicates the average ice extent for the period 1979-2000 for the respective month of each map. Adapted from Richter-Menge et al. 2008 (figures from the National Snow and Ice Data Center Sea Ice Index: nsidc.org/data/ seaice_index.)

form of addressing global climate change or for adaptation by biota and humans to the new conditions they will soon experience in the Arctic marine environment. The changes to the physical system will have ecological repercussions for a long time as species and ecosystems adapt and adjust. What the new Arctic system will look like remains to be seen.

Tipping point mechanisms

The Arctic experiences high interannual variability in many biophysical respects (ACIA 2005). To some extent, this characteristic implies a high degree of flexibility and adaptability to changing conditions. On the other hand, many Arctic species require certain conditions in order to flourish. Warmer air and water may also allow subarctic species to move northwards, competing with Arctic species already stressed by changes in habitat and food webs. The return of "normal" sea ice conditions would in theory allow restoration of Arctic ecosystems, but the rapid retreat of sea ice threatens a long-term directional change in the physical environment. The loss of multi-year sea ice and consequent thinning of the ice pack means,

among other things, that several years are required to restore that feature to the Arctic seascape. It also means higher susceptibility to the rapid retreats of sea ice seen in 2007 and 2008 (Maslanik et al. 2007). In the winter of 2007-08, sea ice thickness was 0.26–0.49 cm below the mean of the previous six years, a reduction of 10-20% in ice thickness (Giles et al. 2008). Further loss of sea ice may make it even more difficult to restore the thickness and extent of ice cover from as recently as the late 20th century. Furthermore, the changes in food webs in the Arctic Ocean and marginal seas may take even longer to change back, if indeed they have not found a new, relatively stable state. Without much prospect for the restoration of sea ice, it appears likely that the Arctic is approaching, if it has not already reached, a major ecological tipping point.

IMPACTS ON BIODIVERSITY

The most visible impact to biodiversity from the loss of sea ice is that of ice-dependent species. The Arctic appears to have had at least some summer sea ice

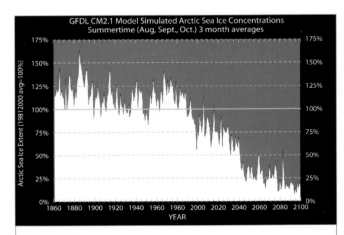

FIGURE 2

Summertime Arctic-wide sea ice extent simulated by the Geophysical Fluid Dynamics Laboratory GFDL CM2.1 model for the historical period 1860 to 2000 and projected for the 21st century following the SRES A1B emissions scenario. Sea ice extent values are normalized (scaled) so that the average for years 1981 to 2000 is equal to 100%. Totally ice-free summer conditions would equal 0% (http://www.gfdl.noaa.gov/the-shrinking-arctic-ice-cap-ar4#maps2d).

for at least 800000 years (Overpeck et al. 2005), time enough for the adaptation of many ice-associated species (Harington 2008). Laidre et al. (2008) evaluated the vulnerability of Arctic marine mammals to climate change, especially the loss of sea ice habitat and associated changes in the food web. They found that narwhal (*Monodon monoceros*) is the most vulnerable species, followed by polar bear (*Ursus maritimus*). Other Arctic marine mammals are likely to be affected, with a general shift in favor of subarctic species (Moore and Huntington 2008). Unfortunately, there are many protected areas on land in the Arctic, but there are few if any marine protected areas (UNEP/GRID-Arendal 2007).

Changes in the Arctic food web are already apparent. The distribution of species is changing along with trophic interactions, due in large part to climate forcing, though other factors are also involved (Mueter and Litzow 2008). Not only are subarctic species moving northwards, but changes in ocean circulation are causing some Arctic species to move south, and appear responsible for the first exchanges of zooplankton between the North Pacific and North Atlantic regions in perhaps 800000 years (Greene et al. 2008). Changes in distributions may also affect disease vectors in both directions, posing an additional threat to species already stressed by habitat loss and other impacts (Burek et al. 2008). Bluhm and Gradinger (2008) identify three plausible results of large-scale biotic change: (a) increased pelagic productivity in the central Arctic basin as more open water allows more sunlight to reach the water column, (b) reduced biomass in coastal and shelf areas due to changes in salinity and turbidity, and (c) increased pelagic grazing leading to reduced vertical flux to benthos. These changes would have far-reaching impacts on Arctic marine ecosystems but where these changes lead is not yet clear.

A major driver is likely to be the change in seasonal patterns of ice cover and productivity. If ice melt occurs earlier in the year in the Southern Bering Sea, the ice-edge bloom will be modest due to lack of sunlight but the later summer bloom will be larger, with the net result that the trophic pathway will favour pelagic species rather than the benthic fauna favoured in colder years (Hunt et al. 2002). On the other hand, in the northern Bering Sea, the spring bloom is large enough to overwhelm the grazing capacity of zooplankton, resulting in a rich benthic ecosystem. For benthic-feeding species such as walrus (*Odobenus rosmarus*) and the endangered spectacled eider (*Somateria fischeri*), the retreat of the summer ice edge causes the animals to swim farther and expend more energy to move between feeding and resting areas and having reduced benthic resources (Grebmeier et al. 2006, Laidre et al. 2008). In the Barents Sea, a complicated relationship among cod (*Gadus morhua*), capelin (*Mallotus villosus*), and euphausiids creates large oscillations in fish stocks, but recent warming tends to push capelin farther north but may favor cod (Stiansen and Filin 2007). If the relative distribution of these fishes changes, new trophic interactions may dominate the system.

ECOSYSTEM SERVICES

The Arctic marine ecosystem in its present form provides a variety of services to humans. On a global scale, the presence of sea ice helps regulate global climate and plays a role in ocean circulation, providing a regulating service. Sea ice reflects incoming sunlight, which in the absence of sea ice is absorbed by the ocean. This effectively replaces one of the brightest most reflective services on the planet with one of the darkest most absorbent ones, leading to further warming both locally and globally (Perovich et al. 2008). Because sea ice is floating, the melting of sea ice will have no effect on sea level (the melting of glaciers and ice caps on land is a different story). The loss of sea ice leads to increased exchange of carbon between air and seawater in the Arctic, since the sea ice no longer functions as a physical barrier. Warming water would hold less carbon dioxide, whereas greater productivity may increase carbon uptake in the water column. The net result is hard to predict (AMAP 2009).

Locally, Arctic marine mammals, seabirds, and fishes provide food and cultural materials for Arctic peoples, a provisioning service and a cultural service (Huntington et al. 1998, AHDR 2004, Hovelsrud et al. 2008). Iconic Arctic species such as the polar bear draw tourists northwards (Forgione and Martin. 2008) and also hold considerable existence value for many people who will never visit the Arctic but enjoy knowing that Arctic species exist.

The changes underway in the Arctic marine environment are likely to change ecosystem services in several ways. Provisioning services will shift, altering traditional patterns of marine resource use. The net change is difficult to assess. For example, a northward shift of Pacific salmon could provide a major new source of food for coastal and riparian settlements, but at the same time some marine mammal hunting opportunities may decrease or be lost. Likewise, an increase in pelagic productivity in the Arctic's marginal seas and improved access to the Arctic Ocean itself could mean a substantial net benefit in the long run for commercial fisheries, depending on which fish species flourish under the new conditions and how management regimes and policies respond (Vilhjálmsson and Hoel. 2005). Based on experiences elsewhere, the advent of commercial fisheries in waters that have not yet been subject to large-scale fisheries would likely have considerable impacts on biodiversity in Arctic waters (National Research Council 2003, Plagányi and Butterworth 2005).

Overall, Arctic ecosystem service degradation is likely to occur due to increased industrial development and commercial shipping, both of which could be facilitated by reduced sea ice cover. Offshore oil and gas development poses the risk of marine oil spills in addition to chronic habitat degradation through noise, bottom disturbance, and pollution (AMAP 2009). Marine shipping poses many of the same threats, dispersed along the full length of major shipping routes through Arctic waters (PAME in press) (Figure 3). Shipping poses an additional threat of introduced species. Increased human activity in general creates a risk of synergistic and cumulative effects, leading to more rapid impacts and potentially to reaching critical thresholds sooner, leaving less time for effective conservation action (PAME in press).

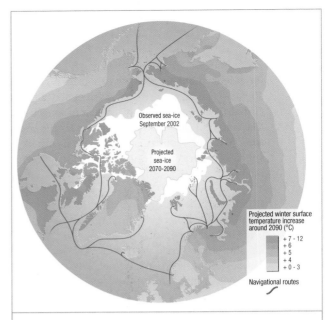

FIGURE 3
Potential shipping routes in the Arctic and projected ice extent (Source: ACIA 2004). Note that recent sea ice retreat has been far more rapid than predicted here. (Map: Hugo Ahlenius, UNEP/GRID-Arendal; http://maps.grida.no/go/graphic/projected-changes-in-the-arctic-climate-2090-with-shipping-routes)

UNCERTAINTIES

The preceding discussion of the Arctic marine environment draws largely on observational data, leaving little doubt that major changes are underway. Future trajectories, on the other hand, are far from certain. The rapid loss of sea ice suggests that general circulation models and sea ice models are at best conservative in their projections of future sea ice decline, indicating that factors as yet not incorporated in the models may play a substantial role in determining what happens next. While reduced sea ice thickness and the loss of multi-year ice imply greater vulnerability and thus continued and potentially accelerated loss of sea ice, it is also possible that other conditions such as cloud cover feedbacks or further changes in ocean circulation may slow or even reverse the decline. Similarly, the response of Arctic species and food webs is highly uncertain. Atlantic cod may flourish in warmer water in the North Atlantic, or lower trophic pathways may shift towards coccolithophores or jellyfish, undermining many of the species used and valued by humans. Nevertheless, as explained below, the greatest uncertainty remains the degree to which global and local actions can be implemented in a timely manner preventing the permanent deterioration of the arctic ecosystem.

LOCAL TO GLOBAL ACTION AND OPPORTUNITIES

Global action

Globally, the largest driver of Arctic change at present is climate change. Addressing it will take global action. As noted earlier, the speed of current change in the Arctic makes it clear that there may be relatively little time left if we are to retain a sizeable sea ice environment. Many scientists believe that a tipping point in sea ice loss would result in an unstoppable reaction of the system. The possibility of refugia remaining in some regions offers the prospect of additional time to act, but the preservation of a small remnant Arctic marine ecosystem is not equivalent to maintaining the large, functional ecosystems that exist today. Among other things, a small area with small populations would be highly susceptible to catastrophic loss, such as disease or anomalous shifts in ocean or atmospheric circulation.

Other global conservation challenges in the region include sound management of commercial shipping and fisheries in international waters. Ideally, appropriate international or multi-lateral regulatory regimes would be developed in advance of large-scale commercial activity so that sensible restrictions could be imposed before poor practices and low environmental standards become the norm. Existing institutions such as the International Maritime Organization should be engaged where possible, with new institutions created where necessary.

Regional and local action

Circumpolar, regional, bilateral, and national actions should include stringent regulation of human activity in Arctic waters to avoid additional stressors on species and ecosystems already experiencing the effects of climate change. Existing treaties and agreements address polar bears, some fisheries, other migratory species, and research and conservation. These can be supplemented by additional cooperation to protect shared animal populations and ecosystems and to use the urgency of the Arctic situation to promote the global actions noted above. For example, the 2001 Stockholm Convention on Persistent Organic Pollutants took global action against that class of chemicals, in part driven by findings of high concentrations in Arctic animals and peoples (Downie and Fenge 2003). In many regions of the Arctic Ocean, oil and gas activities are already underway (AMAP 2009). While environmental regulations are generally strong in Arctic countries, the risk of an oil spill or other disaster will be present so long as petroleum activities occur, and the cumulative impacts of widespread industrial activity will only grow as such activity increases in amount and geographic spread. Taking coordinated action can help preserve the ecosystems that exist today, retaining more options for the future. Regional and national actions are an important part of an effective Arctic marine conservation strategy, but in the long run they will be ineffective in the absence of global action on climate change (Ragen et al. 2008), which is likely to turn Arctic ecosystems into subarctic ecosystems, leaving no home for true Arctic species.

REFERENCES

ACIA. 2004, December. Impacts of a Warming Arctic - Arctic Climate Impact Assessment. Arctic Climate Impact Assessment. Cambridge University Press, Cambridge.

ACIA. 2005. Arctic climate impact assessment. Cambridge University Press, Cambridge.

AHDR. 2004. Arctic human development report. Stefansson Arctic Institute, Akureyri.

AMAP. 2009. Climate change updates. Oslo.

Bluhm, B. A., and R. Gradinger. 2008. Regional variability in food availability for arctic marine mammals. Ecological Applications 18:S77-S96.

Burek, K. A., F. M. D. Gulland, and T. M. O'Hara. 2008. Effects of climate change on Arctic marine mammal health. Ecological Applications 18:S126-S134.

Downie, D. L., and T. Fenge. 2003. Northern lights against POPs: combating toxic threats in the Arctic. McGill-Queen's University Press, Montreal.

Durner, G. M., D. C. Douglas, R. M. Nielson, S. C. Amstrup, T. L. McDonald, I. Stirling, M. Mauritzen, E. W. Born, O. Wiig, E. DeWeaver, M. C. Serreze, S. E. Belikov, M. M. Holland, J. Maslanik, J. Aars, D. A. Bailey, and A. E. Derocher. 2009. Predicting 21st-century polar bear habitat distribution from global climate models. Ecological Monographs 79:25-58.

Forgione, M., and H. Martin. 2008. Now threatened, polar bears are a bigger draw in Churchill, Canada. Los Angeles Times.

Giles, K. A., S. W. Laxon, and A. L. Ridout. 2008. Circumpolar thinning of Arctic sea ice following the 2007 record ice extent minimum. Geophysical Research Letters 35: L22502.

Grebmeier, J. M., J. E. Overland, S. E. Moore, E. V. Farley, E. C. Carmack, L. W. Cooper, K. E. Frey, J. H. Helle, F. A. McLaughlin, and S. L. McNutt. 2006. A major ecosystem shift in the northern Bering Sea. Science 311:1461-1464.

Greene, C. H., A. J. Pershing, T. M. Cronin, and N. Ceci. 2008. Arctic climate change and its impacts on the ecology of the north atlantic. Ecology 89:S24-S38.

Harington, C. R. 2008. The evolution of Arctic marine mammals. Ecological Applications 18:S23-S40.

Holland, M. M., C. M. Bitz, and B. Tremblay. 2006. Future abrupt reductions in the summer Arctic sea ice. Geophysical Research Letters 35: L22502.

Hovelsrud, G. K., M. McKenna, and H. P. Huntington. 2008. Marine mammal harvests and other interactions with humans. Ecological Applications 18:S135-S147.

Hunt, G. L., P. Stabeno, G. Walters, E. Sinclair, R. D. Brodeur, J. M. Napp, and N. A. Bond. 2002. Climate change and control of the southeastern Bering Sea pelagic ecosystem. Deep-Sea Research Part Ii-Topical Studies in Oceanography 49:5821-5853.

Huntington, H. P., J. H. Mosli, and V. B. Shustov. 1998. Peoples of the Arctic: characteristics of human populations relevant to pollution issues. Arctic Monitoring and Assessment Program, Oslo.

Laidre, K. L., I. Stirling, L. F. Lowry, O. Wiig, M. P. Heide-Jorgensen, and S. H. Ferguson. 2008. Quantifying the sensitivity of arctic marine mammals to climate-induced habitat change. Ecological Applications 18:S97-S125.

Maslanik, J. A., C. Fowler, J. Stroeve, S. Drobot, J. Zwally, D. Yi, and W. Emery. 2007. A younger, thinner Arctic ice cover: Increased potential for rapid, extensive sea-ice loss. Geophysical Research Letters 34: L22507.

Moore, S. E., and H. P. Huntington. 2008. Arctic marine mammals and climate change: Impacts and resilience. Ecological Applications 18:S157-S165.

Mote, T. L. 2007. Greenland surface melt trends 1973-2007: Evidence of a large increase in 2007. Geophysical Research Letters 34: L22507.

Mueter, F. J., and M. A. Litzow. 2008. Sea ice retreat alters the biogeography of the Bering Sea continental shelf. Ecological Applications 18:309-320.

National Research Council. 2003. The decline of the Steller sea lion in Alaskan waters: untangling food webs and fishing nets. National Academies Press, Washington.

Nghiem, S. V., Y. Chao, G. Neumann, P. Li, D. K. Perovich, T. Street, and P. Clemente-Colon. 2006. Depletion of perennial sea ice in the East Arctic Ocean. Geophysical Research Letters 33:L17501.

Overpeck, J. T., M. Sturm, J. A. Francis, D. K. Perovich, M. C. Serreze, R. Benner, E. C. Carmack, F. S. C. III, S. C. Gerlach, L. C. Hamilton, L. D. Hinzman, M. Holland, H. P. Huntington, J. R. Key, A. H. Lloyd, G. M. MacDonald, J. McFadden, D. Noone, T. D. Prowse, P. Schlosser, and C. Vörösmarty. 2005. Arctic system on trajectory to new, seasonally ice-free state. EOS 86:309, 312-313.

PAME. in press. Arctic marine shipping assessment. Protection of the Arctic Marine Environment, Akureyri.

Perovich, D. K., J. A. Richter-Menge, K. F. Jones, and B. Light. 2008. Sunlight, water, and ice: Extreme Arctic sea ice melt during the summer of 2007. Geophysical Research Letters 35: L11501.

Plagányi, É. E., and D. S. Butterworth. 2005. Indirect fishery interactions. Pages 19-46 in J. E. R. III, W. F. Perrin, R. R. Reeves, S. Montgomery, and T. J. Ragen, editors. Marine mammal research: conservation beyond crisis. Johns Hopkins, Baltimore.

Ragen, T. J., H. P. Huntington, and G. K. Hovelsrud. 2008. Conservation of Arctic marine mammals faced with climate change. Ecological Applications 18:S166-S174.

Richter-Menge, J., J. Comiso, W. Meier, S. Nghiem, and D. Perovich. 2008. Sea ice. Arctic Report Cards.

Romanovsky, V. E., M. Burgess, S. Smith, K. Yoshikawa, and J. Brown. 2002. Permafrost temperature records: indicators of climate change. EOS 83:589.

Serreze, M. C., J. E. Walsh, F. S. Chapin, T. Osterkamp, M. Dyurgerov, V. Romanovsky, W. C. Oechel, J. Morison, T. Zhang, and R. G. Barry. 2000. Observational evidence of recent change in the northern high-latitude environment. Climatic Change 46:159-207.

Stiansen, J. E., and A. A. Filin. 2007. Joint PINRO/IMR report on the state of the Barents Sea ecosystem 2006, with expected situation and considerations for management.

Stroeve, J., M. M. Holland, W. Meier, T. Scambos, and M. Serreze. 2007. Arctic sea ice decline: Faster than forecast. Geophysical Research Letters 34: L09501.

UNEP/GRID-Arendal. 2007. Protected areas and wilderness (http://maps.grida.no/go/graphic/protected-areas-and-wilderness).

Vilhjálmsson, H., and A. H. Hoel. 2005. Fisheries and aquaculture. Pages 691-780 in ACIA, editor. Arctic climate impact assessment. Cambridge University Press, Cambridge.

Walsh, J. E. 2008. Climate of the arctic marine environment. Ecological Applications 18:S3-S22.

Winton, M. 2006. Does the Arctic sea ice have a tipping point? Geophysical Research Letters 33: L235504.

Appendix 9. MARINE FISHERIES

U. Rashid Sumaila (University of British Columbia, r.sumaila@fisheries.ubc.ca)
William W.L. Cheung (University of East Anglia, william.cheung@uea.ac.uk)
Sylvie Guénette (University of British Columbia, guenette@agrocampus-ouest.fr)

SUMMARY

▸ There is a growing scientific consensus based on models and observations that human impacts including fishing, climate change, pollution, eutrophication and species introductions, could lead to severe changes in the structure of marine trophic webs, causing the loss of marine biodiversity and the depletion of ocean fishery resources.

▸ The combined action of all stressors will increasingly drive marine ecosystem functions towards a tipping point characterized by changes in the composition of marine communities, namely by the collapse of populations of large predators and a shift towards more resilient communities dominated by organisms lower in the food-chain such as jellyfishes.

▸ Currently, the most vulnerable marine species are already under serious threat from overfishing, habitat destruction and other direct human impacts. In addition, negative impacts of climate change, including ocean warming and acidification, over sensitive species and ecosystems such as coral reef and other calcifying organisms constitute an additional threat to marine life.

▸ Some models predict that distribution shift of marine species under climate change would result in high biodiversity impacts in the tropics, polar regions and semi-enclosed seas. Moreover, models project that under current trends in fishing and climate change, potential fisheries catch will redistribute away from tropical countries, that is, parts of the world where food security is a critical issue.

▸ Allowing global ocean fisheries to reach a tipping-point will not only affect marine biodiversity but it will also undermine life on the planet because of the immense importance of the global ocean to biogeochemical cycles.

▸ The implication of reaching the tipping-point for the major marine ecosystem services, particularly fish production, will be severely affected. Total fish catch in the global ocean may be reduced to up to a tenth of its peak amount by 2048, this will result in significant negative economic and social effects, especially, on some of the world's most vulnerable human communities. Experience from previous cases of stock collapses illustrates the scale of the problem, e.g., collapse of the Canadian northern cod stocks.

▸ Global to local scale actions are urgently needed to prevent fisheries from reaching a tipping-point. At the global scale, institutional and governance structures need to be developed to stop overfishing and limit the emission of greenhouse gases. At the national scale, governments need to pursue efforts to stop illegal, unreported and unregulated fishing, manage marine resources appropriately and remove subsidies that that promote overfishing and excessive capacity. The private sector should pledge to be environmentally sustainable and socially responsible. The public at large should demand that politicians and corporate leaders put in place institutions, structures and policies, both market and non-market, to tackle the problems facing global ocean fisheries.

DESCRIPTION

Fisheries resources in the global ocean are already under severe pressure of over-exploitation. Global capture production increased rapidly since 1950 and peaked at around 90 tonnes in the 2000s (FAO 2009) (Figure 1). However, if fisheries production reported from the highly productive and variable Peruvian anchovy catch are excluded from the statistics, global fisheries catch has been gradually declining since the late 1980s (Pauly et al. 2002). Currently, of all the marine fish stocks reported in the catch statistics, 19% are overexploited, 8% are depleted, 52% are fully exploited, 20% are moderately exploited, and only 1% demonstrated signs of recovery from overexploitation. The main drivers of overfishing include excess demand for seafood from growing world population rising incomes and consumption per capita, over-capacity fuelled by adverse subsidies, open access to fisheries resources, short-term economic profits and inadequate governance.

Excessive fishing has serious impacts on the resources, on the habitat and accompanying fauna, and on the long-term functioning and productivity of the oceans (e.g., Pauly et al. 2002, Worm et al. 2006). Overfishing has depleted many large-bodied predatory fishes. Fish catch becomes increasingly dominated by species lower in the food-chain, a phenomenon known as 'fishing down marine foodweb' (Pauly et al. 1998). It also threatens the long-term survival of marine species, particularly those that are vulnerable to fishing (Hutchings and Reynolds 2004). For example, some species that have particularly vulnerability life history or ecology such as certain species of groupers, sharks and rays have been listed under the IUCN Red List of Endangered Species (www.redlist.org) because of over-exploitation, with the international trading of a few fish and invertebrates listed by CITES (the Convention on International Trade in Endangered Species). Besides, over-exploitation results in substantial economic loss to the fishing industries and communities (World Bank and FAO 2008). The long-term sustainability (ecological, economic and social) of many fish stocks in the world is in jeopardy (Pauly et al. 2002, Worm et al. 2006).

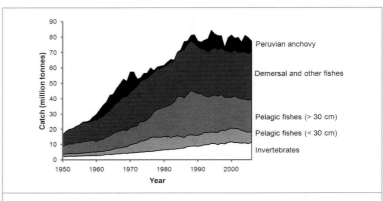

FIGURE 1

Time-series of global reported catch from 1950 to 2004. Data are from the Sea Around Us Project (www.seaaroundus.org). Data are mainly based on the fisheries statistics from the Food and Agriculture Organization of the United Nations (FAO) with modification with more reliable data when appropriate.

Given the current projections of increasing human populations and consumption per capita, it is likely that there will be sustained or increasing demand for food from the ocean. Traditional fisheries resources have generally reached maximum capacity. Exploring global fisheries scenarios using ecosystem models suggest that further increase in fisheries production from the current level may only be achieved by expanding fishing to species that are not preferred by the current markets (e.g., small fish or even jellyfish). This will also involve trade-offs with diversity where increasing landings would result in the decline of mean trophic level of most marine ecosystems (Alder et al. 2007).

The combined effects of overfishing and other human stressors increases the susceptibility of the ecosystem to reach a threshold tipping point where the structure of marine trophic web suffers a sudden drastic change, shifting towards more simplified communities, resulting in biodiversity loss, productivity and disruption of ecosystem functions. The major stressors include climate change, habitat destruction, pollution and introductions of invasive alien species. Observations and model projections show that long term changes in ocean conditions are happening, e.g., ocean warming, acidification, expansion of oxygen minimum zones, retreat of sea ice. Also, increased nutrient inputs from human sources have lead to a large number of hypoxic/anoxic "dead zones" where most animals could not survive. The number of such "dead zones" may increase in the future. Increased shipping and expansion of aquaculture further increased the risk of introduction of invasive species. Particularly, depleted ecosystems may become more susceptible to impacts from these human stressors. There are examples of some heavily impacted ecosystems that have already reached such tipping points. The resulted ecological and socio-economic consequences are large.

IMPACTS ON BIODIVERSITY

The global ocean makes up 99% of the living space on the planet (Mitchell 2009), and covers about 70% of the total surface area of the planet. These numbers coupled with the fact that life on oceans constitutes the foundation of many trophic webs topped by terrestrial organisms, and that oceans play a key role on the regulation of biogeochemical cycles, ascribe a crucial role to oceans regarding the maintenance of life on Earth.

Combinations of myriad human-induced stressors are causing altered marine biodiversity, including reduced species diversity, reduced abundance, changes in latitudinal and depth distribution, altered age and sex structures, altered temporal and spatial spawning patterns, reduced viability of offspring, and reduced genetic diversity.

Genetic level impacts

Fishing tends to select fishes of particular economic importance (e.g., large and older individuals of a species) and can cause mortalities that are often higher than natural predation, and therefore could exert a strong selection force on the exploited fish populations and communities. Two main impacts of overfishing on the genetic diversity that could be expected are the following: (1) changes on the species' phenotypes (i.e., traits, reaction norms, or how individuals respond to changes, and behavior), and (2) reduction or changes in species' genetic variability and heterozygosity. Fisheries-induced changes in life-history are observed in exploited marine populations, e.g., reductions in size at maturity (e.g., rock lobster and Pacific salmon) and reductions in age at maturity (e.g., cod, haddock, flatfish, and Atlantic salmon), and delayed spawning (e.g., herring) – due to the high mortality of larger individuals selected by fishing. Particularly, many of these cases demonstrated that fisheries-induced changes in fishes' life history strategies are not easily reversible, as demonstrated by case studies. For example, the heavily fished New Zealand snapper showed a five times reduction in its effective population and the reduction of its heterozygosity (Hauser et al. 2002). Moreover, large decreases in the spawning aggregation of the orange roughy in New Zealand resulted in significant reduction in genetic diversity (Smith et al. 1991). Such reduction in genetic diversity from over-exploitation may have reached a tipping point over which recovery of genetic diversity is not possible.

Species level impacts

Severe overexploitation can lead to large reduction of the marine animal populations to the extent that they become threatened, endangered, or even locally extinct. Large predatory fishes are particularly vulnerable to overexploitation due to their high economic value, and due to their life history traits. These species tend to be characterized by a large body size, high longevity, high age at maturity and low growth rates (Cheung at al. 2007). All these features contribute to slow recovery rates from overfishing. When subjected to large population declines over a certain threshold, some populations may not be able to recover, and some species may even become threatened with extinction. For example, overfishing has contributed to the listing of 20 species of groupers (e.g. *Epinephelus lanceolatus*, *Mycteroperca rosacea*) as threatened with extinction (critically endangered, endangered or vulnerable) under the IUCN Red List of Endangered Species (Polidoro et al. 2008). Similarly, among the 21 ocean pelagic shark and ray species assessed under the IUCN-World Conservation Union Red List criteria, 11 species (e.g., *Carcharhinus longimanus*, *Alopias superciliosus*) are classified as globally threatened with higher risk of extinction as a result of unsustainable fishing (Dulvy et al. 2008a).

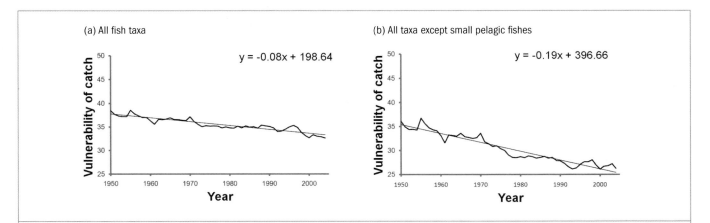

FIGURE 2

Intrinsic vulnerability – a measure of the inherent capacity to response to fishing pressure – of fish in each year's global catch has decreased consistently and significantly since the 1950s because the vulnerable species are depleted early while the ocean becomes increasingly dominated by more resilient species, mainly small fishes and invertebrates that can sustain high fishing pressure. (Cheung et al. 2007): (a) All fish taxa and (b) all fish taxa except small pelagic fishes. When data of small pelagic fish are removed from analysis, the decrease in stocks ability to respond to fishing pressure (see text) becomes more apparent (Source: redrawn from Cheung et al. 2007).

Ecosystem level impacts

Overexploitation and depletion of marine species may pull ecosystems to tipping points. Depleted marine populations may not be able to recover from overexploitation even if fishing stops (Mace et al. 2005), and changes in the structure of marine communities may last for long. Fishing leads to long-term changes in community structure. Since 1950, abundance of large fishes in the global ocean declined and the ocean becomes increasingly dominated by small-bodied, fast-growing species that could sustain human disturbance (Figure 2). Such changes in community structure are irreversible in some cases. For example, the Canadian cod stocks (*Gadus morhua*) collapsed in the late 1980s because of overexploitation. Despite the closure of the fisheries from 1992 until now, there is little sign of population recovery. It is suggested that the depletion of cod and other top predatory species have led to a shift to an ecosystem structure that does not favour cod. The system is now dominated by small pelagics and benthic macroinvertebrates – e.g., the northern snow crab (*Chionoecetes opilio*) and northern shrimp (*Pandalus borealis*).

Combined effects from different human stressors

The risk of surpassing ecosystem tipping points can be substantially increased by the combined impacts from other human stressors. For instance, the depletion of large pelagic predators combined with the loading in nutrients from intensive agriculture and the introduction of a jellyfish invasive species has provoked, through a trophic cascade, a drastic change in the structure of Black Sea communities involving the dominance of jellyfish and severe collapse of fisheries (Daskalov 2002). A recent work by Richardson et al. (2009) discusses the emergent threat of jellyfish outbreaks for marine biodiversity. Several human induced drivers, such as overfishing of predatory fish (which are both predators and competitors of jellyfish), eutrophication and climate change can trigger jellyfish booms. Once jellyfish have the conditions to become dominant, a feedback mechanism that perpetuates their dominance is thought to occur, intensifying the decline of other species. Briefly, in the presence of depleted fish stocks, jellyfish abundance increases, due to low predation and competition. Then, the competitive pressure of jellyfish becomes very strong as jellyfish will compete for food and also predate fish eggs and larvae. Under this scenario, there is an uncontrolled growth of jellyfish and their continuous expansion to neighbouring areas.

Climate change causes long-term changes in ocean conditions, which will have numerous impacts on marine ecosystems (e.g. Easterling et al. 2007, Cheung et al. 2009a). Observations and theory indicate that exploited marine species may respond to ocean warming by shifting their latitudinal and depth ranges (Perry et al. 2005, Dulvy et al. 2008b, Cheung et al. 2009a). Such species responses may lead to local extinction and invasions (Figure 3). Also, the timing and location of biological phenomenon such as plankton blooms have changed following changes in environmental conditions (Edwards and Richardson 2004). Moreover, even more worrying is that climate change is modifying the chemistry of the ocean, which can result in devastating consequences, e.g., ocean acidification is caused by the increased uptake of carbon dioxide into the ocean. Ocean acidification may have large impacts on marine organisms through negatively affecting the calcification of calcium carbonate skeletons and other body structure, as well as other physiological processes.

Specifically, some marine ecosystems are more vulnerability to climate change impacts. For example, coral reef is identified as a very vulnerable ecosystem to climate change through intensified coral bleaching (the loss of symbiotic algae in coral, leading to what is described in the literature as coral bleaching) from ocean warming, reduced light penetration (for photosynthesis) because of rising sea level, and ocean acidification. Such adverse climate change effects reduce the resilience of the ecosystem to other human impacts. This may lead to a rapid shift in ecosystem structure, affecting overall productivity and community structure, and thus the available fisheries resources.

ECOSYSTEM SERVICES

Global oceans provide a broad range of ecosystem services at local to global scales that will be seriously degraded as a result of widespread overfishing and global change. A comprehensive valuation of the global ocean and the habitats it contains has to include direct use values, indirect use values, option values, existence values and bequest values (Berman and Sumaila 2006).

Direct use values may be generated through the consumptive or non-consumptive use of ocean resources such as food fish and whale watching. Indirect use values are related with services that are used as

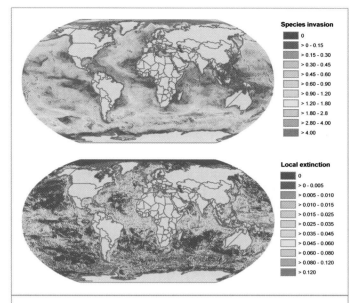

Species invasion

- 0
- > 0 - 0.15
- > 0.15 - 0.30
- > 0.30 - 0.45
- > 0.45 - 0.60
- > 0.60 - 0.90
- > 0.90 - 1.20
- > 1.20 - 1.80
- > 1.80 - 2.8
- > 2.80 - 4.00
- > 4.00

Local extinction

- 0
- > 0 - 0.005
- > 0.005 - 0.010
- > 0.010 - 0.015
- > 0.015 - 0.025
- > 0.025 - 0.035
- > 0.035 - 0.045
- > 0.045 - 0.060
- > 0.060 - 0.080
- > 0.080 - 0.120
- > 0.120

FIGURE 3

Predicted distribution of biodiversity impact due to warming-induced range shifts in marine metazoans by 2050 under the IPCC SRES A1B scenario. Biodiversity impact is expressed in terms of (a) invasion intensity and (b) local extinction intensity, for 1,066 species of fish and invertebrates. Redrawn from Cheung et al. 2009a.

intermediate inputs to the production of goods and services to humans, such as water cycling, waste assimilation and other services leading to clean air and water. Option values are related with the potential services and goods that oceans may provide in the future, even if they are not still identified. This includes many ocean species that have yet to be identified, and also well-known species that can possess characteristics which will have future use or non-use values. For instance, a few decades ago, black cod of the northern Pacific has low economic value because no one would eat it. This situation has changed and now this species evolved into a big export commodity for British Columbia and some USA states (Sumaila et al. 2007a). Finally, existence value is the value conferred by humans on the ecosystem regardless of its use value, this value may arise from aesthetic, ethical, moral or religious considerations, and bequest value is the value ascribed to a resource considering its relevance for the well-being of future generations (Sumaila and Walters 2005).

Marine fisheries generate economic revenues, support livelihoods and provide food for human and cultured animals, and are a major ecosystem service provided by the ocean. Financially, the gross revenue generated directly by global capture fisheries was estimated to be about $US 85 billion in 2004 value (Sumaila et al. 2007b, The World Bank and FAO 2008). Marine fish and shellfish remain as an important source of animal protein. Fish contributes to 15.3% of world's total animal protein intake in 2005 (FAO 2009). In coastal Low-Income Food-Deficient Countries (LIFDCs), fish contributes at least 20% of animal protein intake (FAO 2009, Swartz and Pauly 2008). Global per capita fish consumption has been increasing steadily in the past four decades (FAO 2009). Fishing is the major, and in many cases, the only available livelihood for many coastal communities.

Global fisheries economics may work like a ratchet that drives marine ecosystems to their tipping points. Currently, global fisheries are economically over-fished. It is estimated that the total net profit of the global fisheries is negative and in the order of $US 5 billion in 2004 value (The World Bank and FAO 2008). The negative net profit is mainly caused by the loss of fisheries productivity resulted from over-exploitation of many fisheries resources in the world. However, the fishing sectors receive substantial subsidies from government that amounts to as much as US$ 34 billion globally (Sumaila and Pauly 2006). These subsidies promote and maintain excessive fishing capacity, leading to further over-exploitation of fisheries resources. Given the socio-economic importance of marine fisheries, the implications of the tipping point for human-wellings are big. This can be illustrated by previous cases of fisheries collapses such as the Canadian cod fisheries.

The alteration of ocean conditions, due to climate change, will further increase the vulnerability of countries to the impacts from ecosystems be driven over tipping points. Recent studies suggest that climate change may lead to large-scale redistribution of potential catch with tropical countries suffering substantial losses and high-latitude countries enjoying significant gains (Cheung et al. 2009b). Climate change may further exacerbate the stress on the already over-exploited stocks (e.g., reef-associated species, Hoegh-Guldberg et al. 2007). The combination of overfishing, climate change and other human stresses may drive marine ecosystems toward the tipping point for functional collapse. This may have serious socio-economic consequences for fisheries-dependent communities, particularly the tropical developing countries that are vulnerable to climate change impacts (Allison et al. 2009, Cheung et al. 2010).

UNCERTAINTIES

Despite the uncertainties associated with future projection of changes in marine ecosystems and fisheries, it is very likely that excessive overfishing, particularly in combination with other human stressors, will drive marine ecosystems to tipping points. Assessing the impacts of overfishing on marine biodiversity can be challenging because of the lack of time-series data for the assessment of the conservation status of many marine species, and the difficulty of effectively sampling a sufficient portion of the ocean for the assessment of the status of many marine species. Currently, only a small fraction of marine species have been assessed in terms of their extinction risks using the IUCN Red List of Endangered Species Criteria, although there are various efforts to increase the Red List assessment of major marine species. Moreover, the extent of overfishing impacts on marine biodiversity and habitats through trophic interactions, ecosystem functions, and evolutionary changes of marine species, are only beginning to be explored and understood.

Because of the complex interactions between ecosystem components and human activities, projections from models that predict future changes in ecosystem structure, biodiversity and ecosystem goods and services are uncertain. Particularly, such projections often require the integration outputs from coupled ocean-atmosphere climate models, biogeochemical – lower trophic level-upper trophic level ecosystem models. Development and exploration of such models have only been started recently and the effects of the propagation of uncertainties amongst these models are yet to be properly assessed. Moreover, there are uncertainties over the scenarios of future global changes (e.g., demography, climate, markets). However, there are several examples that signal the risk incurred by weakening the ecosystem structures that develop gradually over long periods, before the tipping point is reached.

LOCAL TO GLOBAL ACTION AND OPPORTUNITIES

The future state of marine biodiversity and fisheries depends on the concerted action of several sectors of society from global to local levels (Sumaila et al. 2008, Gilman and Lundin 2009). The international community and leaders need to undertake actions to deal with global threats, such as climate change impacts, and demand global binding solutions. National governments need to stop illegal, unreported and unregulated fishing and remove subsidies that contribute to harm the environment and undermine our common future (Sumaila et al. 2008). Companies in the private sector should compromise to act according to environmentally and social responsible lines of action. Finally, public at large should demand that politicians and corporate leaders put in place institutions, structures and policies, both market and non-market, to tackle the problems facing global ocean fisheries. More specifically, opportunities for action include:

Global actions
- Co-ordinate international efforts to reduce greenhouse gas emissions, and to increase the adaptive capacity of developing countries to face climate change impacts on fisheries;
- Stop illegal, unreported and unregulated fishing and ban the use of bottom destroying fishing gear;
- Augment progress in the integration of fishery-depended datasets and research survey datasets so that they are made interpretable and can be pooled for large-scale analyses. This is important, because human threats to biodiversity, including from commercial fisheries, occur across large spatial and temporal scales. Therefore, biodiversity and ecosystem monitoring, forecasting and risk assessments, such as improved understanding of tipping point thresholds, require data to be organized in a global, integrated infrastructure, such as provided by the Global Biodiversity Information Facility and Ocean Biogeographic Information System.

Local and regional actions
- Implement comprehensive and integrated ecosystem-based approaches to manage human activities (e.g. aquaculture, fisheries, coastal development) in coasts and oceans, and to manage disaster risk reduction and climate change adaptation;
- Reduce fishing capacity and rebuild over-exploited ecosystems; this could be achieved partly by eliminating subsidies to the fishing industry that promote overfishing and excessive capacity;
- Adopt environmentally-friendly and fuel efficient fishing and aquaculture practices and integrate 'climate-proof' aquaculture with other sectors;

- ‣ Strengthen our knowledge of aquatic ecosystem dynamics and biogeochemical cycles, particularly at local and regional levels;
- ‣ Strengthen the adaptive capacity of local populations to climate change impacts by conducting local climate change assessments of vulnerability and risk and through an investment in raising people's awareness, namely in schools and among stakeholders.

REFERENCES

Alder J., S. Guénette, J. Beblow, W. Cheung, and V. Christensen. 2007. Ecosystem-based global fishing policy scenarios. Fisheries Centre Research Reports 15 (7).

Allison, E. H., A. L. Perry, M. Badjeck, W., Neil Adger, K. Brown, D. Conway, A. S., Halls, G. M., Pilling, J. D., Reynolds, N. L., Andrew, and N. K. Dulvy. 2009. Vulnerability of national economies to the impacts of climate change on fisheries. Fish and Fisheries 10:173-196.

Brander, K. 2008. Tackling the old familiar problems of pollution, habitat alteration and overfishing will help with adapting to climate change. Marine Pollution Bulletin 56:1957-1958.

Cheung, W. W. L., R. Watson, T. Morato, T. J. Pitcher, and D. Pauly. 2007. Intrinsic vulnerability in the global fish catch. Marine Ecology Progress Series 333:1-12.

Cheung, W. W. L., V. W. Y. Lam, J. L. Sarmiento, K. Kearney, R. Watson, D. Zeller, and D. Pauly. 2010. Large-scale redistribution of maximum fisheries catch potential in the global ocean under climate change. Global Change Biology 16:24-35.

Cheung, W. W., V. W. Lam, J. L. Sarmiento, K. Kearney, R. Watson, and D. Pauly. 2009. Projecting global marine biodiversity impacts under climate change scenarios. Fish and Fisheries 10:235-251.

Daskalov, G. M. 2002. Overfishing drives a trophic cascade in the Black Sea. Marine Ecology Progress Series 225:53–63.

Dulvy, N. K., J. K. Baum, S. Clarke, L. J. V. Compagno, E. Cortés, A. Domingo, S. Fordham, S. Fowler, M. P. Francis, C. Gibson, J. Martínez, J. A. Musick, A. Soldo, J. D. Stevens, and S. Valenti. 2008a. You can swim but you can't hide: the global status and conservation of oceanic pelagic sharks and rays. Aquatic Conservation: Marine and Freshwater Ecosystems 18:459-482.

Dulvy, N. K., S. I. Rogers, S. Jennings, V. Stelzenmüller, S. R. Dye, and H. R. Skjoldal. 2008b. Climate change and deepening of the North Sea fish assemblage: a biotic indicator of warming seas. Journal of Applied Ecology 45:1029-1039.

Easterling, W. E., P. K. Aggarwal, P. Batima, K. M. Brander, L. Erda, S. M. Howden, A. Kirilenko, J. Morton, J. F. Soussana, J. Schmidhuber, and others. 2007. Food, fibre and forest products. Climate change 2007: Impacts, adaptation and vulnerability. Contribution of working group II to the fourth assessment report of the intergovernmental Panel on Climate Change:273–313.

Edwards, M., and A. J. Richardson. 2004. Impact of climate change on marine pelagic phenology and trophic mismatch. Nature 430: 881-884.

FAO. 2009. The state of world fisheries and aquaculture 2008. FAO Fisheries and Aquaculture Department. Food and Agriculture Organization of the United Nations, Rome, 2009. 196 pp.

Gilman, E., and C. Lundin. 2009. Minimizing bycatch of sensitive species groups in marine capture fisheries: lessons from commercial tuna fisheries in Q. Grafton, R. Hillborn, D. Squires, M. Tait, and M. Williams, editors. Handbook of marine fisheries conservation and management. Oxford University Press.

Hauser, L., G. J. Adcock, P. J. Smith, J. H. Bernal Ramírez, and G. R. Carvalho. 2002. Loss of microsatellite diversity and low effective population size in an overexploited population of New Zealand snapper (*Pagrus auratus*). Proceedings of the National Academy of Sciences of the United States of America 99: 11742.

Hoegh-Guldberg, O., P. J. Mumby, A. J. Hooten, R. S. Steneck, P. Greenfield, E. Gomez, C. D. Harvell, P. F. Sale, A. J. Edwards, K. Caldeira, N. Knowlton, C. M. Eakin, R. Iglesias-Prieto, N. Muthiga, R. H. Bradbury, A. Dubi, and M. E. Hatziolos. 2007. Coral Reefs under rapid climate change and ocean acidification. Science 318:1737-1742

Hutchings, J. A., and J. D. Reynolds. 2004. Marine fish population collapses: consequences for recovery and extinction risk. BioScience 54: 297-309.

Mace, G., H. Masundire, J. Baillie, T. Ricketts, T. Brooks, and M. Hoffmann. 2005. Biodiversity in R. Hassan, R. Scholes, and N. Ash, editors, Ecosystems and human wellbeing: current state and trends, vol 1. Findings of the condition and trends working group of the Millennium Ecosystem Assessment. Washington, DC: Island Press.

Mitchell, A. 2009. Seasick: ocean change and the extinction of life on Earth. Alanna Mitchell. University of Chicago Press, Chicago.

Pauly, D., V. Christensen, J. Dalsgaard, R. Froese, and F.C. Torres Jr. 1998. Fishing down marine food webs. Science 279: 860-863.

Pauly, D., V. Christensen, S. Guénette, T. J. Pitcher, U. R. Sumaila, C. J. Walters, R. Watson, and D. Zeller. 2002. Towards sustainability in world fisheries. Nature 418:689–695.

Perry, A. L., P. J. Low, J. R. Ellis, and J. D. Reynolds. 2005. Climate change and distribution shifts in marine fishes. Science 308: 1912-1915.

Polidoro, B. A., S. R. Livingstone, K. E. Carpenter, B. Hutchinson, R. B. Mast, N. Pilcher, Y. Sadovy de Mitcheson, and S. Valenti. 2008. Status of the world's marine species. *In* J.-C. Vié, C. Hilton-Taylor, and S. N. Stuart, editors. The 2008 review of the IUCN Red List of Threatened Species. IUCN, Gland, Switzerland.

Richardson, A. J., A. Bakun, G. C. Hays, and M. J. Gibbons. 2009. The jellyfish joyride: causes, consequences and management responses to a more gelatinous future. Trends in Ecology and Evolution 24:312–322.

Smith, P. J., R. Francis, and M. McVeagh. 1991. Loss of genetic diversity due to fishing pressure. Fisheries Research 10: 309-316.

Sumaila, U. R., and C. Walters. 2005. Intergenerational discounting: a new intuitive approach. Ecological Economics 52: 135–142.

Sumaila, U.R., and D. Pauly. 2006. Catching more bait: a bottom-up re-estimation of global fisheries subsidies. Fisheries Centre Research Reports 14:114.

Sumaila, U. R., L. Teh, R. Watson, P. Tyedmers, and D. Pauly. 2008. Fuel price increase, subsidies, overcapacity, and resource sustainability. ICES Journal of Marine Science 65: 832-840.

Sumaila, U. R., J. Volpe, and Y. Liu. 2007a. Potential economic benefits from sablefish farming in British Columbia. Marine Policy 31: 81-84.

Sumaila, U. R., D. Marsden, R. Watson, and D. Pauly. 2007b. Global ex-vessel fish price database: construction and applications Journal of Bioeconomics 9: 39-51.

Swartz, W. and D. Pauly. 2008. Who's eating all the fish? The food security rationale for culling Cetaceans. A report to humane society. Presented at IWC 60, June 23, 2008. Santiago, Chile. 36 pp.

The World Bank and FAO. 2008. The sunken billions – the economic justification for fisheries reform. Agricultural and Rural Development Department. The World Bank. Washington DC. 86 pp.

Worm, B., E. B. Barbier, N. Beaumont, J. E. Duffy, C. Folke, B. S. Halpern, J. B. C. Jackson, H. K. Lotze, F. Micheli, S. R. Palumbi, E. Sala, K. A. Selkoe, J. J. Stachowicz, and R. Watson. 2006. Impacts of Biodiversity Loss on Ocean Ecosystem Services. Science 314:787-790.

Appendix 10. TROPICAL CORAL REEFS

Joana Figueiredo (University of Lisbon, jcfigueiredo@fc.ul.pt)

SUMMARY

▸ Coral reef ecosystems are global biodiversity hotspots that depend on the massive calcium carbonate structures mainly deposited by scleractinian (i.e., "hard") corals. Scleractinian coral distribution is primarily limited by sea-surface temperature, light, depth, ocean pH, sea water salinity, nutrients and sediment loads. These ecosystems are currently threatened by localized stresses such as overfishing and destructive fishing practices, pollution, terrestrial nutrient and sediment run-off, but are increasing impacted by direct and indirect impacts of rising CO_2 concentrations and climate change.

▸ Coral reefs provide a broad range of ecosystems services with high socio-economic value: tourism, fisheries (food and employment), nutrient cycling, climate regulation, protection of the shoreline and other ecosystems (e.g. mangroves), and constitute the habitat for a wide range of species.

▸ Rising atmospheric CO_2 concentrations have already led to a slight acidification of ocean surface waters and are projected to lead to levels of acidification that will severely impede calcium carbonate accretion. Global warming associated with greenhouse gas emissions has resulted in increased sea-surface temperatures, leading to frequent coral bleaching. Acidification and the increased frequency of local and global disturbances are projected to seriously degrade coral reefs world-wide.

▸ If current trends continue coral reef ecosystems may undergo regime shifts from coral to sponge or algae dominated habitats. The tipping point for this phase shift is estimated to be a sea-surface temperature increase of 2°C and/or atmospheric CO_2 concentrations above 480 ppm (estimated to occur by 2050).

▸ Shifts in dominance from corals to sponges or algae would have dramatic consequences for coral reef communities. The reduction of habitat complexity through erosion would reduce the niches for numerous species that rely on corals for shelter, food, substrate, settlement and nursery.

▸ In order to avoid this phase shift, urgent local and global action is necessary. Reducing local stresses, such as the reduction of terrestrial inputs of sediment, nutrients and pollutants, is paramount to promote a higher resistance to disturbance and ensure ecosystem resilience. Fisheries require the sustainable management of marine species and should aim to conserve key functional groups such as herbivores that control algae growth. Marine protected areas networks should be designed and implemented to provide refuges and serve as larval sources to replenish harvested areas outside reserves. Globally, urgent and ambitious action to reduce CO_2 emissions is necessary to limit sea surface temperature increase and water acidification.

DESCRIPTION

Status and Trends

Coral reef ecosystems are found throughout the world's tropical seas and are some of the most productive marine ecosystems. Coral reefs are largely constructed of calcium carbonate deposited over centuries by the activity of scleractinian (i.e., "hard") corals. The largest number of scleractinian coral species occurs in the Indo-Pacific region with around 80 genera and 700 species and constitutes a global biodiversity hotspot. Although scleractinian corals constitute the basic reef structure, reefs are inhabited by a myriad of species that depend on it for substrate, shelter, feeding, reproduction and settlement. The taxonomic groups inhabiting the reefs vary from calcareous algae to gorgonians, soft corals, mollusks, echinoderms, polychaete worms, sponges, and fishes.

Scleractinian coral development is constrained by several physical factors, with temperature the most limiting. Scleractinian corals only develop in locations where the mean annual sea temperature is above 18°C, optimally between 23-25°C, with some corals temporarily tolerating 36-40°C. This thermal tolerance means that hard corals do not develop on tropical coasts where upwelling (cooler water that

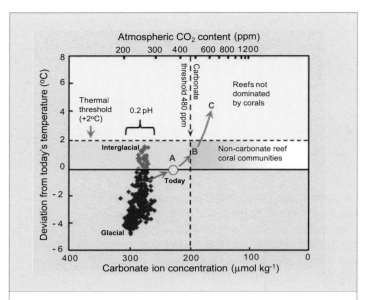

FIGURE 1

Temperature, $[CO_2]_{atm}$, and carbonate-ion concentrations reconstructed for the past 420,000 years. Carbonate concentrations were calculated from CO_2 atm and temperature deviations from today's conditions with the Vostok Ice Core data set, assuming constant salinity (34 parts per thousand), mean sea temperature (25°C), and total alkalinity (2300 mmol kg^{-1}). Temperature, atmospheric CO_2 concentrations and sea-water carbonate-ion concentrations were reconstructed for the past 420,000 years using data from the Vostok Ice Core data set (see Hoegh-Guldberg et al. 2007 for methods). The thresholds for major changes to coral communities are indicated for thermal stress (+2°C) and atmospheric CO_2 concentrations 480 ppm. Points and red arrows indicate projected pathways of temperature and CO_2 concentrations (A = state in ca. 2005, B = projected state in mid-century and C = projected for end of the 21st century in "business as usual scenarios". Source: Hoegh-Guldberg et al. 2007.

surfaces from greater depths) occurs, such as the west coast of South America. Scleractinian corals have a symbiotic relationship with zooxanthellae, endosymbiotic algae that, through photosynthesis provide energy to the coral (almost 90% of coral energy requirements) in the form of glucose, glycerol and amino acids; in return, the coral provides the zooxanthellae with protection, shelter, nutrients (especially nitrogen and phosphorus) and a constant supply of CO_2 required for the photosynthesis. Corals may briefly survive without the algae (for example, during bleaching events when the algae are expelled and the coral appear white after the loss of the pigmented zooxanthellae) but their health will be greatly reduced, particularly for energy-costly processes like lesion repair, growth and reproduction (Fine and Loya 2002). For the zooxanthellae to perform photosynthesis, corals usually inhabit depths above 25 m (maximum 50-70 m depth). A high sediment load, besides clogging the coral feeding structures and smothering them, also increases turbidity and reduces access to light (Anthony and Connolly 2004). This is the main reason why corals are absent in areas where rivers of tropical regions discharge to the oceans, such as the Amazon River. Corals occur in waters with salinity 32-35 ppt and do not support air exposure.

The unsustainable fishing practices on coral reefs can reduce fish populations to unviable levels, and ultimately disturbs all trophic levels. Robbins et al. (2006) found the overharvesting of top predators (i.e. sharks) can impact the entire community since their ecosystem function was diminished. Similarly, on coral reefs, the removal of herbivores is known to upset the competitive balance between coral and algae. In the 80's, a loss of herbivores due to overfishing combined with an acute disease outbreak resulted in considerable coral mortality which resulted in a phase shift from coral-dominated Caribbean reefs to algal-dominated communities (Hughes 1994).

The marine ornamental aquarium trade continues to rely on wild caught organisms (e.g. corals, fish, crustaceans and clams, etc.), particularly from Southeast Asia. Furthermore, many collected organisms die during transportation before arriving at their final destination (mainly U.S.A., Europe and Japan). The removal of reproductive individuals combined with destructive collecting techniques (e.g. cyanide) and damage/death of non-target species damages wild populations and jeopardizes its sustainability (FAO 2009).

Land use activities, namely agriculture, sewage treatment, increased runoff, and coastal zone modification (house and harbour construction in coastal areas, dredging, etc.) contribute with the addition of contaminants, nutrients and sediments to the water (Buddemeier et al. 2004). Toxic or bioactive contaminants (including heavy metals, pesticides/herbicides and fuel) are discharged in the ocean and absorbed in the sediments. The increased nutrient load promotes phytoplankton blooms (which reduces water clarity and light availability) and algal growth that compete with corals. As previously mentioned, increased sediment flux reduces light access (and the ability of zooxanthellae to photosynthesize) and can interfere with coral feeding ability. Coral reef ecosystems can undergo a phase shift from predominantly coral cover to fleshy algae cover, each state having its own inherent resilience and resistance. Nevertheless, there are other possible phase shifts (Bellwood et al. 2004) (Figure 2).

Coral reef ecosystems are declining in productivity and experiencing a dramatic phase shift in dominant species due to intensified human disturbance such as over-harvesting, pollution, increased nutrient and sediment loads and the direct and indirect impacts of climate change, particularly sea-surface temperature increase and ocean acidification (Hughes et al. 2005, Anthony et al. 2007).

Tipping point mechanisms

One of the greatest future threats to the coral reef ecosystems is climate change. Over the 20th century, atmospheric CO_2 concentrations increased from ca. 280 ppm to 367 ppm (IPCC 2007) (Figure 1). Present levels exceed 380 ppm, which is more than 80 ppm above the maximum values of the past 740000 years, if not 20 million years (Hoegh-Gulberg et al. 2007).

Based on IPCC (2007) emissions scenarios, atmospheric CO_2 levels may increase to ca. 460-620 ppm by 2050 and 480-1100 ppm by 2100. The world's oceans are absorbing 25-33% of the CO_2 released by anthropogenic actions, and consequently becoming increasingly acid. When CO_2 dissolves in the water, it forms carbonic acid.

$$H_2O + CO_2 \leftrightarrow H_2CO_3$$

Carbonic acid is unstable and will easily release one or two hydrogen ions to form bicarbonate or carbonate, respectively.

$$H_2CO_3 \leftrightarrow H^+ + HCO_3^- \text{ (bicarbonate)}$$

$$HCO_3- \leftrightarrow H^+ + CO_3^{2-} \text{ (carbonate)}$$

Increased absorption of CO_2 in the oceans alters the relative proportions of the several forms of carbon: dissolved CO_2, carbonic acid, HCO_3^- (bicarbonate) and CO_3^{2-} (carbonate). Increasing the dissolved CO_2 promotes bicarbonate ion formation and decreases carbonate ion formation. This is problematic since calcifying organisms such as scleractinian corals, calcareous algae and many others, combine Ca^{2+} with CO_3^{2-} to accrete their skeletons ($CaCO_3$). A reduction of available CO_3^{2-} ions may slow the calcification rate of calcifying organisms, promote the formation of less dense skeletons that are more susceptible to physical fragmentation during severe weather events and/or accelerate erosion. In the last century, the ocean pH has already dropped 0.1 and seawater carbonate concentrations have been depleted by ~30 $\mu mol\ kg^{-1}$ seawater (IPCC 2007). Recent studies project pH to decline another 0.4 units by the end of the century, with ocean carbonate saturation levels potentially dropping below those required to sustain coral reef accretion by 2050 (Kleypas and Langdon 2006).

In the 20th century, sea surface temperature has increased 0.4-0.8°C, and it is expected to increase an additional 1-3°C (IPCC 2007) in this century, which may severely affect corals symbiotic relationship with the zooxanthellae. Studies have observed the expulsion of zooxanthellae by the coral host when temporarily subjected to higher temperatures, inducing the coral to bleach. As previously mentioned, zooxanthellae are essential to provide energy for the coral to perform more energetically costly processes such as growth, reproduction and lesion repair.

Projected global temperature increases of 1.4-5.8°C by the end of the 21st century are expected to lead to sea level rise of 0.1 to 0.9 m (Buddemeier et al. 2004). Despite the the fact that rate of sea level rise might exceed coral growth rates, most corals are believed to be able to adapt to rising sea level, with the exception of some corals in the lower depth limit. However, the predicted rise of sea level might also cause increased shoreline erosion and in some cases the submersion of islands could increase sediment load in the water.

Some researchers also predict an increase in the frequency and intensity of catastrophic weather events, such as hurricanes/typhoons (Webster et al. 2005), and major alterations to ocean circulation (Harley et al. 2006) due to rising sea surface temperatures. The later phenomenon could alter larval supply and jeopardize population connectivity, gene flow, genetic diversity, risk of extinction and biodiversity.

The macro algae-dominance state can again alternate with a sea urchin barren state. In the later state, if echinoid predators are overfished, the system can degrade completely and become lifeless (Bellwood et al. 2004). The stressors expected to have a greater influence in pushing the system towards a phase shift from coral to algal dominance are those that are gradual and chronic, namely increased sea surface temperatures

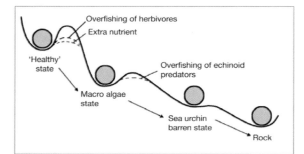

FIGURE 2

A graphic model depicting transitions between ecosystem states. 'Healthy' resilient coral dominated reefs become progressively more vulnerable owing to fishing pressure, pollution, disease and coral bleaching. The dotted lines illustrate the loss of resilience that becomes evident when reefs fail to recover from disturbance and slide into less desirable states. Reprinted by permission from Macmillian Publishers Ltd: [Science] (Bellwood, D.R., T.P. Hughes, C. Folke, and M. Nyström. 2004. Confronting the coral reef crisis. Nature 429:827-833), copyright (2004).

and ocean acidification. Nevertheless, the frequency and intensity of temporary and localized acute stressors (e.g. severe weather, disease) combined with manageable anthropogenic local impacts (e.g., overfishing, pollution, terrestrial runoff) can exacerbate the process and contribute to the loss of resistance and resilience. For instance, increased nutrient input is believed to promote the outbreak of coral predators like crown-of-thorns sea stars (*Acanthaster planci*) (Brodie et al., 2005). If these outbreaks occur more frequently on chronically disturbed reefs, the ability of corals to recover would be seriously compromised.

The tipping point of the coral-algal phase shift appears to occur when sea temperatures exceed the upper thermal tolerance of the coral (~2-3°C above species optimal level), which results in the expulsion of the zooxanthellae, i.e., coral bleaching. Thermal tolerance is species-specific, therefore species will not be affected equally. The optimal temperature for most coral species is 23-25°C (annual average), but some species can tolerate 36-40°C. However, with the expected rise in sea surface temperatures, coral cover and species-richness will likely decrease and undergo a dramatic change from coral to algal dominance (Buddemeier et al. 2004, Hoegh-Guldberg et al. 2007).

If atmospheric CO_2 levels exceed 480 ppm and carbonate ion levels drop below 200 μmol.kg^{-1}, the ability for reef organisms to accrete calcium will be compromised. Simulations have predicted that doubling the pre-industrial CO_2 level to 560 ppm would result in a calcification reduction of 11-37% in corals and 16-44% in calcareous algae (Langdon et al. 2000, Marubini et al. 2003) by 2050. The loss of coral cover and the ability to accrete calcium would hasten erosion and permit algae to outcompete coral recruits for suitable settlement substrate.

IMPACTS ON BIODIVERSITY

Since coral reefs are biodiversity hotspots and centres of endemism (Hughes et al. 2002), the regime shift from coral to algae dominance could potentially result in numerous extinctions (Roberts et al. 2002) and substantial changes in the abundance and distribution of species and communities at local to global scales.

Climate change is predicted to impact adult corals' survival, growth and reproductive output. Increased sea-surface temperatures and high solar irradiance have been reported to cause coral bleaching (release of the symbiotic zooxanthellae), which may lead to death (Anthony et al. 2007) as coral will have less energy available for growth, reproduction, lesion repair, disease resistance and recovery (Fine and Loya 2002). Water acidification is expected to compromise coral growth and/or weaken its calcified structure (Kleypas et al. 1999, Hoegh-Guldberg et al. 2007, Madin et al. 2008). All these threats will increase the risk of extinction of several coral species. Furthermore, as sea surface temperature increases, bleaching events are predicted to become more frequent and severe. Coral bleaching frequently causes immediate loss of live coral and may lead to long-term reduction in topographic complexity due to erosion. However, according to Hughes et al. (2003), reefs will change rather than disappear entirely, with certain species already exhibiting greater tolerance to climate change and coral bleaching than others. We expect a loss of less thermally tolerant coral species (the majority), and a replacement by algae species. This change in dominance and subsequent reduction in habitat topography/complexity will be dramatic for the entire coral reef community (e.g. sponges, crustaceans, molluscs and fishes) as available shelter, settlement substrate, nursery, and/or feeding grounds are projected to gradually disappear due to reduction in calcium accretion that offsets erosion (Almany 2004, Pratchett et al. 2008).

Climate change might also impact coral reef fishes' individual performance, trophic linkages, recruitment dynamics and population connectivity (Munday et al. 2008). Ocean acidification has been reported to impair olfactory discrimination and homing ability of settlement stage marine fish (Munday et al. 2009a). Furthermore, according to Nilsson et al. (2009), elevated sea surface temperatures may cause a decline in fish aerobic capacity (resting and maximum rates of oxygen consumption); however, the degree of thermal tolerance is species-specific. Certain species are likely to persist at higher temperatures, while thermally sensitive species may decline at low latitudes and/or move to higher, cooler latitudes. This differential impact and possible alteration to species relative abundance might have serious consequences for the coral reef community and disturb the trophic chain (Munday et al. 2008).

The expected increased frequency and intensity of catastrophic weather events (such as hurricanes/typhoons) (Webster et al. 2005) and weaker carbonate materials associated with more acidic oceans will increase the vulnerability of coral reefs to mechanical damage. Short term, the reduction of coral size is expected to reduce fecundity. On a longer temporal scale, we expect dramatic shifts in assemblage structure following hydrodynamic disturbances, including switches in species' dominance on coral reefs (Madin et al. 2008). The increased frequency and intensity of severe weather events might rule future reefs to have lower colony abundances and be dominated by small and morphologically simple, yet mechanically robust species, which will in turn support lower levels of whole-reef biodiversity than do present-day reefs (Madin et al. 2008).

Coral reef ecosystems typically develop as patches of shallow habitat that can be separated by long distances. Corals and other sedentary reef organisms' long distance dispersal is achieved through larval dispersal. The predicted alterations to large-scale ocean circulation (Harley et al. 2006) are likely to alter the dynamics of larval supply. Increased sea-surface temperatures and reduced pH are expected to affect larval development, settlement, and cause physiological stress (Bassim and Sammarco 2003). These factors could potentially increase larval mortality, reduce competency time, and consequently, reduce dispersal distances, reef connectivity, gene flow, and biodiversity (Jones et al. 2009, Munday et al. 2009b).

Since corals act as barriers altering wave energy and circulation near-shore, other types of tropical and sub-tropical ecosystems, like mangroves (highly protected nurseries), are predicted to experience some negative impacts as well.

ECOSYSTEM SERVICES

Coral reefs provide an extensive and valuable list of services to humans. Cesar et al. (2003) estimated the global net economic benefit from coral reefs to be US$30 billion year^{-1}. Its aesthetic is the prime reason for attracting millions of tourists annually. The revenue generated from tourism/diving is an important income for many coastal countries, states and islands (e.g., Caribbean islands, Southeast Asia, Australia, Hawaii and the Maldives). In addition, coral reefs support the seafood, recreation and aquarium trade industries. The highly productive coral reefs from Asia provide almost one quarter of the annual total catch and food for nearly one billion people. Reefs also supply building materials, fibres, and pharmaceuticals (Balmford et al. 2002).

The geologic and biologic structure of coral reefs creates a complex habitat that provides food, shelter, and nursery habitat for hundreds of marine species. The high biodiversity is not limited to marine animals; many terrestrial plant and animal species (e.g. birds, humans, etc.) have colonized the coastal environments and islands formed by coral reef communities (Buddemeier et al. 2004).

Corals reefs also provide less visible services such as nutrient cycling, climate regulation and protection for the shoreline and other ecosystems (e.g. mangroves). Reefs reduce wave energy during storm events, preventing beach erosion and protecting human settlements from waves, floods and beach erosion (Buddemeier et al. 2004, Hoegh-Guldberg et al. 2007).

UNCERTAINTIES

The projected increase in carbon dioxide production and temperature over the next 50 years exceeds the conditions under which coral reefs have flourished over the past half-million years (Hughes et al. 2003).

Climate and localized non-climate stresses interact, often synergistically, to affect the health and sustainability of coral reef ecosystems (Buddemeier et al. 2004). Scientists have invested a great deal of resources predicting the impact of several disturbances, but the projections are usually based on studies examining one or a few disturbances at a time. Therefore, it is still difficult to predict the outcome of their possible interactions. For instance, one of the expected scenarios for increased sea-surface temperature is the alteration of ocean currents. This phenomenon alone could produce changes in coral larval supply and potentially alter the connectivity between populations of sedentary species by disrupting the gene flow, genetic diversity, speciation rate, and susceptibility to extinction (Jones et al. 2009). Additionally, rising sea-surface temperatures may negatively impact the reproduction of adult corals and/or the larval viability, survival and competence time (i.e., the period during which larvae are competent to settle and form new colonies is expected to decrease as their metabolic rate accelerates with increasing temperatures). However, the effects of increased sea-surface temperature acting simultaneously on ocean currents and coral reproductive characters remain unclear.

However, some interactions (e.g. increased temperature and calcification rates) might not be negative. Small increases in temperatures, which keep corals below their upper thermal limit, accelerate growth through increased metabolism and the increased photosynthetic rates of zooxanthellae. Under this condition, calcification is increased and corals do not respond as significantly to the decrease in carbonate ion concentration (Carricart-Ganivet 2004). Also, Anthony et al. (2007) conducted laboratory experiments that suggest high sediment concentrations reduced the mortality of certain coral species under high temperature and/or high light (irradiance) potentially by alleviating light pressure and by providing an alternative food source for bleached corals.

One of the greatest uncertainties involves the ability of corals to adapt to rising temperatures and acidification. Relatively modest degrees of adaptation would substantially reduce damage to coral reefs, especially in scenarios with strong climate mitigation (Donner 2009, Weiss 2010). For coral reef fishes, small temperature increases might favour larval development but could be counteracted by negative effects on adult reproduction. Several fish species have a large geographical distribution where they are exposed to various temperatures. When this characteristic is allied to a short life cycle, there might be some potential for adaptation to climate change (Munday et al. 2008).

LOCAL TO GLOBAL ACTIONS AND OPPORTUNITIES

In order to sustain the ecosystem's resistance and, in case of significant change in the ecosystem, allow a faster recovery, local and global action must be taken. International integration of management strategies that support reef resilience need to be vigorously implemented, and complemented by strong policy decisions to reduce the rate of global warming (Hughes et al. 2003).

Globally, the reduction of CO_2 emissions is necessary to minimize increasing sea-surface temperatures and water acidification. The levels of atmospheric CO_2 need to be kept below 480 ppm to avoid an almost irreversible phase shift (Hoegh-Guldberg et al. 2007).

As an international consensus of how to reduce CO_2 emissions remains unclear, Bellwood et al. (2004) advocates that we should accept that climate change will eventually occur, and concentrate our efforts in studying how can we help corals reef ecosystems to counter these disturbances.

If we minimize local human impacts (such as terrestrial run-off, coastal pollution and over exploitation of key functional groups), the stresses associated with climate change are likely to be less severe (Hughes et al. 2003, Buddemeier et al. 2004). Fisheries must be managed to keep populations at sustainable levels and particularly protect the populations of key functional groups such as herbivores (fish and invertebrate grazers such as parrotfish and sea urchin species, respectively; Mumby 2006) that control the algae growth and enable corals to recover from disturbances (Bellwood et al. 2004). The reduction of fishing effort cannot be done without considering the local socio-economic impacts. Fishermen must be provided education/training for new trades (e.g. eco-tourism related activities) and more sustainable fishing practices while considering traditional and/or cultural values. The collection of wild caught organisms for the marine aquarium trade must be reduced and replaced by aquacultured individuals. Aquaculture facilities should be placed in regions that supply the aquarium trade and employ former ornamentals collectors.

Marine reserves appear to be an effective means of reducing local stresses on coral reefs and allowing for rapid recovery from bleaching events (Mumby & Harborne 2010). In addition, the implementation of marine protected areas (MPAs) can provide refuges for living organisms and serve as larval sources for replenishment of harvested areas outside the reserve (Botsford et al. 2009). MPAs should be located where the stresses associated with climate change are likely to be less severe (West and Salm 2003). A successful implementation and management of MPAs will require international conservation efforts across larger spatial and temporal scales that match the biogeographic scales of species distributions and life-histories (Hughes et al. 2003).

In order to generate and maintain the biodiversity of coral reef ecosystems we must assure reef connectivity (Hughes et al. 2005). Coral population connectivity patterns are likely to change due to alterations to oceanic currents, reduced reproductive output, lower larval survival and shorter competence time. Therefore, to retain their efficacy, the design (size and spacing) and management of marine reserves may have to be adjusted to contribute to an effective minimization of climate change and anthropogenic pressures (Almany et al. 2009, Bostsford et al. 2009, Munday et al. 2009b).

REFERENCES

Almany, G.R. 2004. Differential effects of habitat complexity, predators and competitors on abundance of juvenile and adult coral reef fishes. Oecologia 141: 105-113.

Almany, G. R., S. R. Connolly, D. D. Heath, J. D. Hogan, G. P. Jones, L. J. McCook, M. Mills, M., R. L. Pressey, and D. H. Williamson. 2009. Connectivity, biodiversity conservation and the design of marine reserve networks for coral reefs. Coral Reefs 28: 339-351.

Anthony, K. R. N., and S. R. Connolly. 2004. Environmental limits to growth: physiological niche boundaries of corals along turbidity–light gradients. Oecologia 141: 373–384.

Anthony, K. R. N., S. R. Connolly, and O. Hoegh-Guldberg. 2007. Bleaching, energetic, and coral mortality risk: effects of temperature, light and sediment regime. Limnology and Oceanography 52: 716-726.

Balmford, A., A. Bruner, P. Cooper, R. Constanza, S. Farber, R. E. Green, M. Jenkins, P. Jefferiss, V. Jessamy, J. Madden, N. Myers, S. Naeem, J. Paavola, M. Rayment, S. Rosendo, J. Roughgarden, K. Trumper, and R. K. Turner. 2002. Economic Reasons for Conserving Wild Nature. Science 297: 950-953.

Bassim, K.M., and P. W. Sammarco. 2003. Effects of temperature and ammonium on larval development and survivorship in a scleractinian coral (*Diploria strigosa*). Marine Biology 142: 241–252.

Bellwood, D.R., T. P. Hughes, C. Folke, and M. Nyström. 2004. Confronting the coral reef crisis. Nature 429: 827-833.

Botsford, L.W., J. W. White, M. A. Coffroth, C. B. Paris, S. Planes, T. L. Shearer, S. R. Thorrold, and G. P. Jones. 2009. Connectivity and resilience of coral reef metapopulations in MPAs: matching empirical efforts to predictive needs. Coral Reefs 28: 327–337.

Brodie, J., K. Fabricius, G. De'ath, and K. Okaji. 2005. Are increased nutrient inputs responsible for more outbreaks of crown-of-thorns starfish? An appraisal of the evidence. Marine Pollution Bulletin 51: 266–278.

Buddemeier, R.W., J. A. Kleypas, and R. B. Aronson. 2004. Coral reefs and global climate change – Potential contributions of climate change to stresses on coral reef ecosystems. Pew Center on Global Climate Change.

Carricart-Ganivet, J.P. 2004. Sea surface temperature and the growth of the West Atlantic reef-building coral *Montastraea annularis*. Journal of Experimental Marine Biology and Ecology 302: 249– 260.

Cesar, H., L. Burke, and L. Pet-Soede. 2003. The economics of worldwide coral reef degradation. Cesar Environmental Economics Consulting. Arnhem, The Netherlands, 23 pp.

Donner SD. 2009. Coping with Commitment: Projected Thermal Stress on Coral Reefs under Different Future Scenarios. Plos One 4: 1-10.

FAO, 2009. State of world fisheries and aquaculture (SOFIA). Food And Agriculture Organization of the United Nations, Rome. 176pp.

Fine, M., and Y. Loya. 2002. Endolithic algae: an alternative source of photoassimilates during coral bleaching. Proceedings of the Royal Society of London B 269: 1205–1210.

Harley, C. D. G., A. R. Hughes, K. M. Hultgreen, B. G. Miner, C. J. B. Sorte, C. S. Thornber, L. F. Rodriguez, L. Tomanek, and S. L. Williams. 2006. The impacts of climate change in coastal marine systems. Ecology Letters 9: 228-241.

Hoegh-Guldberg, O., P. J. Mumby, A. J. Hooten, R. S. Steneck, P. Greenfield, E. Gomez, C. D. Harvell, P. F. Sale, A. J. Edwards, K. Caldeira, N. Knowlton, C. M. Eakin, R. Iglesias-Prieto, N. Muthiga, R. H. Bradbury, A. Dubi, and M. E. Hatziolos. 2007. Coral reefs under rapid climate change and ocean acidification. Science 318: 1737-1742.

Hughes, T.P. 1994. Catastrophes, phase shifts and large-scale degradation of a Caribbean coral reef. Science 265: 1547-1551.

Hughes, T.P., D. R. Bellwood, and S. R. Connolly. 2002. Biodiversity hotspots, centres of endemicity, and the conservation of coral reefs. Ecology Letters 5: 775-784.

Hughes, T.P., A. H. Baird, D. R. Bellwood, M. Card, S. R. Connolly, C. Folke, R. Grosberg, O. Hoegh-Gulberg, J. B. C. Jackson, J. Kleypas, J. M. Lough, P. Marshall, M. Nyström, S. R. Palumbi, J. M. Pandolfi, B. Rosen, and J. Roughgarden. 2003. Climate change, human impacts, and the resilience of coral reefs. Science 301: 929-933.

Hughes, T. P., D. R. Bellwood, C. Folke, R. S. Steneck, and J. Wilson. 2005. New paradigms for supporting the resilience of marine ecosystems. Trends in Ecology and Evolution 20: 380-386.

IPCC, 2007. Climate Change 2007: The physical science basis. IPCC, Climate Change 2007: the physical science basis. In S. Salomon, D. Qin, M. Manning, M. Marquis, K. Averyt, M. M. B. Tignor, H L. Miller Jr., and Z. Chen, editors, Contribution of Working Group I to the Fourth Assessment Report of the Intergovernmental Panel on Climate Change (IPCC), 989pp.

Jones, G. P., G. R. Russ, P. F. Sale, and R. S. Steneck. 2009. Theme section on Larval connectivity, resilience and the future of coral reefs. Coral Reefs 28: 303-305.

Kleypas, J.A., R. W. Buddemeier, D. Archer, J. Gattuso, C. Langdon, and B. N. Opdyke. 1999. Geochemical consequences if increased atmospheric carbon dioxide on coral reefs. Science 284: 118-120.

Kleypas, J.A., and C. Langdon. 2006. Coral Reefs and changing seawater chemistry. In J. T. Phinney, A. Strong, W. Skirving, J. Kleypas, O. Hoegh-Guldberg, editors, Coral reefs and climate change: science and management, AGU Monograph. Coastal and Estuarine Studies 61: 73-110.

Langdon, C., T. Takahashi, C. Sweeney, D. Chipman, J. Goddard, F. Marubini, H. Aceves, H. Barnett, and M. J. Atkinson. 2000. Effect of calcium carbonate saturation state on the calcification rate of an experimental coral reef. Global Biogeochemical Cycles 14: 639-654.

Madin, J. S., M. J. O'Donnell, and S. R. Connolly. 2008. Climate-mediated mechanical changes to post-disturbance coral assemblages. Biology Letters 4: 490-493.

Marubini, F., C. Ferrier-Pages, and J.-P. Cuif. 2003. Suppression of growth in scleractinian corals by decreasing ambient carbonate ion concentration: a cross-family comparison. Proceedings of the Royal Society B 270: 179-184.

Mumby, P.J., 2006. The impacts of exploiting grazers (Scaridae) on the dynamics of Caribbean coral reefs. Ecological Applications 16(2): 747–769.

Mumby PJ, Harborne AR. 2010. Marine Reserves Enhance the Recovery of Corals on Caribbean Reefs. Plos One 5: 1-7.

Munday, P.L., G. P. Jones, M. S. Pratchett, and A. J. Williams. 2008. Climate change and the future for coral reef fishes. Fish and Fisheries 9: 261-285.

Munday, P. L., D. L. Dixson, J. M. Donelson, G. P. Jones, M. S. Pratchett, G. V. Devitsina, and K. B. Døving. 2009a. Ocean acidification impairs olfactory discrimination and homing ability of a marine fish. Proceedings of the National Academy of Science 106: 1848–1852.

Munday, P. L., J. M. Leis, J. M. Lough, C. B. Paris, M. J. Kingsford, M. L. Berumen, and J. Lambrechts. 2009b. Climate change and coral reef connectivity. Coral Reefs 28: 379–395.

Nilsson, G.E., N. Crawley, I. G. Lunde, and P. L. Munday. 2009. Elevated temperature reduces the respiratory scope of coral reef fishes. Global Change Biology 15: 1405–1412.

Pratchett, M.S., P. L. Munday, S. K. Wilson, N. A. J. Graham, J. E. Cinner, D. R. Bellwood, G. P. Jones, N. V. C. Polunin, and T. R. McClanahan. 2008. Effects of climate-induces coral bleaching on coral reef fishes – Ecological and Economic Consequences. Oceanography and Marine Biology: an Annual Review 46: 251-296.

Robbins, W. D., M. Hisano, S. R. Connolly, and J. H. Choat. 2006. Ongoing collapse of coral-reef shark populations. Current Biology 16: 2314-2319.

Roberts, C.M., C. J. McClean, J. E. N. Veron, J. P. Hawkins, G. R. Allen, D. E. McAllister, C. G. Mittermeier, F. W. Schueler, M. Spalding, F. Wells, C. Vynne, and T. B. Werner. 2002. Marine biodiversity hotspots and conservation priorities for tropical reefs. Science 295: 1280-1284.

Webster, P. J., G. J. Holland, J. A. Curry, and H. R. Chang. 2005. Changes in tropical cyclone number, duration, and intensity in a warming environment. Science 309: 1844-1846.

Weis VM. 2010. The susceptibility and resilience of corals to thermal stress: adaptation, acclimatization or both? Molecular Ecology 19: 1515-1517.

West, J.M., and R. V. Salm. 2003. Resistance and resilience to coral bleaching: implications for coral reef conservation and management. Conservation Biology 17: 956-967.